D0689534

How to Track
Politics
on the
Internet

How to Track Politics on the Internet

Bruce Maxwell
bmaxwell@mindspring.com

CQ PRESS

A Division of Congressional Quarterly Inc.
Washington, D.C.

REF DESK
320.973
M 465h

——————————— *For Barbara* ———————————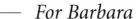

CQ Press
A Division of Congressional Quarterly Inc.
1414 22nd St. N.W.
Washington, DC 20037
(202) 822-1475; (800) 638-1710

www.cqpress.com

© 2000 Congressional Quarterly Inc.

All rights reserved. No part of this publication may be reproduced or transmitted in any form or by any means, electronic or mechanical, including photocopy, recording, or any information storage and retrieval system, without permission in writing from the publisher.

Printed in the United States of America

04 03 02 01 00   5 4 3 2 1

Library of Congress Cataloging-in-Publication Data
In process

ISBN 1-58602-472-X

11/04

SUMMARY CONTENTS

v

CONTENTS

AIDS   78

Animal Rights   85

Business   93

Gay and Lesbian Issues   147

General Government Policy and Reform   151

Gun Control   162

Internet and Telecommunications Policy   194

Labor and Employment   200

Media and Communications Policy   206

Poverty and Welfare   210

Race and Ethnicity   215

Religion   222

Right to Die   227

Senior Issues   230

PREFACE

Will the Internet play a crucial role in the 2000 elections? The experts disagree. But they're unanimous on one point: because of the Internet, the American public can access more political information today than ever before.

How to Track Politics on the Internet is a guide to that information. It describes more than 600 of the best political Web sites, electronic mailing lists, and Usenet news-groups.

The book does not pretend to be an exhaustive catalog of everything political on the Internet. It would be impossible to create such a catalog because the Internet offers an enormous and ever-changing number of political resources. No one knows how many political sites exist, but the number is surely more than 10,000 and may be many multiples of it.

Instead of attempting to cover everything, I've sifted through thousands of political sites, looking for the most useful resources. I've especially focused on sites that are good starting points for researching particular topics.

To be included in this book, a site has to meet a number of criteria. It must provide a substantial amount of useful information, cost nothing to access, and be stable and reasonably easy to navigate.

A site's inclusion in this book does not mean that I condone the views of the group that runs it. Some of the groups are well outside the political mainstream and advocate methods other than the ballot box to achieve their goals. I include them because they are part of the broad political spectrum in the United States, and their words and deeds can have a disproportionate impact on public debate and the political process.

A few of the sites listed are specifically geared toward the 2000 elections. The vast majority are not, though, and will continue to provide useful information about political issues long after the ballots are counted in November 2000.

Most of the sites fall into one of three categories:

- Directories, which are collections of links to sites about a topic. Directories are great because others have already spent hours and hours searching the Internet for resources about certain topics and then have kindly shared the fruits of their labors. For example, the About.com: Animal Rights site (p. 85) has links to hundreds of sites about animal rights issues, all annotated and neatly arranged by topic. It's a fantastic place to start a search for animal rights information on the Internet—far better than typing "animal rights" into a search engine and sorting through the thousands of hits you'll receive.

- Sites that are key resources about a specific topic. If you're interested in Internet issues, for example, the site operated by the Center for Democracy and Technology (p. 194) is a must. It offers a wealth of information about everything from free speech online to protection of the nation's electronic infrastructure from terrorist attacks.

- News sites, especially those devoted to coverage of a specific topic. For example, if you're tracking the national debate over gun control, one of the best sources is the Yahoo! News page about gun control (p. 167). It provides hundreds of stories about gun control published or broadcast from June 1998 to the present by sources such as Reuters, the *New York Times,* the *Detroit News, Time* magazine, and CNN.

Many people helped make this book possible and deserve my hearty thanks. I'm grateful to Dave Tarr for his support of the book and its author through thick and thin, Sharon Lamberton and Ann Davies for their editing, Tom Roche for shepherding the book through the production process, Debra Naylor for creating the design, Joan Stout for writing the index, Grace Hill for coordinating manuscript processing, and Judy Plummer for her publicity work.

As always, I reserve my greatest thanks for my wife, Barbara. She surely ranks among the most tolerant and supportive book widows of all time.

Introduction

Although he was far from the first politician to go online, Republican presidential candidate Bob Dole was the one who really legitimized the Internet as a political tool.

At the end of his first presidential debate with Bill Clinton in 1996, Dole—the World War II veteran and former majority leader of the U.S. Senate—recited the address of his campaign's Web site and encouraged people to visit.

It was the first time a candidate had ever mentioned a Web site in a presidential debate and the surest sign possible that the Internet had arrived on the political scene.

Never mind that Dole got the address wrong (he left out one of the dots, a crucial mistake). It was the thought that counted.

Only four years later as the 2000 campaign blasts into full swing in the United States, it's de rigueur for candidates seeking offices ranging from president to dog catcher to have Web sites. Republican Steve Forbes even announced his candidacy for president on the Internet. Virtually all political parties, ranging from the largest to the most obscure, have Web sites, as do thousands of interest groups, think tanks, trade associations, labor unions, agencies at all levels of government, news organizations that provide political reports, polling firms, private individuals, and just about everyone else involved in the political process.

Perhaps most telling, candidates in their stump speeches have added the Internet to their discussions of enduring issues such as welfare, education, and the economy. They're discussing topics such as electronic privacy, free speech online, protection for children from online pornography, and Internet taxation—all issues that didn't even appear on the political radar only a few years ago.

Of course, some candidates have stumbled over the Internet. Those who flooded the Internet with messages touting their candidacies earned the wrath rather than the votes of Internet users who hate the proliferation of unsolicited e-mail known as spam. And Democratic presidential candidate Al Gore was blasted after he claimed credit for creating the Internet.

Lawmakers in Congress and in statehouses nationwide also have noticed the Internet. They've introduced hundreds of bills to regulate it—or to keep government out of the regulation business.

The use of the Internet as a political tool is not limited to the United States. Political organizations, candidates, and governments around the world have embraced the communications opportunities that the Internet presents. In fact, some of the most interesting political uses of the Internet are occurring in countries such as China, where it has opened—if only slightly—the door that previously blocked all public debate.

The Internet's Impact on Politics

So what does it all mean? Will the Internet become a great democratizing influence that levels the playing field, boosts political participation, creates new opportunities for dialogue between politicians and those they represent, gives voice to the speechless,

How to Use This Book

The first chapter in this book describes a variety of political directories and search engines. All are great starting places in your search for political information on the Internet.

Subsequent chapters are arranged alphabetically by subject. In addition to looking under the appropriate chapter heading, however, be sure to check the index for topics of interest. Sites frequently have documents about numerous subjects and don't fit perfectly into a single category.

Although all sites listed in this book are well worth visiting, I have highlighted sites of special merit with check marks. One check next to a site's name means the site is particularly strong, and two checks mean it's one of the best political sites on the Internet.

The access information for each site follows its description. For most sites, two pieces of information are provided:

- Access method—The tool you use to access the information, such as the World Wide Web, e-mail, or Usenet.

- To access—The site's address on the Internet.

Two other pieces of access information are provided for mailing lists:

- Subject line—The word(s) you must type on an e-mail message's subject line to subscribe to a mailing list. The words you must type are in **bold** type. If this line is blank in the instructions, leave it blank in your message as well.

- Message—The word(s) you must type in an e-mail message's message area to subscribe to a mailing list. The words you must type are in **bold** type. You must replace any words that are in *italics* with the correct information. For example, if the message in the instructions reads **subscribe *listname firstname lastname*** you must type the word **subscribe** followed by the list's name, your first name, and your last name.

and generally restores the political process in the United States, if not around the world? Or is all the fancy talk just a lot of hype?

The answer depends upon whom you ask. In recent books about the Internet's impact on politics, two respected authors came to diametrically opposing conclusions. Gary W. Selnow, a professor of communication at San Francisco State University, took the "pro" position in his book *Electronic Whistle-Stops:*

> [T]he Internet is shaping up to be a serious international medium that will radically alter politics in the United States and abroad, and what's more, it will impact society on a larger level. It stands to change political and ideological alignments, the substance of news available to the population, and the relationships between political leaders and the people.[1]

Richard Davis, a political science professor at Brigham Young University, took the opposite view in *The Web of Politics:*

The most likely Internet users will continue to be the affluent, the most common users of Internet political information will be the already politically interested, and those who will use the Internet for political activity will be primarily those who are already politically active. And that is why the Internet will not lead to the social and political revolution so widely predicted.[2]

The reality is likely somewhere in the middle of these two viewpoints. When you are assessing the Internet's impact on politics, it's crucial to remember that the Internet is a tool—nothing more, nothing less. As with any tool, its power depends upon the context in which it's used. A hammer is a great tool for pounding nails but a lousy one for leveling fresh cement. So it is with the Internet.

What the Internet does best is distribute information. Without question, the Internet has made a huge range of political information available that previously was difficult or impossible to obtain. You can find out who's giving money to political candidates, check the voting records of your representatives in Congress, read the texts of bills being considered by Congress, read the full texts of speeches by candidates (without the news media serving as a filter), subscribe to e-mail alerts on issues ranging from abortion to gun control, find advocacy groups that work on issues that interest you, read political news from a wide variety of media outlets, and much more.

Release of some of this information can have major consequences. For example, the House of Representatives changed the political landscape forever when it placed on the Internet the full text of the report by Independent Counsel Kenneth Starr regarding his investigation of President Bill Clinton's affair with Monica Lewinsky. Millions of people read all or parts of the report within days of its release.

The Internet also is good at mobilizing people, at least in some cases. The most notable example is the 1998 election of Jesse Ventura as governor of Minnesota. Although some commentators have incorrectly attributed Ventura's victory to the Internet, online communication clearly played a role in his election. Perhaps most important was the Jesse Net, an e-mail alert list that had 3,000 subscribers by election day.

In an article following the election, Ventura's webmaster, Phil Madsen, said the Internet was only one tool in the campaign's arsenal:

> Without the Internet, we would have lost the election. The same applies to all other components of the campaign. Take away the debate inclusion, public campaign finance money, campaign office, telephone team, good media relations, public policy research, campaign leadership, quality candidates, a staff that worked well together, eager and hard-working volunteers, etc., etc., etc., and we would have lost as well.[3]

The Internet is especially good at mobilizing people around issues. In March 1999 the chairman of the Federal Deposit Insurance Corporation said that an Internet e-mail campaign caused the agency to withdraw a proposed "Know Your Customer" pol-

Newsletter Provides Free Updates

With new political Web sites going online every day, a book like this has certain limitations. To get around them, I've created a free electronic newsletter called PoliSites to provide weekly updates about politics on the Internet.

Each issue contains descriptions of new political sites and summaries of recent news
stories, reports, and other documents about political use of the Internet. Each summary
links to the full document where it's available.

You can subscribe to PoliSites by sending a blank e-mail message to join-polisites@lists.
silverhammerpub.com or by visiting the newsletter's Web site:
http://silverhammerpub.com

icy. The policy, which was aimed at detecting money laundering, would have required
banks to monitor customers' accounts and report any unusual activity to federal regulators.

The agency received 257,000 comments about the proposed policy, with about
205,000 arriving by e-mail. The overwhelming majority denounced the proposal as an
invasion of privacy. The Libertarian Party was a major force behind the unprecedent-
ed number of comments. It launched a campaign opposing the policy through its Web
site and an e-mail alert list, among other venues. By the end of the campaign, 140,000
people had subscribed to a new party e-mail list about privacy issues, according to the
New York Times.[4]

The Internet also is good at helping groups or individuals publicly express their
views, no matter how modest their resources. Free Internet access and Web space are
available to anyone who can access a computer at home, school, work, or a library,
making it possible to create a simple Web site at no charge. This is a boon for third parties, small organizations with limited budgets, and individuals who otherwise might
not be able to get their message out because of high printing and distribution costs for
traditional political literature.

This is not to say, however, that the Internet levels the playing field between those
who are well funded and those of modest means. Simply creating a Web site does not
guarantee that anyone will visit. Well-funded site owners can buy advertising for their
site and engage in a wide range of other promotional activities that draw in visitors—
and cost money. The well-established also have a built-in advantage simply because
the public tends to gravitate to what it knows. Thus Al Gore's campaign site automatically receives far more hits than Web sites operated by any third-party presidential candidate.

The Internet is lousy at creating true two-way communication between candidates
and voters. Sure, most candidates' Web sites ask visitors to vote in online polls, send in
their views by e-mail, or engage in other "interactivity." Unfortunately, it's all a sham.
The dirty secret is that campaigns ignore the polls and e-mail opinions from online

visitors—except to harvest e-mail addresses for future campaign mailings. Results from online polls are not scientific and thus are of no use to a campaign, and candidates lack the time and resources to engage in one-on-one e-mail conversations with voters. A few campaigns have instituted online "town meetings," where a handful of visitors get to interact with the candidate online, but such opportunities are rare.

The Internet also fails miserably (at least so far) in creating useful forums for members of the public to discuss political issues. Dozens of Usenet newsgroups allow people to express their views about various political topics, but they commonly erupt in flame wars that scare away any rational discussion.

The Internet and Voting

A huge push is under way to allow voting online. Proponents claim that instituting Internet voting would re-ignite interest in politics, remove obstacles to voting, and vastly expand the number of people who cast ballots. Only 49 percent of the voting age population voted in the 1996 presidential election, according to the Federal Election Commission, so low turnout is a serious problem in American elections.

But even setting aside the numerous problems associated with online voting—security breaches that could lead to massive fraud and lack of computer access by the poor being just two—there is no evidence that allowing Internet voting would actually increase voter participation.

The best evidence comes from the National Voter Registration Act, which went into effect in 1995. The law allows people to mail in their voter registration forms or to register when they obtain driver's licenses or apply for Aid to Families with Dependent Children, food stamps, Medicaid, and other social services. The law was intended to make voter registration easier.

So far the results have been underwhelming. The Census Bureau found that the percentage of the voting-age population registered to vote actually dropped 2.3 percent between 1992 and the 1996 election, the first that took place after the law took effect. The Federal Election Commission, using slightly different statistical methods, found a 1.8 percent increase in registration in the forty-three states and the District of Columbia covered by the new law.[5]

Whichever number you accept, making registration easier had little effect on voter registration numbers. The same would be true of Internet voting. Why? Because the reasons people don't bother to vote have nothing to do with the supposed difficulty of the process. Rather, they stem from disenchantment with the political system.

The Census Bureau documented this attitude in the 1996 election, when it asked people who were registered to vote but didn't appear at the polling place why they failed to do so. Some 16.6 percent said they weren't interested in the election, and 13 percent said they didn't like the candidates. Another 21.5 percent said they had no time off or were too busy (another way of saying they weren't interested), and 4.4 percent forgot to vote (again, a way of saying they weren't interested). Added together, those four responses accounted for 55.5 percent of all people who didn't vote. Only 4.3 percent said they failed to vote because they had no transportation to the polls.[6]

What these numbers point to is a lack of interest in voting, not a lack of opportunity. But with a political system that churns out Tweedledee and Tweedledum candidates, campaigns that focus on not making mistakes instead of articulating a vision, a political "debate" geared toward polarization instead of consensus building, and a corrupt campaign finance system that makes elected officials the servants of special interests instead of their constituents, is it any wonder that people don't vote? Fixing these and other systemic problems in American politics would likely boost voter participation, but they have nothing to do with the Internet.

Notes

1. Gary W. Selnow, *Electronic Whistle-Stops: The Impact of the Internet on American Politics* (Westport, Conn.: Praeger, 1998), xxii.
2. Richard Davis, *The Web of Politics: The Internet's Impact on the American Political System* (New York: Oxford University Press, 1999), 168.
3. Phil Madsen, "Notes Regarding Jesse Ventura's Internet Use in His 1998 Campaign for Minnesota Governor," Dec. 7, 1998. http://www.jesseventura.org/internet/netnotes.htm (Dec. 10, 1998).
4. Rebecca Fairley Raney, "Flood of E-Mail Credited with Halting U.S. Bank Plan." *New York Times on the Web,* March 24, 1999. http://search.nytimes.com/search/daily/bin/fastweb? getdoc+site+site+89761+0+wAAA+FDIC (Oct. 30, 1999).
5. Lynne M. Casper and Loretta E. Bass, "Voting and Registration in the Election of November 1996," *Current Population Reports* (Washington, D.C.: U.S. Census Bureau, July 1998), 2.
6. Ibid., 3.

1

Directories and Search Engines

✓ Democracy Network (DNet)

The Democracy Network (DNet) has quickly established itself as a key source of information about local, state, and federal political candidates. DNet is operated by the Center for Governmental Studies, a nonpartisan think tank in California, in cooperation with the League of Women Voters.

To find information for a particular state, you just click on a national map. During election season, candidates are invited to post statements, biographical materials, policy papers, and other materials on the page for their state. Each state's page also provides links to state political parties, nonpartisan state election information, candidates for all federal and statewide offices, federal and statewide elected officials, and state newspapers.

On the national level, DNet provides links to selected sites and news articles about the 2000 presidential election and to sites operated by national political parties.

Vital Stats:

Access method: WWW
To access: http://www.dnet.org

✓ Liszt: Politics

This page offers information about more than 250 Internet mailing lists concerning various political topics. Information provided for each list varies in amount but often includes subscription instructions and a brief description.

The lists are divided into more than two dozen categories, including action alerts, activism, conservative, economics, environment, government, human rights, international, labor, regional, specific issues, and women.

Vital Stats:

Access method: WWW
To access: http://www.liszt.com/select/Politics

✓✓ NIRA's World Directory of Think Tanks

Detailed information about more than 200 think tanks around the world is provided at this site, which is operated by the National Institute for Research Advancement in Japan.

You can access the information by choosing World Directory of Think Tanks on the home page. The think tanks are arranged by country. Most of the think tanks are from the United States, although an excellent selection of think tanks from other countries also is provided.

The information available about each think tank varies in amount but often includes the Web site address, postal address, telephone number, fax number, history, areas of research, geographic focus, titles of publications, number of staff, names of key researchers and their specialties, budget figures, and titles of periodicals published.

For a current list of links to think tanks around the world, at the home page choose Links to Think Tanks and Other Policy Research Resources. The list just provides links, but it's updated regularly.

The site also provides links to several other think tank directories on the Internet.

Vital Stats:

Access method: WWW
To access: http://gate.nira.go.jp/ice/index.html

✓ Open Directory Project: Issues

The Open Directory Project provides this page, which has links to more than 6,000 Web sites about various political issues. The top page has links to a few general sites. It also leads to separate pages about dozens of specific subjects, each of which typically provides dozens or hundreds of links.

The topics covered include abortion, animal welfare, censorship, children, church-state relations, civil liberties, corporate operations, crime and justice, disabilities, economics, education, end of life, environment, free speech, gun control, health, housing, human rights, hunger, immigration, international trade policy, militia movement, peace, population, poverty, privacy, property rights, science and technology, sexual politics, terrorism, violence, war and defense, welfare and workfare, women, and youth rights.

Each link is briefly annotated.

Vital Stats:

Access Method: WWW
To access: http://dmoz.org/Society/Issues

✓✓ Policy.com

Policy.com's highlight is its thousands of links to policy-related position papers, reports, press releases, newspaper and magazine articles, government documents, and court decisions from a huge array of organizations across the political spectrum.

The links are located in the Issues Library, where they're divided into hundreds of topics. Some of the top-level subjects include agriculture, civil rights, communications and technology, constitutional issues, crime, defense policy, economics, education, elections, government reform, health, immigration, regulatory reform, Social Security, society and values, trade, and urban renewal. You can browse the documents by topic or search them by organization, keywords, title, author, and date.

Another key feature is a collection of annotated links to Web sites operated by thousands of organizations involved in public policy. Separate lists provide links to think tanks, advocacy groups, associations, foundations, businesses, universities, U.S. government agencies, foreign governments, international organizations, and media outlets.

The site also offers daily news stories about policy issues from the Associated Press and summaries of articles from major policy magazines.

Vital Stats:

Access method: WWW
To access: http://www.policy.com

✓✓ Political Advocacy Groups

Created by a political science librarian at California State University, this site is much more than just a collection of links to hundreds of Web sites operated by political advocacy groups. Besides supplying links, the site also provides the e-mail address, postal address, telephone number, fax number, and a brief description of each group from the group's own Web site. This additional information greatly increases the links' value.

The links are divided into several dozen subject categories, including African Americans, animal rights, Arab Americans, children, consumer advocacy, corporate accountability and responsibility, environment, government reform, international affairs, land resources, Native Americans, religion, voting and elections, and water resources.

Vital Stats:

Access method: WWW
To access: http://reinert.creighton.edu/advocacy/index.htm

Political Information

This site is a gateway to a massive amount of political information on the Internet. It's operated by a private company.

The site's highlight is a targeted search engine that lets you search more than 5,000 political and policy Web sites. The engine indexes sites operated by the news media, issue advocacy organizations, political interest groups, trade associations, political parties, and others, and lets you search more than 275,000 documents. The search index is updated every two or three weeks.

One caution: The engine uses some unorthodox syntax, so it's a good idea to click on Improve Your Search to learn the details. For example, to search by phrase you must connect all the words with dashes.

A separate engine lets you search political news from dozens of sources, including the *Los Angeles Times, Roll Call, Hill News, Boston Globe, Newsday, Washington Post,* CNN, MSNBC, ABC News, and PBS. The database is updated every two hours.

Another highlight is a directory of links to political sites across the Internet. The directory has more than 1,500 links, which are arranged into more than 200 categories. The top-level categories are campaigns, news, government information, grassroots, issues, parties and organizations, and research tools.

You also can sign up at the site to receive a newsletter by e-mail about political use of the Internet

Vital Stats:

Access method: WWW
To access: http://www.politicalinformation.com

✓ Political Resources on the Net

This site presents links to more than 16,000 politics-related Internet sites around the world. The links lead to sites operated by political parties, organizations, governments, media outlets, and others. You can browse the links by region or country, and you also can search the whole site.

Vital Stats:

Access method: WWW
To access: http://www.agora.stm.it/politic

✓ Political Science and Public Policy Resources

Operated by a librarian at Michigan State University, this page has links to hundreds of politics-oriented Internet sites. The links are divided into more than a dozen subjects, including breaking news, public policy resources sorted by subject, think tanks, U.S. political parties and groups, journals and magazines, campaign information, political science associations, and public opinion polls.

Vital Stats:

Access method: WWW
To access: http://www.lib.msu.edu/harris23/govdocs/pol_sci.htm

---

✓✓ Political Science Resources: United States Politics

This site from the University of Michigan Documents Center offers links to hundreds of Web sites about politics and elections in the United States. The annotated links are divided into more than twenty categories, including campaign finances, elections, lobby groups, news sources, political parties, primaries, public policy issues, statistics, and think tanks.

Vital Stats:

Access method: WWW
To access: http://www.lib.umich.edu/libhome/Documents.center/
                             psusp.html

✓ Political Site of the Day

As its name implies, each day this site highlights a single political site on the Internet. It provides a link to the featured site and a one-sentence description. The sites are selected for their quality, so this is a good place to check for new or especially interesting political sites.

The home page lists picks for the previous two weeks. The library offers hundreds of links to sites selected since July 1995. The library links are listed by month, but there is no way to search by subject.

Vital Stats:

Access method: WWW
To access: http://www.aboutpolitics.com

✓✓ Politics1

Politics1 offers more than 1,000 links to political sites, all neatly arranged and annotated. The obvious care taken in building the site and its thoroughness have quickly made Politics1 one of the premier political sites on the Internet.

Perhaps the highlight is the section about U.S. presidential candidates. For each candidate, Politics1 provides a link to the official campaign site, links to unofficial and opposition sites, biographical details, a partial list of endorse-ments, and information about any books written by or about the candidate. Dozens of candidates are covered, ranging from announced major party candidates to obscure independents. The presidential section also has a handy calendar of all presidential primaries and caucuses and links to other sites that offer information about the presidential election.

Another impressive section offers extensive state political links. For each state, there are links to Web sites of the candidates for governor, U.S. Senate, and U.S. House of Representatives; state election offices; state newspapers; and state political parties.

Politics1 also provides a huge list of links to sites operated by major and minor political parties (along with a detailed description of each party), links to dozens of issue-oriented Web sites, and links to numerous sources of political news.

Finally, Politics1 publishes an extremely useful e-mail newsletter called Politics1 Report.

Vital Stats:

Access method: WWW
To access: http://www.politics1.com

✓✓ Project Vote Smart

Project Vote Smart is a political junkie's dream come true. Through thousands of pages of original material and links to other sites, it provides a huge array of information about campaigns, elections, political leaders, and government.

Perhaps its most impressive section provides extensive information about more than 13,000 candidates for president, Congress, governor, and state legislator. For each candidate, the site provides a biography, positions on issues, voting record, campaign finance data, contact details, and ratings by various special interest groups.

Another highlight is the CongressTrack section, which provides information about the status of major bills, floor schedules for the House and Senate, details about how individual members voted on bills, congressional committee information, and links to all the major Internet sites about Congress.

Project Vote Smart also offers a superb collection of links to sites about dozens of political issues. Some of the topics covered include abortion, AIDS, animal issues, campaign finance, citizen participation, civil liberties, crime, defense, education, foreign policy, gender issues, government reform, gun control, health care, immigration, labor, media and communications, taxes, tobacco, and violence.

Other highlights include links for each state to sites run by courts, governments, interest groups, the news media, political parties, and think tanks; the text of ballot initiatives from states around the country; results from past federal and state elections; lesson plans and resources for teachers and students; links to political news sources, online political magazines, and think tanks; and a political source book for reporters.

Project Vote Smart is the major program of the Center for National Independence in Politics. The center is a nonpartisan, nonprofit organization that provides voters with information about issues and candidates.

Vital Stats:

Access method: WWW
To access: http://www.vote-smart.org

✓ WebActive

WebActive provides more than 2,000 annotated links to Web sites aimed at progressive political activists. The links are divided into more than forty subjects, including AIDS/HIV issues, animal rights, children's issues, civil rights, elections and politics, food and nutrition, health care, housing and shelter, human rights, international affairs, labor, media watch organizations, nonviolence and physical safety, peace, religion, and social justice. You also can browse the links alphabetically or search them using keywords.

WebActive also offers broadcasts of progressive radio programs, including Pacifica Network News, RadioNation, Democracy NOW!, Hightower Radio, and CounterSpin.

WebActive is provided by RealNetworks, the makers of RealAudio and other computer software.

Vital Stats:

Access method: WWW
To access: http://www.webactive.com

Web White & Blue

After lying dormant since the 1998 election, Web White & Blue was still in the planning phase for the 2000 election when this book was being written. The site is sponsored by the Markle Foundation, among other organizations.

In 1998 the site provided links to just under four dozen of what it considered the best election directories and voter information sites on the Internet. The links were divided into six categories: voter info, issues, election news, campaigns, your state, and participate. Although the site's exact focus in 2000 is still unknown, it's expected once again to provide links to a select number of political Web sites.

Vital Stats:

Access method: WWW
To access: http://www.webwhiteblue.org

✓ Yahoo! Issues and Causes

This page from Yahoo! provides links to more than 3,000 Web sites about various political issues and causes. The links are divided into dozens of subjects, including abortion, affirmative action, campaign finance reform, climate change policy, church and state, conservation, the death penalty, euthanasia, firearms policy, global warming, health care policy, human rights, immigration reform, Internet policy, language policy, militia movement, population, poverty, race relations, Social Security reform, stadium taxes, tax reform, term limits, and weapons disarmament and nonproliferation.

Vital Stats:

Access method: WWW
To access: http://dir.yahoo.com/Society_and_Culture/
                         Issues_and_Causes

2

Government

FEDERAL

Directories

✓✓ Federal Government Resources on the Web

This site offers a great collection of annotated links to federal government Internet sites. It's operated by the University of Michigan Documents Center, which is part of the University of Michigan Library.

The links are divided into more than a dozen categories: agency directories and Web sites, bibliographies, budget, civil service, copyright, executive branch, executive orders, General Accounting Office, grants and contracts, historic documents, judicial branch, laws and constitution, legislative branch, Office of Management and Budget, patents, president, regulations, taxes, and White House.

The site also has a special set of links to government documents related to recent news events. To reach the Government Documents in the News page directly, use the address http://www.lib.umich.edu/libhome/Documents.center/docnews.html.

Vital Stats:

Access method: WWW
To access   http://www.lib.umich.edu/libhome/Documents.center/
                       federal.html

✓ The Federal Web Locator

The Federal Web Locator provides links to hundreds of Web sites operated by federal agencies and departments. The links are divided into seven categories: federal legislative branch; federal judicial branch; federal executive branch (with departments); federal independent establishments and government corporations; federal government consortium and quasi-official agencies; federal boards, commissions, and committees; and nongovernmental federally related sites. You can browse through the listings by category or search for agency or organization names using keywords.

The Federal Web Locator is operated by the Illinois Institute of Technology's Chicago-Kent College of Law. The institute also operates the State Web Locator (p. 40).

Vital Stats:

Access method: WWW

To access: http://www.infoctr.edu/fwl

✓ Frequently Used Sites Related to U.S. Federal Government Information

This excellent site provides links to dozens of federal Web sites that are among those used most frequently by government documents librarians. It's operated by the Federal Documents Task Force of the Government Documents Round Table, which is associated with the American Library Association.

The annotated links are divided by subject: business and economics; census; Congress; consumer information; copyright, patents, and trademarks; crime and justice; education; foreign countries; health and welfare; impeachment; laws and regulations; major indexes; natural resources; president and executive branch; scientific and technical reports; statistics; the Supreme Court; tax forms; travel; and voting and elections.

Vital Stats:

Access method: WWW

To access: http://www.library.vanderbilt.edu/central/staff/fdtf.html

---

✓✓ INFOMINE

The government page at INFOMINE is an attempt by librarians to tame federal information on the Internet and catalog the available resources. While any such effort is by definition incomplete, INFOMINE is a great place to start a search for government information on the Internet. INFOMINE is provided by librarians at the University of California.

The links are divided into thousands of subjects, and you can browse the links by subject, title, or keywords. You also can search the listings. Each listing provides an excellent description of what's available at the linked site. INFOMINE's What's New section is a particularly useful resource for keeping up with new government Internet sites.

Vital Stats:

Access method: WWW

To access: http://www.infomine.ucr.edu/search/govpubsearch.phtml

✓✓ United States Government Information

The United States Government Information site is one of the best places to start a search for federal information on the Internet. It offers hundreds of annotated links to federal Internet sites, divided by dozens of subjects.

Some of the subjects available include affirmative action and civil rights, climate and weather, consumer information, crime, demographics and statistics, economic and business information, education, elections, environment, foreign affairs and international aid, health and medical information, historic documents and exhibits, legislation, patents and trademarks, and welfare and welfare reform.

The site is operated by the Government Publications Library at the University of Colorado, which deserves three cheers for putting together this great resource.

Vital Stats:

Access method: WWW
To access: http://www-libraries.colorado.edu/ps/gov/us/federal.htm

---

✓✓ U.S. Government Documents Ready Reference Collection

This site provides links to dozens of the most requested federal government publications. It's operated by the Documents Service Center at Columbia University Libraries.

The links are divided into the following categories: agriculture, business and economics, census, crime and justice, education, energy, environment, foreign countries, general sources, government and law, health, military, minerals and mining, science and engineering, and transportation.

The site has links to electronic versions of the *Catalog of U.S. Government Publications, County and City Data Book, Statistical Abstract of the United States, Agriculture Fact Book, Census of Manufactures, Commerce Business Daily, Monthly Labor Review, Occupational Outlook Handbook, Social Security Handbook, State and Metropolitan Area Data Book, Compendium of Federal Justice Statistics, Hate Crime Statistics, Immigration to the United States, Sourcebook of Criminal Justice Statistics, Terrorism in the United States, Uniform Crime Reports of the United States, Digest of Education Statistics, Annual Energy Outlook, Code of Federal Regulations, Congressional Record, Federal Register, Where to Write for Vital Records, Arms Control and Disarmament Agreements,*

National Military Strategy of the United States, and *World Military Expenditures and Arms Transfers,* among many others.

Vital Stats:

Access method: WWW
To access: http://www.cc.columbia.edu/cu/libraries/indiv/dsc/
                   readyref.html

Congress

Committee Hearings

This bare-bones site, which is operated by the House of Representatives, offers transcripts of selected hearings by House committees. What's available varies widely by committee: some committees have posted transcripts from 1997 to the present, some have posted a few transcripts from 1997 or 1998 but haven't updated anything since, and some committees have posted nothing at all.

The hearings are separated by committee, but unfortunately there is no search engine. This means you have to browse manually through each committee's offerings to find what you want.

Vital Stats:

Access method: WWW
To access: http://commdocs.house.gov/committees

Committee on Rules

This site has a huge collection of materials about the legislative process. It's operated by the Committee on Rules in the House of Representatives.

The site's highlight is dozens of reports by the Congressional Research Service. Some of the available titles are *Legislative Research in Congressional Offices: A Primer; How to Follow Current Federal Legislation and Regulations; Hearings in the House of Representatives: A Guide for Preparation and Conduct; Investigative Oversight: An Introduction to the Law, Practice, and Procedure of Congressional Inquiry; How Measures are Brought to the House Floor: A Brief Introduction; A Brief Introduction to the Federal Budget Process;* and *Presidential Vetoes 1789–1996: A Summary Overview.*

The site also has the full text of the House rules manual, descriptions of House procedures, and a guide to the federal budget process.

Vital Stats:

Access method: WWW
To access: http://www.house.gov/rules

Congress Today

This site's highlight is a searchable database of congressional votes from 1996 to the present. You can search it by member, subject, or month. C-SPAN operates the site.

Other highlights include schedules of House and Senate actions for the current day, a calendar of House and Senate committee hearings for the current month, a congressional directory, and a Write to Congress feature that helps you send e-mail to the members of Congress who represent you.

Vital Stats:

Access method: WWW
To access: http://congress.nw.dc.us/c-span

The Hill

The Hill, a weekly newspaper that covers Capitol Hill, is published each Wednesday. On its Web site, the paper offers selected news stories, columns, articles about political campaigns, and classified ads.

The most impressive feature at the site is HillLinks, a very handy congressional directory. The directory offers no original information, but through a well-chosen set of links it provides extensive information about each member of Congress, including a biography, campaign finance reports, a list of legislation sponsored, ratings by special interest groups, and personal financial disclosure reports.

Another interesting feature on the Resources page of this site is a list of political action committees run by politicians, commonly referred to as leadership PACs. Through links, the newspaper provides campaign finance reports for each committee.

Vital Stats:

Access method: WWW
To access: http://www.hillnews.com

HillSource

The HillSource site, operated by the House Republican Conference, provides digests of activities in the U.S. House of Representatives, publications about Republican positions on various issues, press releases from House Republican leaders, and media advisories.

Vital Stats:

Access method: WWW
To access: http://hillsource.house.gov

✓ Library of Congress Information System (LOCIS)

LOCIS allows you to track bills and resolutions introduced in the U.S. Congress from 1973 to the present. The Library of Congress operates the site.

The legislative databases provide tracking and descriptive information for every bill introduced. Each database covers a separate Congress, and you can search the databases separately or together.

For each bill, the database lists the official title, the bill number, the sponsor(s), the committee(s) where it was referred, the subcommittee(s) where it was referred, all actions taken regarding the bill, and a detailed summary of the legislation. The database does not include the full texts of bills or information about how specific members of Congress voted.

Most information in the legislative databases is current. For example, bill numbers, official titles, sponsors, and status changes are added within forty-eight hours. However, indexing terms and digests are recorded later, sometimes several weeks after the bill is added to the database.

You can search the legislative databases by subject, member's name, keywords, bill number, public law number, and committee name.

Vital Stats:

Access method: Telnet
To access: telnet://locis.loc.gov
Availability: Most parts of LOCIS are available twenty-four hours a day
                          except from 5:00 P.M. Saturday to noon Sunday, EST.
                          However, some catalog commands are unavailable
                          Sunday through Friday from 9:30 P.M. to 6:30 A.M. LOCIS
                          also is unavailable on national holidays.

The Majority Whip

The Majority Whip site provides minute-by-minute accounts of activities on the floor of the U.S. House of Representatives, with links to bills that are being debated. The site is operated by House majority whip Tom DeLay.

The site also has a House calendar, speeches by DeLay, and electronic versions of *The Whipping Post* and *The Whip Notice,* which report on upcoming House activities. *The Whipping Post* is published daily when Congress is voting, and *The Whip Notice* is published weekly when Congress is in session. Both publications also are available through e-mail subscriptions.

Vital Stats:

Access method: WWW
To access: http://majoritywhip.house.gov

The Office of the Clerk On-line Information Center

This site, which is operated by the Office of the Clerk of the U.S. House of Representatives, has records of all roll-call votes taken in the House since 1990. The votes are recorded by bill, so compiling a particular representative's voting record is a lengthy process.

The site also contains lists of committee assignments, a telephone directory for members and committees, mailing label templates for members and committees, rules of the House, information about the types of documents that are available from the Legislative Resource Center, federal election statistics from 1920 to the present, electoral college results from 1789 to the present, biographies of Speakers of the House, biographies of women who have served since 1917, and a virtual tour of the House Chamber.

Vital Stats:

Access method: WWW
To access: http://clerkweb.house.gov

Roll Call Online

Roll Call is a biweekly newspaper that covers the people and politics of Capitol Hill. The paper posts its top stories online every Monday and Thursday, along with editorials, election news, commentary, cartoons, and classified ads. The paper's Web site also offers a searchable congressional directory.

Vital Stats:

Access method: WWW
To access: http://www.rollcall.com

✓✓ THOMAS

Through original documents and links to other sites, THOMAS is a one-stop source for congressional information. The Library of Congress operates the site.

THOMAS's biggest highlight is its collection of searchable databases. They offer the full text of all bills introduced in Congress from 1989 to the present; summaries of bills introduced in Congress since 1975; information about the status of all bills; and reports by House and Senate committees.

You can search most of the bills databases by keyword, subject term, bill or amendment number, stage in legislative process, date, sponsor or cosponsor, and committee where the bill was referred.

Two special pages provide links to the hottest bills currently or recently considered by Congress. The Congress in the News page provides links to bills that received lots of news coverage, and the Major Legislation page has links to bills deemed especially significant by the Congressional Research Service. Both pages are arranged by topic.

Some of the site's other highlights include the full text of the *Congressional Record* dating back to 1990, publications titled *How Our Laws Are Made* and *Enactment of a Law,* and links to hearing schedules and oversight plans by House and Senate committees.

Vital Stats:

Access method: WWW
To access: http://thomas.loc.gov

✓ The United States Senate

The United States Senate site has everything from a virtual tour of the U.S. Capitol to explanations of the legislative process.

This site offers senators' voting records (divided by bill), schedules of upcoming committee meetings and hearings, a list of pending items on the Senate floor, the Senate legislative calendar, the *Standing Rules of the Senate,* and a list of committee reports issued during the previous week.

It also provides contact information for senators, links to the home pages of those senators and committees that are online, a glossary of Senate terms, and a bibliography of publications about the Senate.

Vital Stats:

Access method: WWW
To access: http://www.senate.gov

✓✓ U.S. Government Printing Office

This site's highlight is GPO Access, a collection of databases that provide a huge amount of federal information. Much of the information concerns Congress, but there are also lots of documents from the executive and judicial branches.

GPO Access includes dozens of databases. Some of the most interesting congressional databases provide the full text of bills introduced in Congress, the *Congressional Record,* daily House and Senate calendars, selected House and Senate reports, and General Accounting Office reports.

Other important databases offer the federal budget, the *Code of Federal Regulations,* the U.S. Code, the *Federal Register,* the *Economic Report of the President,* an electronic version of the most recent *United States Government Manual,* and Supreme Court decisions from 1937 to 1975.

The site also has the full text of the *Statistical Abstract of the United States;* a database containing the *Monthly Catalog of United States Government Publications;* more than 150 subject bibliographies that list publications, periodicals, and electronic products available for sale by the GPO; a database listing federal depository libraries; information about U.S. government bookstores around the country; and much, much more.

Vital Stats:

Access method: WWW
To access: http://www.access.gpo.gov

✓ U.S. House of Representatives

The U.S. House of Representatives site provides a wealth of congressional information. It has up-to-the-minute reports about current actions on the House floor, schedules of upcoming floor and committee votes and hearings, a link to the full texts of bills introduced in Congress, and a link to the *Congressional Record.*

The site also provides the full text of *How Our Laws Are Made,* the House ethics manual, the Declaration of Independence, the U.S. Constitution, and amendments to the Constitution that have been proposed but not yet ratified, as well as links to Web pages operated by House members and committees.

Vital Stats:

Access method: WWW
To access: http://www.house.gov

✓ U.S. Legislative Branch

This page, maintained by the Library of Congress, provides a superb collection of links to sites about Congress and the legislative process.

The links are grouped into the following topics: about Congress, official congressional Internet sites, congressional mega sources, members, committees, congressional organizations, e-mail addresses, congressional schedules, congressional calendars, floor proceedings, legislation, U.S. Code, House and Senate Rules, *Congressional Record* and journals, roll call votes, executive business of the Senate, legislative process, congressional news and analysis, the history of Congress, and visitor information.

Many of the main topics are divided by sub-topics. For example, the legislation topic is divided into the following sub-topics: about legislation; comprehensive sites for bills, amendments, and laws; Congress this week; major bills and amendments; appropriations bills; bills in conference; bill and amendment summaries and status; full text of legislation; discharge petitions; laws enacted; bills vetoed by the president; and line item vetoes.

Vital Stats:

Access method:	WWW
To access:	http://lcweb.loc.gov/global/legislative/congress.html

Courts

✓ The Federal Court Locator

The Federal Court Locator provides opinions from the Third Circuit Court of Appeals. It also has links to sites that offer opinions from all the other circuit courts, dozens of U.S. district courts, and the U.S. Supreme Court.

The Federal Court Locator is operated by the Villanova University School of Law. Villanova also operates the State Court Locator (p. 37).

Vital Stats:

Access method:	WWW
To access:	http://vls.law.vill.edu/Locator/fedcourt.html

✓ FindLaw

The FindLaw site provides a searchable database of U.S. Supreme Court opinions from 1893 to the present. It's operated by FindLaw, a private company.

You can browse the database by year and *United States Reports* volume number, and you can search it by citation, party name, and keywords. Presented in

HTML format, the cases have hyperlinks to previous decisions that have been loaded on the site.

The FindLaw site also has recent Supreme Court news from Reuters, links to lots of other Internet sites that offer Supreme Court information, and a copy of the U.S. Constitution that has hyperlinks to relevant Supreme Court decisions through June 29, 1992.

Vital Stats:

Access method: WWW
To access: http://www.findlaw.com/casecode/supreme.html

✓✓ Legal Information Institute

This site's highlight is its collection of U.S. Supreme Court decisions from May 1990 to the present. New decisions are posted the same day they're released by the Court. Cornell Law School's Legal Information Institute operates the site, and also operates a mailing list called liibulletin that sends out syllabi of Supreme Court decisions as they're placed on the Internet.

In addition to recent Supreme Court decisions, the site offers nearly 600 historic pre-1990 Supreme Court decisions in cases involving such topics as abortion, administrative law, copyright and trademarks, and school prayer; the Court's current calendar; a schedule of oral arguments; Supreme Court rules; and pictures, biographies, and lists of decisions by current Court members.

Of particular interest is a page that has links to recent newsworthy decisions of state and federal courts around the United States. To reach the page directly, use the address http://www.law.cornell.edu/focus/liieye.htm.

Other highlights include:

- A search engine that provides access to decisions of all U.S. Circuit Courts of Appeals. For most circuits, opinions from 1995 to the present can be searched.

- Links to constitutions, statutes, judicial opinions, and related legal materials from countries around the world.

- Links to state legal materials. Where available, for each state there are links to the constitution, statutes, pending bills, legislative directories, judicial opinions, and regulations, among other materials.

- The full text of the U.S. Code.

- The *Federal Rules of Evidence* and the *Federal Rules of Civil Procedure.*

Vital Stats:

Access method: WWW
To access: http://www.law.cornell.edu

liibulletin

The liibulletin is a mailing list that sends out syllabi of U.S. Supreme Court decisions as they're placed on the Internet, along with instructions about how to obtain the full texts of the decisions. The list is operated by Cornell Law School's Legal Information Institute.

Vital Stats:

Access method: E-mail
To access: Send an e-mail message to listserv@listserv.law.cornell.edu
Subject line:
Message: **subscribe liibulletin *firstname lastname***

White House

E-Mail to the White House

You can send e-mail to the president, the vice president, the first lady, and the vice president's wife through the Internet. But don't expect to develop a regular e-mail correspondence with the White House.

That's because there's no system for e-mail replies from the White House. You'll get an e-mail acknowledgment when you send a message, but you won't get a personalized response. If you want a personal response, you have to include your postal address in your message.

Here are the White House addresses:

- President Bill Clinton: president@whitehouse.gov

- Vice President Al Gore: vice.president@whitehouse.gov

- First Lady Hillary Rodham Clinton: first.lady@whitehouse.gov

- Vice President's Wife Tipper Gore: mrs.gore@whitehouse.gov

If you prefer, you can send e-mail to the White House through electronic forms located at http://www.whitehouse.gov/WH/EOP/html/principals.html.

Vital Stats:

Access method: E-mail
To access: Send e-mail messages as described

✓ The Impeachment of President Clinton

This page from the University of North Texas Libraries offers a great selection of documents related to Independent Counsel Kenneth Starr's investigation of President Bill Clinton.

Through documents loaded at the site and links to other sites, it provides Starr's initial report and supplemental materials, a transcript of Clinton's grand jury testimony, White House responses to Starr's report, a letter from Starr in which he did not rule out further impeachment referrals, remarks by Clinton at the Religious Leaders Breakfast, the independent counsel statute, Senate impeachment rules, House of Representatives resolutions and reports, various documents from the 1974 impeachment inquiry involving Richard Nixon, and other documents.

Vital Stats:

Access method:	WWW
To access:	http://www.library.unt.edu/govinfo/impeach/ impeachpage.html

Welcome to the White House

This site offers a huge collection of White House documents, such as speeches by the president and transcripts of press briefings. You can search all the White House documents released since the beginning of the Clinton administration, the contents of this site, executive orders, recordings of the president's Saturday radio addresses, and White House photographs.

The site also has links to federal Internet sites (arranged by agency and topic), information about White House offices and agencies such as the Council of Economic Advisers and the Office of Management and Budget, portraits and biographies of each president and first lady, and the White House for Kids, a section that offers basic information about the president, the vice president, and children and pets who have lived in the White House.

Vital Stats:

Access method:	WWW
To access:	http://www.whitehouse.gov

✓ White House Publications

Through this Web page, you can sign up to receive new White House publications automatically by e-mail. The Quick Interface option lets you subscribe to documents in more than twenty categories, and the Custom Interface option lets you fine-tune your subscription to specific documents.

Categories available include computers and communications; daily press briefings; economy; education; environment; everything; executive acts; foreign affairs; government activities; healthcare; instructions (FAQs); international security and defense; justice and crime; legislation; party politics; personnel announcements; policy briefings; remarks by the president, vice president, and first lady; science; science and technology; social issues; speeches on major topics; and technology.

Vital Stats:

Access method: WWW
To access: http://www.pub.whitehouse.gov/publications/
                  subscription-registration.html

STATE

Court Web Sites

The National Center for State Courts provides this directory, which has links to more than 150 Web sites operated by state and local courts around the United States. The links are divided by state. The directory also provides a small selection of links to sites operated by foreign courts.

Vital Stats:

Access method: WWW
To access: http://www.ncsc.dni.us/court/sites/courts.htm

Full-Text State Statutes and Legislation on the Internet

This page is a directory of links to state constitutions, statutes, legislation, and administrative rules that are available on the Internet. The links are divided by state. The page is maintained by a private individual.

Vital Stats:

Access method: WWW
To access: http://www.prairienet.org/~scruffy/f.htm

---

gov.topic.info.systems.epub, GOVPUB

Readers of the gov.topic.info.systems.epub newsgroup, which is mirrored on the GOVPUB mailing list, discuss practical and policy issues involved in putting state and local government information online. Some of the issues discussed include freedom of information laws, government use of electronic publishing, Internet voting, and privacy policies.

Vital Stats:

Access methods: Usenet newsgroup, e-mail list
To access
  (Usenet):   news:gov.topic.info.systems.epub
To access
  (mailing list): Send an e-mail message to listserv@listserv.nodak.edu
Subject line:
Message: **subscribe GOVPUB *firstname lastname***

Internet Sites of the State Legislatures

This directory provides links to Web sites operated by every state legislature in the United States. For some states, the links are broken down by chamber or party. The site also has links to dozens of Web sites operated by legislators from various states. The directory is provided by the National Conference of State Legislatures.

Vital Stats:

Access method: WWW
To access: http://www.ncsl.org/public/sitesleg.htm

✓ NGA Online

The National Governors' Association operates this site, which offers lots of useful information about political issues affecting the states.

The best feature is a collection of pages about key state issues. The pages vary in what they offer, but they commonly have a brief summary of the issue, links to related NGA publications, testimony about the topic, links to articles and reports from federal agencies and other sources, and links to Web sites about the topic operated by advocacy groups, government agencies, and research centers.

The issues pages cover more than two dozen topics, including children and families, cleanup of nuclear weapons facilities, education reform, electric industry restructuring, environmental regulatory programs, health insurance trends, juvenile crime, managed care oversight and quality, rural health, school violence, smart growth, telecommunications and information services, welfare reform, and workforce development.

Another set of pages tackles federal-state issues. Each page provides background about the topic, describes recent actions by Congress and the administration, and discusses the effects of federal actions on the states. There are pages about trends in private health insurance coverage, the tobacco settlement, improving the information technology workforce, youth mentoring programs, open spaces, underground storage tanks, and rural health care delivery.

Other highlights include updates about congressional activities affecting the states on issues ranging from education to Medicare reform; office addresses, telephone numbers, and Web site links for each governor; biographies of each governor; links to the press release page at each governor's Web site; lists of states with gubernatorial elections in the next two years; results from gubernatorial elections around the country; and state-of-the-state and inaugural addresses by many governors.

Vital Stats:

Access method: WWW
To access: http://www.nga.org

✓ State and Local Government on the Net

If you're trying to track down Internet sites operated by state and local governments in the United States, this site is the place to start. It offers thousands of links, separated by state.

The number of links varies by state, but most states have dozens. For most states, the site has links to the official state home page, as well as official pages for the governor, secretary of state, attorney general, legislature, courts, executive branch departments and agencies, boards and commissions, regional governments, counties, and cities.

Besides the state links, there are links to sites operated by tribal governments, governments of U.S. territories, multistate organizations, and state and local government associations. Piper Resources, a private firm, operates the site.

Vital Stats:

Access method: WWW
To access: http://www.piperinfo.com/state/states.html

✓✓ State and Local Government on the Web

This page from the University of Michigan Documents Center provides links to dozens of the best state and local government sites on the Internet. Many of the sites are directories of sites about specific topics.

The state links are divided by more than a dozen subjects: associations, bibliographies, comprehensive listings of state Internet sites, congressional delegations by state, courts, forms, jobs, laws, legislatures and proposed legislation, Michigan, statistics, tax forms, and think tanks. The local links are divided by three topics: associations, comprehensive listings of local Internet sites, and municipal codes.

Vital Stats:

Access method: WWW
To access: http://www.lib.umich.edu/libhome/Documents.center/
                              state.html

✓ The State Court Locator

The State Court Locator provides links to Web sites operated by state and local courts around the country. The links are divided by state.

The available links vary by state, but for many states there are links to state supreme court opinions, court of appeals decisions, court libraries, court rules, and county and municipal courts.

The State Court Locator is operated by the Villanova University School of Law. Villanova also operates the Federal Court Locator (p. 29).

Vital Stats:

Access method: WWW
To access: http:/vls.law.vill.edu/Locator/statecourt/index.htm

---

State Government Home Pages

Each state government has a home page that serves as a gateway into its Internet sites. These home pages are a great way to quickly learn what kinds of information a state has placed online.

Home pages typically offer dozens of links to sites about the governor and executive branch, the legislature, courts, tourism, business opportunities, libraries, schools, and many other subjects. Most home pages only offer links to other official government sites, although some also provide links to private sites.

Vital Stats:

Access method: WWW
To access: See State Home Pages (in box, p. 38)

State Legislative Look Up

Do you know who represents you in the state legislature? If you don't, this page from Common Cause can help. Just type your zip code in the box, and the site will provide the names of your state representative and senator, along with their postal addresses, telephone numbers, fax numbers, e-mail addresses, and Web page addresses where available. You also can search the site by state or by the legislator's name.

Vital Stats:

Access method: WWW
To access: http://www.commoncause.org/
                    cgi-bin/congress.pl?cf=ccause/stateleg.cf

State Home Pages

Alabama http://www.state.al.us

Alaska http://www.state.ak.us

Arizona http://www.state.az.us

Arkansas http://www.state.ar.us

California http://www.ca.gov

Colorado http://www.state.co.us

Connecticut http://www.state.ct.us

Delaware http://www.state.de.us

Florida http://fcn.state.fl.us/gsd

Georgia http://www.state.ga.us

Hawaii http://www.hawaii.gov

Idaho http://www.state.id.us

Illinois http://www.state.il.us

Indiana http://www.state.in.us

Iowa http://www.state.ia.us

Kansas http://www.state.ks.us

Kentucky http://www.state.ky.us

Louisiana http://www.state.la.us

Maine http://janus.state.me.us/
homepage.asp

Maryland http://www.mec.state.md.
us/mec

Massachusetts http://www.magnet.
state.ma.us

Michigan http://www.migov.state.
mi.us

Minnesota http://www.state.mn.us

Mississippi http://www.state.ms.us

Missouri http://www.state.mo.us

Montana http://www.mt.gov

Nebraska http://www.state.ne.us

Nevada http://www.state.nv.us

New Hampshire http://www.state.
nh.us

New Jersey http://www.state.nj.us

New Mexico http://www.state.nm.us

New York http://www.state.ny.us

North Carolina http://www.sips.state.
nc.us

North Dakota http://www.state.nd.us

Ohio http://www.ohio.gov

Oklahoma http://www.oklaosf.state.
ok.us

Oregon http://www.state.or.us

Pennsylvania http://www.state.pa.us

Rhode Island http://www.state.ri.us

South Carolina http://www.state.sc.us

South Dakota http://www.state.sd.us

Tennessee http://www.state.tn.us

Texas http://www.state.tx.us

Utah http://www.state.ut.us

Vermont http://www.cit.state.vt.us

Virginia http://www.state.va.us

Washington http://access.wa.gov

West Virginia http://www.state.wv.us

Wisconsin http://www.state.wi.us

Wyoming http://www.state.wy.us

✓✓ stateline.org

Anyone interested in public policy at the state level should bookmark this marvelous site and check it daily. Through original articles, links to stories from newspapers around the country, and state-level data obtained from sources such as the U.S. Census Bureau, it provides an excellent collection of state policy information. It's operated by the Pew Center on the States.

The site's highlight is its daily summaries of state policy stories from newspapers nationwide. The 60–100 summaries posted on a typical day all have links to the full stories. New summaries are posted each weekday at 11 A.M. eastern standard time.

You also can search the story archive by keyword or date range. A search for stories about a particular state typically returns between several dozen and several hundred articles.

Another key feature is the Issues page, which leads to information about health care, welfare reform, taxes and budget, education, and utility deregulation. For each issue, there's background information, comparison data for the fifty states, links to Web sites about the issue, and links to newspaper stories about state actions regarding the issue.

Another feature not to be missed is the States page. For each state, it provides a link to the state's home page on the Internet, information about the governor, party breakdowns in the state legislature, policy-related news stories, and extensive data that you can use to rank the state in relation to others on a variety of topics. The site has statistics about such topics as average auto insurance costs, median household income, number of executions, percentage of people living in poverty, per capita federal and state tax burden, per inmate spending, state corrections expenditures, state environmental agency budgets, state prison incarceration rate per 100,000 residents, and the unemployment rate.

The site also operates a superb current awareness service that you can sign up for at http://www.stateline.org/maillistsignup.cfm. The service alerts you by e-mail when a major news story is posted at the site about a particular state or issue that you choose. The available issues are campaign finance, education, gambling, guns, health care, land use and sprawl, prisons and corrections, taxes and budget, utility deregulation, and welfare reform.

Vital Stats:

Access method: WWW
To access: http://www.stateline.org

StateSearch

StateSearch is designed to be a topical clearinghouse to state government information on the Internet. It's operated by the National Association of State Information Resource Executives.

The site provides more than 2,300 links to sites operated by state agencies and departments. The links are arranged by more than two dozen topics: administration and finance; agriculture; arts commissions; auditors; constitutions; corrections; criminal justice; disabilities agencies; economic development and commerce; education; employment services; energy, environment, and natural resources; governors; health and human services; home pages; information technology; judiciary; legal opinions; legislatures; lieutenant governors; older adult services; other; public safety/state policy; purchasing/procurement; regulation and licensing; revenue; state libraries; statutes; tourism; transportation; treasurers; and year 2000 offices.

The site was experiencing some technical difficulties when this book was being written, but they may be cleared up by the time you access it.

Vital Stats:

Access method: WWW
To access: http://www.nasire.org/stateSearch

StatesNews

Much of the information at this site, which is operated by the Council of State Governments, is available only to state government officials and members of their staffs. However, each weekday the site posts public links to dozens of articles about state actions from newspapers around the country. The public also can access updates about congressional actions that affect the states.

Although the links are divided by subject, they are not archived.

Vital Stats:

Access method: WWW
To access: http://www.statesnews.org

✓ The State Web Locator

The State Web Locator provides links to hundreds of Web sites operated by government officials and agencies in the fifty states, the District of Columbia, Puerto Rico, the Virgin Islands, and the Mariana Islands.

The number of links varies among the states, but often there are dozens of links for a particular state. For many states, the site provides links to the state home page and pages for the governor, lieutenant governor, secretary of state, attorney general, legislature, and individual departments and agencies.

The State Web Locator is operated by the Illinois Institute of Technology's Chicago-Kent College of Law. The institute also operates the Federal Web Locator (p. 20).

Vital Stats:

Access method: WWW
To access: http://www.infoctr.edu/swl

LOCAL

Linkages in the Urban Politics Section

This page provides links to dozens of Web sites related to cities and urban politics. The links are divided by subject: agencies; associations; cities on the Net; city listings; city sites; community activism, politics, and legislation; data and datasets; news media; policy issues and urban services; and research organizations. The page was created by the Urban Politics section of the American Political Science Association.

Vital Stats:

Access method: WWW
To access: http://thecity.sfsu.edu/~urbanpol/links.html

---

munisource

This site from the Maritime Municipal Training and Development Board in Canada provides links to more than 3,500 official city and county Web sites in thirty-three countries. Most of the links are to sites in Canada and the United States.

Vital Stats:

Access method: WWW
To access: http://www.munisource.org

National Association of Counties

A database at this site provides basic information about every county in the United States. For each county, the site lists the population, names of county officials, and the county government's address, telephone number, and fax number, besides providing links to the county's Web site (where available) and to other Internet sites that have data about the county. The National Association of Counties operates the site.

The site also offers legislative fact sheets and research publications about everything from airport improvements to county referendums, a weekly report about congressional actions that affect counties, descriptions of model county programs, a code of ethics for county officials, links to codes from dozens of counties, links to hundreds of Web sites operated by counties, and much more.

Vital Stats:

Access method: WWW
To access: http://www.naco.org

National Association of Towns and Townships

This small site from the National Association of Towns and Townships offers descriptions of the association's legislative priorities and excerpts from a monthly report about recent federal actions that affect local communities.

Vital Stats:

Access method: WWW
To access: http://www.natat.org/natat/Default.htm

National League of Cities

This site from the National League of Cities offers a small collection of issue papers. They provide background about the topic, describe its effect on cities, list recent congressional actions, and suggest actions that city officials can take. There are papers about electric utility deregulation, financial services reform, juvenile justice, and enhanced 911 service, among other topics.

The site also has press releases about new reports from the league, although the reports themselves are not online.

Vital Stats:

Access method: WWW
To access: http://www.nlc.org

Official City Sites

This site provides links to thousands of city and county Web sites, most of which are operated by city and county governments. The United States links, which dominate the site, are divided by state. There also are small groups of links to city sites in Australia, Canada, France, Germany, Japan, the Netherlands, and the United Kingdom. Private individuals operate the site.

Vital Stats:

Access method: WWW
To access: http://officialcitysites.org/country.htm

The U.S. Conference of Mayors

This site's highlight is the *U.S. Mayor Newspaper,* the official publication of the U.S. Conference of Mayors. Each issue has dozens of articles about issues that cities are facing, actions by mayors, and recent federal actions that affect cities.

The Mayors at a Glance database is another nice feature of this site. The information available varies for each mayor, but it frequently includes a photograph, telephone number, e-mail address, date of next election, city population, and link to the city's Web site. The database is fairly comprehensive but does not have information about every U.S. mayor. You can search the database by mayor's last name, city, state, or city population size.

The site also has press releases and a huge collection of links to Web sites operated by city governments around the United States. The links are divided by state.

Vital Stats:

Access method: WWW
To access: http://www.usmayors.org/USCM/home.html

FOREIGN

Address Directory—Politicians of the World

This site provides the names and postal addresses of the national leader and provincial governors in 195 countries around the world. Where available, it also provides the telephone number, fax number, e-mail address, and Web address for each politician.

Two separate pages list the e-mail addresses of dozens of heads of state and postal addresses, telephone numbers, and fax numbers of foreign affairs ministries worldwide.

Vital Stats:

Access method: WWW
To access: http://www.trytel.com/~aberdeen

Chiefs of State and Cabinet Members of Foreign Governments

For each country in the world, this electronic publication from the Central Intelligence Agency lists the names of the chief of state, cabinet members, the ambassador to the United States, and the representative to the United Nations. The CIA constantly updates the publication, so the information is very current.

Vital Stats:

Access method: WWW
To access: http://www.odci.gov/cia/publications/chiefs

Constitution Finder

Through documents loaded here and links to other sites, the Constitution Finder provides access to constitutions for dozens of nations. Drafts of constitutional documents also are provided for some countries. Most of the constitutions are in English, but some are in other languages. The T. C. Williams School of Law at the University of Richmond operates the site.

Vital Stats:

Access method: WWW
To access: http://www.urich.edu/~jpjones/confinder

The Electronic Embassy

Basic information about every foreign embassy in Washington, D.C., is available from the Electronic Embassy. For each embassy, where available the site offers the street address, telephone number, fax number, e-mail address, and a link to the embassy's Web site. Embassy sites often are great sources of information about the country that the embassy represents.

Vital Stats:

Access method: WWW
To access: http://www.embassy.org

✓ Foreign Government Information

This excellent directory arranges links to documents about foreign governments and issues by subject, providing easy access to a wide range of information about international affairs. The directory is produced by the government publications department at the University of Colorado at Boulder Libraries.

The links cover dozens of topics, including business and economic information, climate change, conflicts, elections, governments, health, human rights, labor statistics, law, military expenditures, news, terrorism, and treaties. The links primarily lead to documents produced by foreign governments, U.S. government agencies, international organizations such as the United Nations, and public policy groups.

Vital Stats:

Access method: WWW
To access: http://www-libraries.colorado.edu/ps/gov/for/foreign.htm

---

✓✓ Governments on the WWW

Whether you're seeking general or specific information about foreign governments, this extraordinary directory should be your first stop on the Internet. A private individual operates the site.

The directory has more than 14,000 links to sites operated by foreign parliaments, ministries, courts, embassies, city councils, public broadcasting corporations, central banks, multinational organizations, and political parties in 220 countries and territories.

You can access the links by country or type of institution. The number of links varies by country, based on the country's level of Internet development. Countries like Afghanistan have only a few links, for example, while France and other countries with greater Internet access have hundreds of links. The site names are listed in the directory in their original language, but the webmaster has helpfully translated them into English as well.

If you prefer to look for links by type of institution instead of country, check out the pages for elections, heads of state, multinational organizations, parliaments, political parties, and tourism, among others.

Vital Stats:

Access method: WWW
To access: http://www.gksoft.com/govt

✓✓ Inter-Parliamentary Union

The PARLINE database at this site provides an astounding amount of detailed information about every national parliament in the world. The site is operated by the Inter-Parliamentary Union, a world organization of parliaments that works closely with the United Nations.

For each parliamentary chamber, the database provides basic membership data, a description of the electoral system, results of the most recent elections, information about the presidency of the chamber, information about the mandate and status of members of parliament, postal address, telephone number, fax number, and a link to the chamber's Web site. A simple query retrieves all the information about a particular nation's parliament, and advanced search functions allow you to compare parliaments or search the entire database using keywords.

The site also offers reports about abuses of the human rights of parliamentary members in various countries; detailed data about the number of women in national parliaments in each country and worldwide; the PARLIT database, which contains bibliographic references to thousands of books and articles about national parliaments and electoral systems; links to Web sites operated by parliaments around the world; press releases; and documents about the IPU's activities in a number of areas, including promoting representative democracy and sustaining development.

Vital Stats:

Access method: WWW
To access: http://www.ipu.org

International Constitutional Law

The International Constitutional Law site provides national constitutions for dozens of countries, all translated into English. Draft constitutions and related documents also are available for some countries.

As a bonus, the site provides a brief explanation of events leading up to adoption of the constitution in each country. The site, which is managed by Wuerzburg University in Germany, also has links to other Internet sites that provide constitutions.

Vital Stats:

Access method: WWW
To access: http://www.uni-wuerzburg.de/law/home.html

✓ Political Science Resources: Foreign Politics

Links to some of the best Internet sites about foreign politics are provided by this page, which was created by the University of Michigan Documents Center. The links are divided into four major categories: comprehensive political sources, elections, individual country politics, and military affairs. Many of the links lead to directories of political sites.

Vital Stats:

Access method: WWW
To access: http://www.lib.umich.edu/libhome/Documents.center/
                   psfp.html

Web Sites on National Parliaments

From the Andoran Parliament to the Welsh National Assembly, this directory provides links to dozens of sites about national parliaments in countries around the world. Many of the sites are operated by the parliaments themselves, although some are operated by academics or other individuals or groups who monitor parliamentary activity.

The directory also has links to sites of a few international and regional parliamentary institutions such as the Assembly of the Western European Union and the United Nations, in addition to links to several other parliamentary directories. The directory is operated by the political science department at the University of Minnesota.

Vital Stats:

Access method: WWW
To access: http://www.polisci.umn.edu/information/parliaments

✓ Yahoo! Government: Countries

This page from Yahoo! (p. 17) provides links to governmental and political Web sites in more than 140 countries, from Afghanistan to Zimbabwe.

For many countries, the site provides dozens of links. What's available varies by country, but often there are links to sites maintained by the offices of the national leader, the legislature, embassies and consulates, national departments and agencies, and political parties.

Vital Stats:

Access method: WWW
To access: http://dir.yahoo.com/government/countries

3

International Organizations

Europa

The European Union operates this site, which is available in nearly a dozen languages. Its highlight is an extensive collection of information about EU institutions, including the European Parliament, Council of the European Union, European Commission, European Investment Bank, and European Central Bank. Links to Web sites operated by the institutions also are provided.

The site also has selected official EU documents, a database containing press releases from various EU institutions, a history of the organization, treaties that created the EU, various publications with background information about the EU, details about citizen rights conferred by the union, extensive statistical indicators for EU countries, newsletters, and links to Web sites operated by the fifteen EU countries.

Vital Stats:

Access method: WWW
To access: http://europa.eu.int

✓ Governments on the WWW: Multi-Governmental Organizations

This page at the Governments on the WWW site (p. 46) provides links to Web sites operated by a wide range of international organizations, from the European Union to the Arctic Council. The links are divided by continent. There's also a section of links to organizations like the United Nations that serve more than one continent.

Vital Stats:

Access method: WWW
To access: http://www.gksoft.com/govt/en/multi.html

✓✓ International Agencies and Information on the Web

This directory from the University of Michigan Documents Center is a great place to start a search for information about international organizations on the Web.

It begins by providing links to similar directories. Next, it has nicely annotated links to Web sites of dozens of inter-government organizations. The links are arranged alphabetically. The page concludes with numerous links to sites about international treaties.

Vital Stats:

Access method: WWW
To access: http://www.lib.umich.edu/libhome/Documents.
                  center/intl.html

International Monetary Fund

Dozens of International Monetary Fund reports are available in full text at this site. Some of the available titles include *Economic Adjustment and Reform in Low-Income Countries, Perspectives on Regional Unemployment in Europe, Ukraine—Recent Economic Developments,* and *How Persistent Are Shocks to World Commodity Prices?*

   The site also provides the text of various agreements between the IMF and individual member countries, reports about individual countries by IMF staff, fact sheets about such topics as the Asian financial crisis and composition of a support package for Brazil, background information about the IMF, speeches by IMF officials, transcripts of various press conferences and meetings, and press releases.

Vital Stats:

Access method: WWW
To access: http://www.imf.org

North Atlantic Treaty Organization

The NATO Web site provides updates about the alliance's current military operations, extensive background information about NATO, and various NATO treaties and political documents. The site is available in English and French.

   Other highlights include hundreds of photographs from NATO meetings and exercises, a large collection of documents about NATO's relationship with the United States, biographies and photographs of NATO's major officials and commanders, press releases and transcripts of press conferences, speeches by NATO officials, the full text of the *NATO Review* magazine from 1991 to the present, links to government and military Web sites operated by NATO member nations, and the full text of the *NATO Handbook,* which has chapters about everything from opening up the alliance to its military command structures.

Vital Stats:

Access method: WWW
To access: http://www.nato.int

Organization of American States

The official site of the Organization of American States, which was created in 1948 by a charter signed by twenty Latin American republics and the United States, offers documents about issues affecting the Americas. Most documents are available in both English and Spanish.

Highlights of the site include a calendar of upcoming elections in the Americas, publications about OAS observations of elections in such countries as Guatemala and Nicaragua, a link to documents about the Summit of the Americas, resolutions and declarations by the OAS general assembly, and speeches by the OAS secretary general.

The site also has the OAS charter, many inter-American treaties, model laws about drug control and transnational bribery, a newsletter, and background information about the OAS.

Vital Stats:

Access method: WWW
To access: http://www.oas.org

Pan American Health Organization

The Pan American Health Organization site offers numerous publications about health issues affecting residents of the Americas and the Caribbean. Publications are available about adolescent health, AIDS/HIV, diabetes, emerging and re-emerging diseases, environmental health, gender and health, malnutrition, sanitation, sexually transmitted diseases, tobacco, and vaccines, among many other subjects. The site is provided in English and Spanish.

Other highlights of the site include background information about PAHO, which is affiliated with the World Health Organization and the United Nations; a list of PAHO publications that you can order, and the full text of the book

Health in the Americas, which has political and health profiles of every nation in the Americas and the Caribbean.

Vital Stats:

Access method: WWW
To access: http://www.paho.org

UN System

This directory is a gateway to the dozens of Web sites operated by various United Nations agencies. The site is provided in English and French.

As an aid to finding information, the directory leaves a lot to be desired. For example, the secretary-general and the Security Council are not listed because they don't have separate Web sites. If you want to access their documents, you must know to click on the link to United Nations Headquarters.

Vital Stats:

Access method: WWW
To access: http://www.unsystem.org

✓✓ United Nations Home Page

Available in English, French, Spanish, Russian, Chinese, and Arabic, this site is the mother lode for United Nations information. It's far too extensive to describe in detail, but here are a few highlights of what's available:

- Reports, resolutions, and other documents from the Security Council, secretary-general, and General Assembly.
- An annotated list of documents that the UN has released in the previous two months.
- The United Nations System Pathfinder, which provides bibliographic data for major UN publications indexed by subject. The Pathfinder also has links to those documents that are available online. Some of the subjects covered include disarmament, economic development, environment, human rights, international law, international security and peacekeeping, population, and social development.
- Numerous documents about land mines, including casualty data and reports about land mine problems in individual countries.
- Documents from past, current, and upcoming UN conferences.
- Background information about the United Nations, including the UN Charter, the Universal Declaration of Human Rights, a history of the United

Nations, a list of major UN achievements, biographies of past and present secretaries-general, a list of UN member states, and a virtual tour of UN headquarters.

- Links to the home pages of permanent missions to the United Nations in New York and e-mail addresses for the missions.
- Press releases and transcripts of press briefings.

Vital Stats:

Access method: WWW
To access: http://www.un.org

The World Bank

Poverty and development are the focus of this site from the World Bank. The site has a huge collection of information about individual regions and countries of the world, all of it available in English, Spanish, and French.

The site also has development news, information about World Bank projects, links to Web sites operated by World Bank projects in various countries, summaries or the full text of numerous World Bank publications, an excellent group of materials for teachers and students arranged by country and topic, an index of mailing lists about various development issues, speeches, a media guide that lists World Bank experts by topic, and much more.

Vital Stats:

Access method: WWW
To access: http://www.worldbank.org

World Health Organization

Articles, reports, and international statistics about dozens of health topics are provided at this official World Health Organization site. Each topic has its own page with links to the relevant documents.

Some of the topics covered include aging, asthma, blindness and deafness, cancer, cardiovascular diseases, chemical safety, children's vaccination, cholera, chronic rheumatic diseases, dengue, diabetes, drinking water quality, dysentery, electronic and magnetic fields, environmental health, food and nutrition, hepatitis, HIV/AIDS, influenza, malaria, measles, mental health, occupational health, polio, reproductive health, solid and hazardous wastes, tobacco use, tuberculosis, and women's health.

The site also offers the full text of WHO's annual *World Health Report,* fact sheets about everything from tobacco dependence to strengthening mental health promotion, a catalog of WHO publications that you can order, press releases, and a database of WHO policies.

Vital Stats:

Access method: WWW
To access: http://www.who.org

World Trade Organization

The World Trade Organization explains its role in world trade matters at its Web site, which is available in English, Spanish, and French.

Many of the articles and other documents are indexed by the following trade topics: development, dispute settlement, environment, goods, government procurement, intellectual property, policy reviews, research and analysis, and services.

The site also has a database containing selected official WTO documents, special links to WTO documents released within the previous thirty days, world trade statistics, background information about the organization, and press releases.

Vital Stats:

Access method: WWW
To access: http://www.wto.org

4

Political Candidates

Al Gore 2000

The Web site of Democratic presidential candidate Al Gore has transcripts of dozens of Gore's speeches about such topics as crime, the economy, education, faith and values, and foreign policy.

The site also has documents outlining Gore's position on various issues, separate pages for Gore's campaign offices in New Hampshire and Iowa, an interactive Town Hall where visitors can post questions and comments, answers to selected Town Hall questions, a section for children that has games and other activities, background information about Gore's family, information about how to receive campaign updates by e-mail, press releases, photographs, and videos.

Vital Stats:

Access method: WWW
To access: http://www.algore2000.com

Bill Bradley for President

The Web site of Democratic presidential candidate Bill Bradley provides links to campaign finance reports that Bradley filed with the Federal Election Commission. It also has details about Bradley's position on numerous issues, a biography, excerpts from Bradley's books, transcripts of campaign speeches, information about how to receive campaign updates by e-mail, press releases, photographs, videos, and suggestions for activities by campaign volunteers.

Vital Stats:

Access method: WWW
To access: http://www.billbradley.com

Bush for President

The Web site of Republican presidential candidate George W. Bush has information about Bush's accomplishments as governor of Texas, summaries of Bush's position on various issues, biographical information about Bush and his wife, a list of state and federal office holders who support Bush, links to Bush's separate campaign site in Iowa, and press releases.

Vital Stats:

Access method: WWW
To access: http://www.georgewbush.com

McCain 2000

Republican presidential candidate John McCain, a major advocate of campaign finance reform, lists every contribution to his campaign by individuals and political action committees at his Web site. Each listing includes the contributor's name and state, and the amount of the donation. Contributions as low as one dollar are listed.

The site also has biographical information about McCain, campaign news, information about how to get campaign updates by e-mail, press releases, transcripts of speeches, quotations from recent newspaper articles about McCain, addresses and telephone numbers for the national campaign headquarters and field offices, and position papers about education, foreign policy, Social Security, and tax relief.

Vital Stats:

Access method: WWW
To access: http://www.mccain2000.com

Orrin Hatch for President

The Web site of Republican presidential candidate Orrin Hatch was still being developed when this book was being written. In its early days, the site explained how to receive campaign updates by e-mail and listed contact information for the campaign headquarters.

Vital Stats:

Access method: WWW
To access: http://www.orrinhatch.org

Patrick J. Buchanan for President

The Web site of independent presidential candidate Pat Buchanan offers recordings and transcripts of speeches, video clips, brief descriptions of Buchanan's position on various issues, and information about how to receive campaign updates by e-mail.

The site also has press releases, a campaign calendar, stories about Buchanan from various media outlets, contact information for the campaign headquarters and field offices, and links to online polls where Internet users can vote.

Vital Stats:

Access method: WWW
To access: http://www.gopatgo2000.com

Politics1: Presidency 2000

If you're looking for Web sites of presidential candidates in 2000, this page is a great place to start. It has links to Web sites operated by dozens of Democratic, Republican, third-party, and independent presidential candidates, both announced and unannounced. The page is part of Politics1 (p. 14).

The page is particularly fun to peruse because it provides profiles of every candidate—even obscure independents who can most charitably be described as inhabiting the outer fringes of American politics. The page also has links to other Web sites that provide information about the 2000 presidential campaign.

Vital Stats:

Access method: WWW
To access: http://politics1.com/p2000.htm

Project Vote Smart: Presidential Information

This section of Project Vote Smart (p. 15) presents information about more than 150 candidates for the presidency in 2000, ranging from major Democratic and Republican candidates to obscure third-party and independent contenders.

The amount of information available about each candidate varies. For many candidates, Project Vote Smart offers a photograph, basic biographical information, contact information for the campaign, and a link to the campaign's Web site (if one exists). Listings for some candidates also provide information about the candidate's voting record, evaluations by special interest groups, and links to campaign finance data.

You can browse the candidate information alphabetically by last name or by political party. A useful calendar of primary and caucus dates for the 2000 election also is provided.

Vital Stats:

Access method: WWW
To access: http://www.vote-smart.org/ce/p_index/
                 p_index.phtml?category=President

P2000: Race for the White House

Through original files and links, this site provides extensive information about all major and some minor presidential candidates. The amount of information about each candidate varies, but the site often provides an extensive biographical profile, a link to the official campaign site, links to financial reports filed with the Federal Election Commission by the campaign and the candidate's political action committee, links to other Web sites connected to the candidate, and a link to archived versions of the candidate's Web site from previous campaigns.

The site also has links to news media sites about the 2000 campaign, links to political party sites, and other campaign information.

Vital Stats:

Access method: WWW
To access: http://gwu.edu/~action/P2000.html

The Steve Forbes 2000 National Online Headquarters

Republican presidential contender Steve Forbes announced his candidacy on the Internet, and his Web site says Forbes is running "America's first full-scale Internet campaign." As befits that claim, the site is more extensive than are those of other presidential candidates.

The site has lengthy descriptions of Forbes's positions on such topics as taxation and education, and provides speeches, videos, sound files of radio commentaries by Forbes, and links to more than a dozen online presidential polls. It also has a calculator that visitors can use to determine how they'd make out under Forbes's proposal for a flat income tax.

The site also provides excerpts from news stories about the Forbes campaign, a biography of Forbes, press releases, e-mail postcards, and campaign banners and logos that can be placed on Web sites.

Vital Stats:

Access method: WWW
To access: http://forbes2000.com

Whitehouse 2000

This site offers more than 100 links to sites about the candidates in the 2000 presidential election. Instead of limiting itself to the official site for each candidate, Whitehouse 2000 also provides links to unofficial sites and parody sites where available.

This site also has links to many campaign-related sites that offer humor, polls, party platforms, and campaign news.

Vital Stats:

Access method: WWW
To access: http://www.niu.edu/newsplace/whitehouse.html

5

Political
Issues

ABORTION

Abortion Clinics OnLine

This site provides a directory of abortion clinics around the United States, and also has a few listings for clinics in Australia, Austria, Belgium, Canada, England, and Spain. Listings are available for private physicians' offices, state-licensed abortion clinics, surgical centers, and hospital abortion services. Contact information is provided for each clinic, and there are links to Web sites operated by many clinics.

The site also provides articles about various aspects of abortion rights, links to dozens of articles about different birth control methods, and links to dozens of other Web sites about abortion and women's health. It's operated by a private individual who is a consultant to abortion providers.

Vital Stats:

Access method: WWW
To access: http://www.gynpages.com

The Abortion Rights Activist

This pro-choice site, which is operated by a private individual, offers yearly reports detailing violent attacks against abortion clinics and abortion providers. Reports are available from 1995 to the present.

The site also has a list of abortion providers and clinic workers who have been killed, documents from the trials of people convicted of attacking clinics or abortion providers, links to abortion information at other pro-choice sites, links to information for pro-choice activists, and links to dozens of pro-choice and pro-life Internet sites.

Vital Stats:

Access method: WWW
To access: http://ww1.cais.com/agm/main/index.html

The Alan Guttmacher Institute: Abortion

This page at the site of the Alan Guttmacher Institute has statistics and policy papers about abortion. The institute, which supports family planning, conducts research about abortion, sexual activity, contraception, childbearing, and related topics.

The most impressive publication is *The Status of Major Abortion Related Laws in the States,* which provides detailed information about the types of abortion restrictions imposed by each state. You can examine the data by type of restriction or state.

The policy papers examine various aspects of abortion in the United States and around the world. Some of the available titles include *Abortion in Context: United States and Worldwide, The Role of Contraception in Reducing Abortion, Late-Term Abortions: Legal Considerations, The Limitations of U.S. Statistics on Abortion, An Overview of Clandestine Abortion in Latin America,* and *Teenagers' Right to Consent to Reproductive Health Care.*

The page also offers statistics about induced abortion worldwide, abortion in the United States, and teenage sexual activity and abortion.

Vital Stats:

Access method:	WWW
To access:	http://www.agi-usa.org/sections/abortion.html

---

alt.abortion, alt.support.abortion, talk.abortion

Participants in the alt.abortion, alt.support.abortion, and talk.abortion news-groups discuss all facets of the abortion issue, including when life begins, contraception, adoption, and recent abortion news events. Many messages are cross-posted among the three newsgroups, so you usually just have to read one to keep up on the discussion.

Vital Stats:

Access method:	Usenet newsgroups
To access:	news:alt.abortion, news:alt.support.abortion, news:talk.abortion

---

American Civil Liberties Union: Reproductive Freedom

News about current abortion-related legislation highlights this section of the American Civil Liberties Union's site (p. 97), which is run by its Reproductive Freedom Project. Many ACLU letters to Congress regarding the legislative proposals also are included.

The section also has links to other pro-choice sites and ACLU position papers on topics such as parental involvement laws, bans on partial-birth abortions, abortion counseling, contraception, abortion restrictions, reproductive rights of minors, and reproductive freedom and welfare reform.

Vital Stats:

Access method: WWW
To access: http://www.aclu.org/issues/reproduct/hmrr.html

The Center for Reproductive Law and Policy

This site has news about reproductive rights bills pending before Congress and articles about topics such as state and federal restrictions on funding abortions. It's operated by the Center for Reproductive Law and Policy, which engages in litigation, research, and public education in support of reproductive freedom, including access to contraception and abortion.

One of the most interesting sections of the site has news about legal cases in which the center is involved. The lawsuits address many issues, but most are challenges to partial-birth abortion bans, federal bans on abortion funding, mandatory counseling laws, and laws requiring parental notice before minors can have abortions.

The site also offers dozens of fact sheets about reproductive rights in the United States and other countries. Some of the topics covered include references to family planning in world constitutions, reproductive rights of adolescents, reproductive rights of refugees, abortion laws around the world, and parental consent and notification laws.

Finally, the site provides electronic versions of the monthly *Reproductive Freedom News*, which has articles about recent legislative and legal actions involving reproductive rights in the United States and other countries. The site archives issues of the newsletter from 1997 to the present, and you also can sign up to receive new issues by e-mail.

Vital Stats:

Access method: WWW
To access: http://www.crlp.org

EMILY's List

This Web site has background information about EMILY's List, which raises millions of dollars for pro-choice Democratic women candidates for federal and statewide offices, provides technical assistance to campaigns, and seeks to mobilize Democratic women voters.

The site also has profiles of candidates the group has endorsed in the 2000 election, databases listing women in Congress and state legislatures, a database listing women that EMILY's List has helped elect, information about how to submit a résumé if you'd like to be a staff member in the campaign of a pro-choice Democratic woman, results of polls of women voters, a newsletter, and press releases.

Vital Stats:

Access method: WWW
To access: http://www.emilyslist.org

Ethics Updates: Abortion

Primarily through links, this section of the Ethics Updates site provides access to a wide range of documents about abortion. Ethics Updates is maintained by Lawrence Hinman, director of the Values Institute at the University of San Diego.

It offers links to all the major Supreme Court decisions about abortion, recent and current legislation, papal documents, selected Web sites, and articles from various publications. It also has a list of selected philosophical literature about abortion.

Vital Stats:

Access method: WWW
To access: http://ethics.acusd.edu/abortion.html

The Kaiser Daily Reproductive Health Report

Each issue of the *Kaiser Daily Reproductive Health Report* has summaries of stories from various newspapers, magazines, and other sources. Many of the stories concern abortion, but others discuss contraception, family planning, Medicaid, sexually transmitted diseases, sex education, teenage pregnancy, and managed care. If the full text of the article is online, the summary provides a link.

Each daily issue typically offers summaries of eight articles, and an archive lets users search all previous editions. The archive also allows users to search stories from *Abortion Report* and *American Health Line* from July 1989 to the present. Both are published by the National Journal Group, which prepares the *Kaiser Daily Reproductive Health Report* for the Henry J. Kaiser Family Foundation.

Vital Stats:

Access method: WWW
To access: http://report.kff.org/repro

The Lambs of Christ

This site is operated by the Lambs of Christ, a militant anti-abortion group known for blockading abortion clinics. The group is led by Father Norman Weslin, who has been arrested more than sixty times during abortion protests.

The site has numerous documents outlining the group's opposition to abortion, sermons by Weslin, background information about Weslin, a transcript of Weslin's testimony in one of his trials, and related information.

Vital Stats:

Access method: WWW
To access: http://www.thelambsofchrist.com

Missionaries to the Unborn

Missionaries to the Unborn is a radical anti-abortion group. A prime feature on its home page is a picture of Adolph Hitler, labeled "Jew Killer," that transforms into a picture of a doctor who performs abortions, labeled "Baby Killer."

The Alternative Links page is one of the site's most interesting pages. It provides links to Web sites operated by dozens of groups that oppose abortion. Most of the groups are quite radical, and some advocate violence against abortion clinics and doctors.

The Prisoners of Christ List page also is worth a look. It carries extensive information about individuals who have been incarcerated because of their anti-abortion activities, including attacks against abortion clinics and doctors.

The site also has dozens of photos of aborted fetuses, news about attacks against abortion clinics, and dozens of articles about various aspects of the abortion controversy.

Vital Stats:

Access method: WWW
To access: http://www.mttu.com/main.htm

naral-news

Subscribers to the naral-news mailing list receive national and affiliate news from the National Abortion and Reproductive Rights Action League, a pro-choice group. There is no discussion. NARAL also operates a Web site.

Vital Stats:

Access method: E-mail
To access: Send an e-mail message to
                    subscribe-naral-news@lists.client-mail.com
Subject line:
Message:

National Abortion and Reproductive Rights Action League

One of the highlights at this site is the Congressional Voting Record on Choice, a database that returns the voting record of your senators and representative on abortion and reproductive rights legislation. The site is operated by the National Abortion and Reproductive Rights Action League, a pro-choice group.

Another highlight is a report titled *Who Decides? A State-by-State Review of Abortion and Reproductive Rights,* which for each state provides data about access to abortion, abortion positions of top state leaders, and summaries of abortion statutes and regulations. It's supplemented by pages for each state that summarize current legislative activity regarding abortion, family planning services, sex education, and related topics.

The site also provides an analysis of 1998 U.S. Senate, House, and gubernatorial races in which NARAL believes choice was a deciding factor; dozens of fact sheets about topics such as family planning and reproductive choices, clinic violence, abortion rights, state and federal abortion legislation, and scientific research; the full texts of major Supreme Court decisions about abortion; information about NARAL's Campus Organizing Project; and links to Web sites of other pro-choice groups.

NARAL also operates the naral-news mailing list.

Vital Stats:

Access method: WWW
To access: http://www.naral.org/home.html

National Abortion Federation

This site from the National Abortion Federation, the professional association for abortion providers in the United States and Canada, offers numerous publications for people considering abortion. They include a publication titled *Unsure About Your Pregnancy? A Guide to Making the Right Decision for You,* a guide to choosing an abortion provider, and fact sheets about medical abortion, surgical abortion, abortion safety, post-abortion issues, abortion and breast cancer, and RU 486, among other issues.

The site also has a newsletter describing new abortion legislation that has been introduced at the national and state levels, a guide to supporting community abortion providers, statistics about attacks against abortion clinics and providers, background information about the Freedom of Access to Clinic Entrances Act, a list of selected NAF member clinics, links to other pro-choice Web sites, and press releases.

Vital Stats:

Access method: WWW
To access: http://www.prochoice.org

National Pro-Choice Directory

This directory provides contact information for hundreds of pro-choice groups across the United States. It's maintained by the *Body Politic,* a pro-choice magazine.

For each group, the directory provides the street address, telephone number, and fax number, and where available the e-mail and Web addresses. The directory begins with national organizations and then provides separate pages listing groups in each state.

Vital Stats:

Access method: WWW
To access: http://www.bodypolitic.org/dir/home.htm

National Right to Life Committee

At this site, the pro-life National Right to Life Committee offers news about national abortion legislation, descriptions of state homicide laws that recognize unborn children as victims, and articles analyzing campaign reform legislation that the NRLC believes would stifle free speech.

The site also has electronic versions of the *National Right to Life News* dating from December 1997 to the present. Each monthly issue has more than a dozen articles, many about legislative and legal issues related to abortion.

Other features include articles and congressional testimony about partial-birth abortion, descriptions of abortion techniques, and information about abortion alternatives.

Vital Stats:

Access method: WWW
To access: http://www.nrlc.org

The New York Times: Abortion

Dozens of selected *New York Times* articles about state and federal abortion laws, protests, court decisions, fetal tissue research, and other abortion-related subjects are available through this page at the newspaper's Web site. Most articles date from January 1997 to the present, but a small collection of articles also is provided from the newspaper's coverage of the 1973 *Roe v. Wade* decision by the Supreme Court legalizing abortion.

The page also has a United States map that you can click on to read about the circumstances under which individual states provide public financing for abortion, in addition to links to selected Supreme Court decisions about abortion.

You must register to access the *New York Times* site, but registration is free.

Vital Stats:

Access method: WWW
To access: http://www.nytimes.com/library/national/
                   abortion-index.html

Open Directory Project: Abortion

The abortion page at the Open Directory Project (p. 11) offers more than 150 links to abortion sites on the Web, all selected by human volunteers. Each link is briefly annotated.

The abortion page has a few links to general sites, but most of the links are divided into two categories: pro-choice and pro-life. The page also provides useful links to related pages about abortion alternative services, pregnancy, teen sexuality, and family planning.

Vital Stats:

Access method: WWW
To access: http://dmoz.org/Society/Issues/Abortion

Operation Save America

News about protests against abortion clinics, a campaign to remove what Operation Save America considers child pornography from bookstores, efforts to return the Bible to school classrooms, and suits by the attorney general against Operation Rescue are featured at this site. It also has an archive of Operation Save America's newsletter that contains issues dating back to July 1995.

Operation Save America is the new name for Operation Rescue, and many of the site's documents pertain to Operation Rescue.

Vital Stats:

Access method: WWW
To access: http://www.operationsaveamerica.org

Planned Parenthood

This site offers news about recent actions by Congress, federal agencies, and state legislatures regarding abortion and other reproductive health issues. It's operated by the Planned Parenthood Federation of America, a pro-choice group.

The site also has listings by state of laws that restrict access to abortion, numerous publications about birth control and sexual health, guides for parents about how to talk to their children about sexuality and birth control, and fact sheets about various aspects of abortion, birth control, international family planning, and teen pregnancy and abortion.

Vital Stats:

To access:
Access method: WWW
To access: http://www.plannedparenthood.org

Project Vote Smart: Abortion

This page at Project Vote Smart (p. 15) provides links to several dozen of the most important Web sites about abortion. Each link has a brief description.

Vital Stats:

Access method: WWW
To access: http://www.vote-smart.org/issues/ABORTION

Pro-Life Action League

This site is operated by the Pro-Life Action League, an anti-abortion group that drew national attention in April 1998 when a jury found the group and its director, Joseph Scheidler, guilty of engaging in racketeering activity aimed at shutting down abortion clinics nationwide. The verdict came in a case filed by the National Organization for Women.

The site has updates about appeals and other proceedings in the NOW legal case, information about sidewalk counseling the league conducts outside abortion clinics, stories by former abortion providers, abortion statistics, press releases, links to related sites, and selected chapters from Scheidler's book, *Closed: 99 Ways to Stop Abortion.*

Vital Stats:

Access method: WWW
To access: http://www.prolifeaction.org

Pro-Life Virginia

This site is operated by Pro-Life Virginia, a militant anti-abortion group. Its leader, the Rev. Donald Spitz, has publicly praised the killers of doctors who perform abortions.

A page titled American Hero honors Paul Hill, who awaits execution on Florida's Death Row for the 1994 killing of Dr. John Britton, a doctor who performed abortions, and his escort. The page includes a lengthy document written by Hill titled "Why I Shot an Abortionist."

The site also has most of the text of *The Army of God Manual,* a classic anti-abortion book that describes dozens of methods for attacking abortion clinics and advocates violence to stop abortion; articles supporting violence written by John Brockhoeft, who was imprisoned for arson attacks on abortion clinics; and the texts of two "defensive action statements" supporting the use of force to stop abortion. Each statement has the names of the people who signed it and their affiliations.

Vital Stats:

Access method: WWW
To access: http://www.armyofgod.com

✓ Public Agenda Online: Abortion

This section of the Public Agenda site provides a large collection of materials about various aspects of the abortion controversy. Public Agenda is a nonprofit, nonpartisan organization that researches and reports on public issues.

Among other highlights, the section provides an overview of the abortion issue, a digest of recent reports and news articles about abortion (with links to the full texts of the documents where available), numerous facts about abortion, links to recent studies, lots of results from public opinion polls about abortion, and contact information (including links to Web sites) for some of the major groups involved in the abortion controversy.

Vital Stats:

Access method: WWW
To access: http://www.publicagenda.org/issues/
                      frontdoor.cfm?issue_type=abortion

Susan B. Anthony List

This site is operated by the Susan B. Anthony List, a group that supports pro-life women candidates for Congress. It has information about training offered to campaign staff, candidates, and activists; a brief description of the group's political action committee; transcripts of one-minute radio commentaries by the group; and press releases.

Vital Stats:

Access method: WWW
To access: http://www.sba-list.org

The Ultimate Pro-Life Resource List

As implied by its name, this site's highlight is a collection of links to Web sites operated by more than 200 pro-life organizations around the world. The site is operated by a husband and wife team.

Besides the links, the site offers dozens of articles about RU 486, partial-birth abortion, adoption assistance, euthanasia, and related topics.

Vital Stats:

Access method: WWW
To access: http://www.prolifeinfo.org

Yahoo! Health: Abortion

Links to more than 150 Web sites about abortion are available through this page at Yahoo! (p. 17). A few links to general abortion sites are provided, but the vast majority of the links are divided into two categories: pro-choice and pro-life.

Vital Stats:

Access method: WWW
To access: http://dir.yahoo.com/Health/Reproductive_Health/Abortion

✓ Yahoo! News: Abortion

This page at Yahoo! (p. 17) offers news stories about abortion, either through links or articles archived at the site.

The main set of links provides dozens of selected stories from April 1998 to the present. Stories are provided from newspapers such as the *Los Angeles Times, Miami Herald, Irish Times (Ireland), Sun Sentinel, Washington Post, Denver Post, Arizona Republic, New York Times,* and *Philadelphia Inquirer;* wire services such as Reuters and the Associated Press; and TV networks such as Court TV, the BBC, CNN, ABC, and CBS.

If you select Yahoo! News Search on the left side of the screen, a comprehensive list of stories about abortion published within the past week is returned. The list typically includes dozens of stories from sources such as the Associated Press, Reuters, and ABC.

Vital Stats:

Access method: WWW
To access: http://headlines.yahoo.com/Full_Coverage/US/
            Abortion_News

AIDS

ACT UP/New York

This site is operated by the New York chapter of ACT UP (AIDS Coalition to Unleash Power), a group that favors direct action to end the AIDS crisis. It has documents explaining ACT UP's organization and political views, civil disobedience training materials, reports about more than a dozen direct actions by ACT UP activists, numerous documents and links about AIDS treatment, information about ACT UP meetings in New York, and links to Web sites operated by other ACT UP chapters and other AIDS groups.

Vital Stats:

Access method: WWW
To access: http://www.actupny.org

AIDS Action

Political aspects of the AIDS crisis are the focus of this site. It's operated by AIDS Action, a network of 3,200 community-based organizations that serve HIV-positive Americans.

The site has a report about the records of the candidates in the 2000 presidential election regarding AIDS issues, alerts about new AIDS-related bills introduced in Congress, links to the full texts of AIDS-related legislation currently before Congress, details about the voting record of every current member of Congress on AIDS legislation, information about federal appropriations for AIDS, and press releases.

It also offers a page where you can sign up for the AIDS Action e-Network, which distributes newsletters, policy updates, and other news by e-mail.

Vital Stats:

Access method: WWW
To access: http://www.aidsaction.org

AIDSACT

Subscribers to the AIDSACT mailing list discuss political aspects of the AIDS crisis. The list is aimed at AIDS activists. It's operated by ACT UP/New York, which also has a Web site.

Vital Stats:

Access method:	E-mail
To access:	Send an e-mail message to listproc@critpath.org
Subject line:	
Message:	**subscribe AIDSACT** *firstname lastname*

American Civil Liberties Union: HIV/AIDS

Reports about HIV partner notification statutes, premarital HIV screening requirements, and HIV name-reporting laws highlight this page at the American Civil Liberties Union's site (p. 97).

The page also has news about AIDS-related legal cases in which the ACLU is involved, congressional testimony about various AIDS bills by ACLU officials, annual reports by the ACLU's AIDS Project, and press releases about AIDS issues.

Vital Stats:

Access method:	WWW
To access:	http://www.aclu.org/issues/aids/hmaids.html

✓ The Body: A Multimedia AIDS and HIV Information Resource

The Body is one of the best Internet sites about AIDS. It offers thousands of documents, both original and from other sources, about topics such as AIDS demographics, treatment policy, education and prevention, health insurance policy, mandatory testing and reporting, and experimental drugs, among many others. It's operated by Body Health Resources Corporation with support from several drug companies.

The site also has links to dozens of articles about AIDS activism from various publications, political action alerts, news from recent conferences, links to Web sites operated by many major AIDS organizations, and lots more.

Vital Stats:

Access method:	WWW
To access:	http://www.thebody.com

Internet Bookmarks for AIDS

This directory provides links to hundreds of Web sites about AIDS. The links are divided into more than twenty categories, including advocacy, alternative therapies, conference reports, dissidents, education and prevention, international, news services, newsletters and magazines, and treatment. The directory is part of the New Mexico AIDS InfoNet, which is a project of the New Mexico AIDS Education and Training Center at the University of New Mexico School of Medicine.

Vital Stats:

Access method: WWW
To access: http://www.aidsinfonet.org/999-bookmarks.html

JAMA HIV/AIDS Information Center

This site offers a wide range of useful information, including abstracts and the full texts where available of articles about HIV/AIDS from the *Journal of the American Medical Association* and other medical journals. The site is sponsored by JAMA.

Other offerings include daily news briefings, articles from conferences, ethics guidelines for treating AIDS patients, contact information for national HIV/AIDS organizations and state and local hotlines, links to dozens of other AIDS-related Internet sites, and more.

Vital Stats:

Access method: WWW
To access: http://www.ama-assn.org/special/hiv/hivhome.htm

The Kaiser Daily HIV/AIDS Report

Each issue of the *Kaiser Daily HIV/AIDS Report* has summaries of articles from various newspapers, magazines, medical journals, television networks, and other sources. If the full text of the article is online, the summary provides a link.

Each issue typically provides summaries of five to eight articles about topics such as public health and education, global issues, managed care, protease inhibitors, needle exchange, and names reporting. A searchable archive provides access to previous issues, in addition to stories from *American Health Line* published from March 1992 to the present. *American Health Line* is published by the National Journal Group, which prepares the *Kaiser Daily HIV/AIDS Report* for the Henry J. Kaiser Family Foundation.

Vital Stats:

Access method: WWW
To access: http://report.kff.org/aidshiv

✓ Looking for the Light: The AIDS Epidemic

This extraordinary site from the *New York Times* traces the progress of the AIDS epidemic through hundreds of articles published in the newspaper from 1981 to the present.

The main feature is a year-by-year timeline that uses selected stories from the *Times* to chronicle major events in the epidemic. Additional AIDS stories from each year of the crisis are available through separate pages.

Vital Stats:

Access method: WWW
To access: http://www.nytimes.com/library/national/science/aids/
                          aids-index.html

MEDLINEplus: AIDS

This page from the National Library of Medicine provides links to AIDS resources across the Internet operated by federal agencies, medical organizations, universities, hospitals, and other groups. It also allows users to search the MEDLINE database for bibliographical information about AIDS-related articles from medical journals and other publications.

Vital Stats:

Access method: WWW
To access: http://medlineplus.nlm.nih.gov/medlineplus/aids.html

---

National Institutes of Health Office of AIDS Research

The National Institutes of Health Office of AIDS Research plans, coordinates, evaluates, and funds all NIH AIDS-research activities. Its Web site provides the NIH plan for HIV-related research, descriptions of HIV and AIDS research being conducted at NIH, the report of the NIH AIDS Research Program Evaluation Task Force, a fact sheet about AIDS research and minority populations, and press releases.

Vital Stats:

Access method: WWW
To access: http://www.nih.gov/od/oar

PreventioNews

The PreventioNews mailing list distributes AIDS-related documents from the Centers for Disease Control and Prevention and other federal agencies.

One of the documents distributed is the *CDC HIV/STD/TB Prevention News Update.* Each daily issue has summaries of articles from scientific journals and the news media about HIV/AIDS, other sexually transmitted diseases, and tuberculosis. The list also distributes selected articles from the *Morbidity and Mortality Weekly Report,* fact sheets, conference announcements, and news about funding opportunities.

Vital Stats:

Access method: E-mail
To access: Send an e-mail message to
                                preventionews-subscribe@cdcnpin.org
Subject line:
Message:

Project Vote Smart: AIDS

This page at the Project Vote Smart site (p. 15) provides links to more than thirty of the best Web sites about AIDS. Each link is briefly annotated.

Vital Stats:

Access method: WWW
To access: http://www.vote-smart.org/issues/AIDS

---

sci.med.aids, AIDS

The moderated sci.med.aids newsgroup, which is mirrored on the AIDS mailing list, is one of the most popular online discussion forums about AIDS. Participants commonly discuss prevention, treatment, conferences, and related topics. News about AIDS from the federal Centers for Disease Control and Prevention also is frequently posted.

Vital Stats:

Access methods: Usenet newsgroup, E-mail
To access
    (Usenet):   news:sci.med.aids
To access
    (mailing list):   Send an e-mail message to majordomo@wubios.wustl.edu
Subject line:
Message: **subscribe aids *e-mail address***

U.S. Food and Drug Administration: HIV and AIDS

This site is a directory of HIV and AIDS information provided by the U.S. Food and Drug Administration. The information is divided into the following categories: milestones, testing information, barrier products, news releases, speeches, HIV/AIDS meetings, HIV/AIDS therapies, clinical trials and drug development, FDA/state AIDS health fraud task forces, HIV/AIDS articles and brochures, and other HIV/AIDS Web sites. Information in some of the categories, such as meetings and news releases, was seriously outdated when this book was being written.

Vital Stats:

Access method: WWW
To access: http://www.fda.gov/oashi/aids/hiv.html

White House Office of National AIDS Policy

This site offers very limited information about federal AIDS policy. It provides a list of administration accomplishments in fighting AIDS, transcripts of speeches and reports from White House AIDS events, selected statements and congressional testimony about AIDS by various administration officials, and a good collection of links to other Web sites about AIDS.

Vital Stats:

Access method: WWW
To access: http://www.whitehouse.gov/ONAP

Yahoo! Health: AIDS/HIV Organizations

This page at Yahoo! (p. 17) provides links to more than 100 Web sites operated by AIDS/HIV organizations. The main page has links to several dozen organizations, and other pages available through the main page provide links in the following categories: awareness and prevention; children; fundraising; lesbian, gay, and bisexual; political action; prison inmates; research and treatment; support services; and youth.

Vital Stats:

Access method: WWW
To access: http://dir.yahoo.com/health/diseases_and_conditions/
            aids_hiv/organizations

Yahoo! News: AIDS/HIV

This page at Yahoo! (p. 17) offers several dozen selected news stories about AIDS and HIV through links or articles archived at the site.

Stories are provided from the BBC, Associated Press, CNN, Reuters, *Washington Post, Chicago Tribune, San Francisco Examiner, Los Angeles Times,* and the *New York Times,* among other sources. The page also provides links to some of the best AIDS sites on the Internet.

Vital Stats:

Access method: WWW
To access: http://fullcoverage.yahoo.com/fc/Health/AIDS___HIV

ANIMAL RIGHTS

✓✓ About.com: Animal Rights

This site, which is part of the About.com network, may be the best place on the Internet to start a search for information about animal rights. Its highlight is a collection of links to hundreds of sites and individual documents across the Internet. The links have brief annotations and are neatly arranged by more than two dozen topics, including action alerts, alternatives to testing, animal parts trade, bullfighting, circus animals, cruelty-free shopping, farm animals, hunting, newsgroups and mailing lists, puppy mills, and rescue and adoption.

The site also has articles, a calendar of animal rights alerts and events, a bulletin board and chat room, and a list of recommended books.

Vital Stats:

Access method: WWW
To access: http://animalrights.about.com

Altweb: Alternatives to Animal Testing

Altweb provides answers to frequently asked questions about alternatives to animal testing, the full texts of various laws and regulations about animal testing, and news about everything from upcoming meetings to the latest technology developments. It's operated by the Center for Alternatives to Animal Testing at Johns Hopkins University.

The site also offers the full texts of books titled *The Principles of Humane Experimental Technique* and *Animals and Alternatives in Testing: History, Science, and Ethics*, a report from the National Agricultural Library titled *Directory of Resources on Alternatives and Animal Use in the Life Sciences*, a searchable database with information about alternative procedures, summaries of articles from journals about alternatives to animal testing, a glossary of terms, and links to dozens of related sites.

Vital Stats:

Access method: WWW
To access: http://altweb.jhsph.edu

Animal Care

This site's highlight is a searchable database that provides information about all animal dealers, breeders, researchers, exhibitors, and transporters who are regulated by the federal government. Each listing includes basic contact information and an abbreviated history of the facility's latest inspections. The site is operated by Animal Care, the office in the U.S. Department of Agriculture that enforces the Animal Welfare Act and the Horse Protection Act.

The site also has rules and regulations under the two laws, public notices and proposals, press releases, and background information about the Animal Care office and its responsibilities.

Vital Stats:

Access method: WWW
To access: http://www.aphis.usda.gov/ac

✓ Animal Rights Resource Site

Some of the highlights at this site include recent news stories about animal rights from the Associated Press, answers to frequently asked questions about various animals rights issues and organizations, and dozens of articles and essays about topics including animals and conservation, the animal rights movement, animal rights theory and philosophy, entertainment animals, farm animals, hunting, and laboratory animals. The site is part of the EnviroLink Network.

The site also has subscription information for dozens of electronic mailing lists devoted to animal rights, links to dozens of online petitions about animal rights, links to numerous calendars of animal rights events, details about jobs and internships available at various animal rights groups, and links to a huge range of Web sites, including sites run by groups that oppose the animal rights movement.

For those who like to chat, the site also has nearly two dozen message boards about action alerts, animal rescue, animals in entertainment, factory farms, fur, hunting and trapping, research and testing, and wildlife issues.

Vital Stats:

Access method: WWW
To access: http://arrs.envirolink.org

Animal Welfare Information Center

Through original documents and links to other sites, the Animal Welfare Information Center provides extensive information about animal care and use in research, teaching, and testing. The site, which is operated by the National Agricultural Library, is aimed at animal dealers, breeders, researchers, exhibitors, and transporters who are regulated by the federal government.

The site's highlights include the full texts of the federal Animal Welfare Act and regulations under the law, other federal animal care legislation and policies, links to lots of documents and Web sites about alternatives to animal testing, numerous documents about the humane care and use of farm animals, and dozens of bibliographies about various animal welfare topics.

Vital Stats:

Access method: WWW
To access: http://www.nal.usda.gov/awic

Animal Welfare Legislation and Policies

This page, a part of Primate Info Net, provides links to numerous laws and regulations about animal welfare. The site is operated by the Wisconsin Regional Primate Research Center at the University of Wisconsin–Madison.

Most of the links lead to United States laws and regulations, either state or federal, although a few links lead to laws in Switzerland, Germany, and Canada. The page also provides links to guidelines from a dozen organizations regarding the care and use of research animals.

Vital Stats:

Access method: WWW
To access: http://www.primate.wisc.edu/pin/welfare.html

AR-Wire

The moderated AR-Wire mailing list is aimed at animal rights activists. It distributes announcements about animal rights events such as conferences, protests, liberations, and court trials of activists in the United States and other countries. There is no discussion.

Vital Stats:

Access method: E-mail
To access: Send an e-mail message to waste@waste.org
Subject line:
Message: **subscribe ar-wire**

Foundation for Biomedical Research

This site is operated by the Foundation for Biomedical Research, which represents institutions that use animals in research. The site has answers to frequently asked questions about the use of animals in research, along with articles about the role of animals in medical research, the use of certain types of animals such as cats and dogs in research, regulations that govern research, animal protection groups, and related topics.

Vital Stats:

Access method: WWW
To access: http://www.fbresearch.org

Frontline-News

The Frontline-News mailing list distributes news about animal rights activism, including direct actions, arrests of activists, court trials, and police and government responses to activists. The list is operated by anonymous animal rights activists who are at least loosely associated with the Animal Liberation Front. ALF is a militant animal rights group that engages in direct actions such as releasing animals from fur farms.

Vital Stats:

Access method: E-mail
To access: Send an e-mail message to waste@waste.org
Subject line:
Message: **subscribe frontline-news**

Fur Commission USA

This site features dozens of articles about attacks against fur farms by animal rights activists, federal legislation introduced to increase penalties for attacks on fur facilities, and arrests of animal rights activists. It's operated by Fur Commission USA, a nonprofit group that represents mink and fox farmers in the United States.

It also has articles contrasting animal welfare and animal rights philosophies, brief descriptions of selected attacks on the fur industry and other animal users from 1997 to the present, extensive quotes from animal rights activists, and information about animal rights activists who are being sought by law enforcement authorities.

Other highlights include a video about the day-to-day operations on a fur farm, fact sheets about fur farming and the fur industry, a list of recommended books and articles, links to other fur industry sites, and a large collection of reports by the federal government, the fur industry, and others about animal rights, conservation and sustainable use, forestry, and livestock.

Vital Stats:

Access method: WWW
To access: http://www.furcommission.com

Humane Society of the United States

A pull-down menu at this site provides easy access to extensive information about animal welfare, organized by dozens of issues. The site is operated by the Humane Society of the United States.

Some of the issues covered include animal fighting, animal testing, circuses, dolphin-safe tuna, factory farming, fur, hunting and trapping, international animal issues, legislation, trade in wildlife, whaling, and zoos. The types of information available vary by issue, but the site often provides an overview of the issue, fact sheets, news articles, tips for activists, videos, and links to additional information.

The site also has information about current animal welfare legislation being considered in Washington and state capitals, news articles about animal issues, details about current Humane Society campaigns, and press releases.

Vital Stats:

Access method: WWW
To access: http://www.hsus.org

No Compromise

News articles at this site describe recent arson attacks against facilities that support the fur industry and releases of animals from fur farms, research laboratories, and other facilities. It's operated by *No Compromise,* a New Jersey magazine that supports the Animal Liberation Front and other militant animal rights groups.

The site also has feature articles from the magazine, numerous articles about how activists can fight the government, an international directory of militant animal rights groups, and links to dozens of related sites for activists.

Vital Stats:

Access method: WWW
To access: http://www.nocompromise.org

Office of Animal Care and Use

This site is designed for use by National Institutes of Health employees, but it offers technical information that's helpful to anyone interested in the use of animals in biomedical research. Eighteen of the twenty-five NIH components use animals in their research.

The site's highlights include a lengthy publication from the National Research Council titled *Guide for the Care and Use of Laboratory Animals,* numerous NIH policy manuals on caring for animals and using them in research, and links to lots of related sites.

Vital Stats:

Access method: WWW
To access: http://oacu.od.nih.gov

Open Directory Project: Animal Welfare

The animal welfare page at the Open Directory Project (p. 11) provides links to more than 400 Web sites about topics including animal rights, animal experiments, circuses, farming, fur farming, and hunting. Each link is briefly annotated.

Vital Stats:

Access method: WWW
To access: http://dmoz.org/Society/Issues/Animal_Welfare

PETA Online

This site is operated by People for the Ethical Treatment of Animals, the most prominent group in the animal rights movement. It offers fact sheets, videos, and other materials about current PETA campaigns on vegetarianism, Proctor & Gamble, fur, circuses, college action, consumer products, and animal experimentation, among other topics.

The site also has action alerts, articles from PETA's *Animal Times* magazine, a special section for children, press releases, and links to other animal rights sites.

Vital Stats:

Access method: WWW
To access: http://www.peta.com

Project Vote Smart: Animal Issues

This page at Project Vote Smart (p. 15) has links to several dozen selected Web sites about animal issues. The sites are operated by the American Association for Laboratory Animal Science, Animal Industry Foundation, Animal Legal Defense Fund, Association of Veterinarians for Animal Rights, Dolphin Alliance, Farm Animal Reform Movement, Foundation for Biomedical Research, Humane Society of the United States, and the National Anti-Vivisection Society, among other groups. Each link is briefly annotated.

Vital Stats:

Access method: WWW

To access: http://www.vote-smart.org/issues/ANIMAL

---

talk.politics.animals

Participants in the very active—and very opinionated—talk.politics.animals newsgroup discuss topics such as hunting, vegetarianism, and medical research involving animals, among others.

Vital Stats:

Access method: Usenet newsgroup

To access: news:talk.politics.animals

---

uk.politics.animals

The newsgroup uk.politics.animals is devoted to discussions of animal rights issues in the United Kingdom. Much of the discussion focuses on hunting, including the sabotaging of hunts.

Vital Stats:

Access method: Usenet newsgroup

To access   news:uk.politics.animals

Yahoo! Science: Animal Rights

This page at Yahoo! (p. 17) provides links to hundreds of sites about animal rights. The main page has links to several dozen general sites, and other pages available through the main page provide links in the following categories: animal experimentation, bullfighting views, cat declawing, circus animals, dog tail docking, endangered species, fishing views, humane and rescue societies, hunting views, magazines, opposing views, organizations, petitions, vegetarianism, Web directories, and zoos.

Vital Stats:

Access method: WWW
To access: http://dir.yahoo.com/Science/Biology/
                Zoology/Animals__Insects__and_Pets/Animal_Rights

BUSINESS

Business for Social Responsibility

Business for Social Responsibility is an organization that includes companies of all sizes. At its Web site, the group offers extensive reports about dozens of business issues. Each report provides an explanation of the issue, news about recent developments, examples of good policies, links to related resources, and other information.

Topics covered include business and ethics, child labor, community economic development, community involvement, corruption and bribery, discrimination, diversity, domestic partner benefits, downsizing, environment, forest friendly practices, global community involvement, green building design, human rights, minority and women business development, religion in the workplace, shareholder engagement, sustainable business practices, volunteerism, wages, waste reduction, and water conservation.

You must register to access the reports, but registration is free.

Vital Stats:

Access method: WWW
To access: http://www.bsr.org/ResourceCenter

Business-Industry Political Action Committee (BIPAC)

BIPAC is a political action committee that seeks to elect pro-business candidates to Congress. At its Web site, the group offers documents outlining a business political strategy for the 2000 election, information about candidates BIPAC is supporting in the 2000 election, ratings of the voting records of all House and Senate members, a summary of BIPAC's involvement in the 1998 election, and press releases.

Vital Stats:

Access method: WWW
To access: http://www.bipac.org

Corporate Watch

If you're willing to slog through this rather chaotic site, it provides a large amount of information about the power of transnational corporations. The site is a project of the Transnational Resource and Action Center, an organization that studies the social and environmental effects of corporate activities around the world.

The site has fact sheets and studies about transnational corporations, action alerts, news stories from various sources about the activities of corporations worldwide, analyses of various trade and investment agreements, a book by the Public Interest Research Group in New Delhi titled *An Activist's Guide to Research and Campaign on Transnational Corporations,* and feature articles about corporations and climate change, corporations in public schools, sweatshops, the global politics of tobacco, the future of the Internet, and gender, labor, and environmental justice on the U.S.-Mexico border.

Various sections of the site also contain lists of links to related Web sites. The most interesting list divides the links by issues such as advertising, consumer activism and boycotts, food, forests, high tech and electronics industry, international development, Internet activism, mining, nuclear, social investment, sweatshops, toxics and chemical industry, and wise use movement.

Vital Stats:

Access method: WWW
To access: http://www.corpwatch.org

Manufacturing Central

The National Association of Manufacturers operates this site, which provides briefs describing NAM's position on dozens of political issues. Some of the topics covered include affirmative action, air quality standards, campaign finance, China trade, deficit reduction, electronic commerce, encryption and computer security, environmental justice, ergonomics, export controls, Family and Medical Leave Act, global climate change, health care reform, labor, lobbying disclosure, mental health, minimum wage, mining law reform, nuclear waste disposal, OSHA, striker replacement, Superfund, tax reform, and Vietnam trade.

The site also has a weekly legislative update and press releases. A portion of the site that's restricted to NAM members provides daily Washington news updates, legislative alerts, and voting records for members of Congress.

Vital Stats:

Access method: WWW
To access: http://www.nam.org

Open Directory Project: Corporate Operations

Links to several dozen Web sites about corporate accountability and responsibility are provided on this page at the Open Directory Project (p. 11). It also leads to another page with links to more than four dozen sites about allegedly unethical firms.

Vital Stats:

Access method: WWW
To access: http://dmoz.org/Society/Issues/Corporate_Operations

Open Directory Project: Socially Responsible Investing

More than 600 links to Web sites related to socially responsible investing are provided by this page at the Open Directory Project (p. 11). The top page provides links to general sites, and it also leads to separate pages about green design issues, multinational corporations, publicly traded socially responsible companies, recent news, and sweatshops, among other topics.

Vital Stats:

Access method: WWW
To access: http://dmoz.org/Business/Investing/Socially_Responsible

Project Vote Smart: Business

This page at Project Vote Smart (p. 15) has links to more than two dozen Web sites about business issues. The sites are operated by the American Bar Association, Business for Social Responsibility, Business-Industry Political Action Committee, Corporate Watch, Multinational Monitor, National Cooperative Business Association, National Federation of Independent Business, Public Affairs Council, and U.S. Chamber of Commerce, among other organizations. Each link is briefly annotated.

Vital Stats:

Access method: WWW
To access: http://www.vote-smart.org/issues/BUSINESS

U.S. Chamber of Commerce

The U.S. Chamber of Commerce is one of the most prominent business lobbying groups in Washington. At its Web site, the chamber outlines its positions and priorities on a vast range of political issues.

Among the issues discussed are airport funding, electronic monitoring of employees, environmental and regulatory reform, government privatization, health care, legal reform, Social Security, tax policy, trade, and workforce development.

The site also offers news about legislative actions on chamber issues, much of it presented through a monthly news publication titled *uschamber.com*.

Vital Stats:

Access method: WWW
To access: http://www.uschamber.org

U.S. Department of Commerce

The U.S. Department of Commerce site primarily serves as a gateway into Web sites operated by the department's various components, including the Bureau of the Census, Bureau of Economic Analysis, Bureau of Export Administration, Economic Development Administration, Economics and Statistics Administration, International Trade Administration, Minority Business Development Agency, Patent and Trademark Office, and the Technology Administration, among others.

The site also provides news about the status of current appropriations bills and Commerce-related legislation, databases containing phone numbers and e-mail addresses of department employees, congressional testimony by Commerce officials, speeches by Commerce Secretary William Daley, and press releases.

Vital Stats:

Access method: WWW
To access: http://www.doc.gov

Yahoo! Business: Trade Associations

This page at Yahoo! (p. 17) provides links to Web sites operated by nearly 200 trade associations, including the American Plastics Council, Distilled Spirits Council of the United States, Health Insurance Association of America, National Association of Chain Drug Stores, and the Steel Manufacturers Association, among others.

Vital Stats:

Access method: WWW
To access: http://dir.yahoo.com/business_and_economy/
                             organizations/trade_associations

CIVIL LIBERTIES

ACLU Action Network

Subscribers to the ACLU Action Network mailing list receive periodic e-mail alerts about civil liberties bills or issues before Congress and the executive branch. The list is operated by the American Civil Liberties Union, which also has a Web site.

Vital Stats:

Access method:	E-mail
To access:	Send an e-mail message to lyris@lists.aclu.org
Subject line:	
Message:	**subscribe action**

ACLU NewsFeed

The ACLU NewsFeed mailing list distributes news releases from the national office of the American Civil Liberties Union and the group's state affiliates. The ACLU also operates a Web site.

Vital Stats:

Access method:	E-mail
To access:	Send an e-mail message to lyris@lists.aclu.org
Subject line:	
Message:	**subscribe news**

✓ American Civil Liberties Union

The American Civil Liberties Union site offers a huge quantity of materials about various civil liberties issues. Most are divided on the home page by subject, including criminal justice, cyber liberties, death penalty, drug policy, free speech, HIV/AIDS, immigrant rights, lesbian and gay rights, national security, police practices, prisons, privacy, racial equality, religious liberty, reproductive rights, student rights, voting rights, women's rights, and workplace rights.

The types of materials available for each subject vary. However, they often include news articles, fact sheets, reports, and links to related Web sites.

Other highlights at the site include articles about civil liberties bills currently before Congress, information about the rights of students in school, a student organizing manual, dozens of recent Supreme Court decisions in civil liberties cases where the ACLU was a party, and press releases.

The ACLU also operates two electronic mailing lists: ACLU Action Network and ACLU Newsfeed.

Vital Stats:

Access method: WWW
To access: http://www.aclu.org

Citizens Flag Alliance Inc.

The Citizens Flag Alliance seeks passage of a constitutional amendment that would make it illegal to physically desecrate the American flag. Most of the more than 100 organizations that belong to the alliance represent veterans.

The site has news about recent congressional actions regarding the flag amendment, a detailed history of the issue since the Supreme Court's 1989 ruling that flag burning is free speech protected by the First Amendment, a list of selected flag desecration acts since 1994, answers to more than two dozen frequently asked questions, a list of congressional co-sponsors of the flag amendment bill, and press releases.

Visitors also can sign up at the site to receive e-mail bulletins regarding the flag amendment.

Vital Stats:

Access method: WWW
To access: http://www.cfa-inc.org

✓ Electronic Privacy Information Center

A number of Internet sites offer excellent collections of information about electronic privacy, but the Electronic Privacy Information Center is arguably the best of the bunch. EPIC is a public interest research center in Washington, D.C.

The site has news about privacy-related legislation, court cases, reports, hearings, and other topics; a tracking system for privacy, speech, and cyber-liberties bills introduced in Congress; scanned images of previously classified government documents obtained by EPIC under the Freedom of Information Act; links to dozens of tools for protecting online privacy; news about court cases in which EPIC is involved; and a large guide to privacy organizations, publications, Web sites, mailing lists, newsgroups, and conferences.

One of the site's most interesting sections is located in the EPIC Policy Archives and simply labeled Privacy. It leads to separate pages about dozens of privacy topics, including air travel privacy, caller ID, children's privacy, cookies, counter-terrorism, cryptography policy, international privacy, Internet privacy, medical records, national ID cards, online databases, personal and consumer information, video surveillance, and wiretapping and electronic surveillance. The resources available at each page vary but often include original documents, links to other important documents about the topic, and links to related Web sites.

EPIC also publishes the EPIC-News electronic mailing list.

Vital Stats:

Access method:	WWW
To access:	http://www.epic.org

EPIC-News

The EPIC-News mailing list distributes the *EPIC Alert,* a newsletter published once or twice a week by the Electronic Privacy Information Center, which also operates a Web site. Each issue typically contains a half-dozen stories about topics such as Internet free speech, medical privacy, wiretapping and surveillance, encryption, copyright, and child protection online, in addition to a calendar of upcoming conferences and other events.

Vital Stats:

Access method:	E-mail
To access:	Send an e-mail message to epic-news@epic.org
Subject line:	**subscribe**
Message:	

Federal Trade Commission: Privacy

Numerous documents about personal information privacy are offered on this page at the Federal Trade Commission's site.

Some of the highlights include the consumer publications *Site-Seeing on the Internet: A Consumer's Guide to Travel in Cyberspace* and *Sharing Your Personal Information: It's Your Choice,* the full text of the Children's Online Privacy Protection Act of 1998, transcripts from meetings about protecting children online, extensive information about how to protect yourself from identity theft,

Self-Regulation and Privacy Online: A Federal Trade Commission Report to Congress, and transcripts of congressional testimony about privacy by FTC officials

Vital Stats:

Access method: WWW
To access: http://www.ftc.gov/privacy

---

free! The Freedom Forum Online

This site has hundreds of news articles about First Amendment freedoms, including free speech, freedom of religion, freedom of assembly, and freedom of the press. New articles are added to the site daily. It's operated by the Freedom Forum, a foundation that focuses primarily on free press and free speech issues.

The site also provides the full texts of nearly two dozen Freedom Forum reports. Some of the available titles include *State of the First Amendment, Business Journalism in the New Information Economy, Polls and Scandal from Nixon to Clinton, Indictment: The News Media & the Criminal Justice System,* and *Deities & Deadlines.*

Other highlights include numerous articles about technology's effect on freedom, daily summaries of news stories about the media, and articles critiquing the media.

Vital Stats:

Access method: WWW
To access: http://www.freedomforum.org

Free Expression Network Clearinghouse

This site provides links to news articles and press releases about various free expression topics issued by such organizations as the American Civil Liberties Union, Center for Media Education, Electronic Privacy Information Center, Freedom Forum, Human Rights Watch, National Coalition Against Censorship, and People For the American Way, among others.

The home page has links to the most recent articles. Other pages provide links divided by topic: censorship, in court, in Congress, Internet, and schools. Each topic typically has dozens of articles dating back to early 1998.

Vital Stats:

Access method: WWW
To access: http://www.freeexpression.org

Open Directory Project: Civil Liberties

Links to more than 200 Web sites about civil liberties are available through this page at the Open Directory Project (p. 11). The main page provides links to more than two dozen general sites, and it also leads to separate pages about forfeiture, free speech, press freedom, and privacy. Each link is briefly annotated.

Vital Stats:

Access method: WWW
To access: http://dmoz.org/Society/Issues/Civil_Liberties

Privacy Rights Clearinghouse

A collection of very substantial fact sheets about topics such as cell phone privacy, telemarketing, credit reports, employee monitoring, medical privacy, wiretapping, Social Security numbers, employment background checks, identity theft, and children in cyberspace highlights this site. It's run by the Privacy Rights Clearinghouse, which is affiliated with the Utility Consumers' Action Network, a nonprofit consumer organization in San Diego.

The site also has speeches, testimony, and issue papers; a group of original materials and links about identity theft; and links to other privacy sites.

Vital Stats:

Access method: WWW
To access: http://www.privacyrights.org

Project Vote Smart: Civil Liberties

This page at Project Vote Smart (p. 15) supplies links to just under two dozen selected Web sites devoted to civil liberties. The sites are operated by the American Civil Liberties Union, Americans United for Separation of Church and State, Baptist Joint Committee on Public Affairs, Electronic Frontier Foundation, and the Privacy Rights Clearinghouse, among other groups. Each link is briefly annotated.

Vital Stats:

Access method: WWW
To access: http://www.vote-smart.org/issues/CIVIL_LIBERTIES

CRIMINAL JUSTICE

alt.activism.death-penalty

Participants in the very active alt.activism.death-penalty Usenet newsgroup debate the merits of the death penalty—at least during those moments when they're not engaging in venomous personal attacks on each other.

Vital Stats:

Access method: Usenet newsgroup
To access: news:alt.activism.death-penalty

Bureau of Justice Statistics

A large collection of statistics about crime, victims, criminal offenders, and the justice system is just one of the highlights of this site. It's operated by the Bureau of Justice Statistics, which is part of the U.S. Department of Justice.

The site also offers hundreds of reports about various criminal justice topics. Some of the available titles include *Age Patterns of Victims of Serious Violent Crime, Capital Punishment, The Costs of Crime to Victims, Drug-Related Crime, Felony Sentences in the United States, Female Victims of Violent Crime, Guns Used in Crime, Homicide Trends in the United States, Indicators of School Crime and Safety, Indigent Defense, Juvenile Felony Defendants in Criminal Courts, Mental Health and Treatment of Inmates and Probationers, Probation and Parole in the United States, Profiles of Jail Inmates, Sex Offenses and Offenders, Sourcebook of Criminal Justice Statistics, State Prison Expenditures, Truth in Sentencing in State Prisons, Women in Prison, Workplace Violence,* and *Young Black Male Victims.*

The site also has press releases and links to related Web sites.

Vital Stats:

Access method: WWW
To access: http://www.ojp.usdoj.gov/bjs

Death Penalty Information Center

Although this site seriously needs a redesign, it provides a huge amount of information about the death penalty. It's operated by the Death Penalty Information Center, a group that opposes the death penalty.

The site's highlight may be its collection of reports about various death-penalty topics. Some of the available titles include *The Death Penalty in Black & White: Who Lives, Who Dies, Who Decides; Innocence and the Death Penalty: The Increasing Danger of Executing the Innocent; Killing for Votes: The Dangers of Politicizing the Death Penalty Process; With Justice for Few: The Growing Crisis in Death Penalty Representation;* and *Racial Disparities in Federal Death Penalty Prosecutions.*

Some of the other highlights include annual reports about the death penalty, data about each inmate executed in the United States since 1976, statistics about the number of countries that have abolished the death penalty and those with the most executions, and a list of books about the death penalty.

Vital Stats:

Access method: WWW
To access: http://www.essential.org/dpic

Justice Information Center

The Justice Information Center offers hundreds of reports about criminal and juvenile justice, links to other Internet sites that have similar information, and a database that provides summaries of reports, articles, books, and other items about criminal justice. The center is a service of the National Criminal Justice Reference Service.

The publications are divided into ten categories: corrections, courts, crime prevention, criminal justice statistics, drugs and crime, international issues, juvenile justice, law enforcement, research and evaluation, and victims of crime. The reports were prepared by the National Institute of Justice, Bureau of Justice Statistics, Office for Victims of Crime, and other organizations.

Some of the available titles include *Arrestees and Guns: Monitoring the Illegal Firearms Market, Assessing the Exposure of Urban Youth to Violence, Boot Camps for Juvenile Offenders, Community Policing Strategies, Crime and Policing in Rural and Small-Town America, Drug Enforcement and Treatment in Prisons, Gangs, HIV in Prisons, Improving Literacy Skills of Juvenile Detainees, Managing Adult Sex Offenders in the Community, Partnerships to Prevent Youth Violence, Policing Drug Hot Spots, A Policymaker's Guide to Hate Crimes, Prison Sentences and Time Served for Violence, Responding to Child Sexual Abuse, Trial Court Performance Standards,* and *Working as Partners with Community Groups.*

Vital Stats:

Access method: WWW
To access: http://www.ncjrs.org

Justice Information Electronic Newsletter (JUSTINFO)

JUSTINFO is a biweekly electronic newsletter primarily aimed at criminal justice professionals. It's published by the National Criminal Justice Reference Service, which also operates the Justice Information Center Web site (p. 103).

The newsletter provides information about international criminal justice issues, juvenile justice, criminal justice resources on the Internet, federal legislation, funding for criminal justice programs, and new products, publications, and services from NCJRS.

Vital Stats:

Access method: E-mail
To access: Send an e-mail message to listproc@ncjrs.org
Subject line:
Message: **subscribe justinfo** *firstname lastname*

Mothers Against Drunk Driving

The Mothers Against Drunk Driving site has ratings of drunk driving laws in each state, position statements, extensive statistics about drunk driving, information about the proposed National Victims' Constitutional Amendment, news stories about alcohol use and abuse, brochures about drunk driving, and links to lots of related Web sites.

Vital Stats:

Access method: WWW
To access: http://www.madd.org

National Coalition to Abolish the Death Penalty

The highlight of this site is its extensive descriptions of the death-penalty cases of inmates who face impending execution. It's operated by the National Coalition to Abolish the Death Penalty.

The site also has statistics about the number of executions and commutations by state since 1976, data about the race of defendants executed since 1976, a directory of groups that oppose the death penalty, a list of legal organizations that provide help to inmates on Death Row, and links to other death-penalty Web sites.

At the site, you also can sign up to receive e-mail alerts about impending executions.

Vital Stats:

Access method: WWW
To access: http://www.ncadp.org

Open Directory Project: Crime and Justice

The crime and justice page at the Open Directory Project (p. 11) provides links to more than 150 Web sites, all briefly annotated.

The page provides links to a few general sites, and other pages available through it provide links in the following categories: alleged miscarriages of justice, asset forfeiture, death penalty, gangs, law enforcement, police brutality, police monitoring, political prisoners, prisons, and war crimes.

Vital Stats:

Access method: WWW
To access: http://dmoz.org/Society/Issues/Crime_and_Justice

Project Vote Smart: Crime

This page at Project Vote Smart (p. 15) provides links to several dozen Web sites about crime and criminal justice.

The sites are operated by the American Probation and Parole Association, Bureau of Justice Statistics, Crime Free America, Death Penalty Information Center, Families Against Mandatory Minimums, National Center on Institutions and Alternatives, National Prison Project of the ACLU, National Victims' Constitutional Amendment Network, and the Sentencing Project, among others. Each link is briefly annotated.

Vital Stats:

Access method: WWW
To access: http://www.vote-smart.org/issues/CRIME

✓ Public Agenda Online: Crime

This section of the Public Agenda site has extensive information about crime and criminal justice topics. Public Agenda is a nonprofit, nonpartisan organization that researches and reports on public issues.

The site provides digests of recent reports and news stories (with links to the full texts where available), links to recent studies, statistics on various criminal justice topics, results from numerous public opinion polls about crime and criminal justice, and contact information (including links to Web sites) for major organizations involved in criminal justice.

Vital Stats:

Access method: WWW
To access: http://www.publicagenda.org/issues/
                  frontdoor.cfm?issue_type=crime

United States Sentencing Commission

This site provides reports to Congress by the United States Sentencing Commission about cocaine and federal sentencing policy, mandatory minimum penalties, penalties for fraud crimes involving elderly victims, sentencing policy for money laundering offenses, penalties for intentionally exposing people to HIV, sex crimes against children, telemarketing fraud, and penalties for computer fraud and vandalism offenses, among other subjects.

The site also has a manual containing the federal sentencing guidelines, amendments to the guidelines, federal sentencing statistics by state, transcripts of public hearings, *Federal Register* notices, information about state sentencing commissions, testimony at congressional hearings, and press releases.

Vital Stats:

Access method: WWW
To access: http://www.ussc.gov

U.S. Department of Justice

The U.S. Department of Justice site offers a huge, eclectic assortment of information, including documents from the *U.S. v. Microsoft* antitrust case, reports by the Justice Department inspector general about subjects such as the alleged role of the Central Intelligence Agency in bringing cocaine into the United States, and reports about the Branch Davidian standoff in Waco, Texas.

Other highlights include a report about the availability of bomb-making information on the Internet, numerous press releases and other documents about computer crime, federal guidelines for searching and seizing computers, briefs filed with the Supreme Court by the solicitor general, the texts of numerous documents released by the Justice Department under the Freedom of Information Act, reports and statistics from the Drug Enforcement Administration, speeches and congressional testimony by the attorney general and other Justice Department officials, and links to other Justice Department Web sites.

Vital Stats:

Access method: WWW
To access: http://www.usdoj.gov

✓ Yahoo! News: Death Penalty

Through links and articles archived at the site, this page at Yahoo! (p. 17) provides access to several dozen news stories about the death penalty.

The main set of links provides dozens of selected stories from early 1998 to the present. Stories are provided from the *Washington Post, Chicago Tribune, Miami Herald, Christian Science Monitor, Boston Globe, New York Post, Dallas Morning News,* CNN, Reuters, and the Associated Press, among other sources.

If you select Yahoo! News Search on the left side of the screen, you'll automatically launch a search for stories about the death penalty published within the last two weeks. A search typically returns dozens of stories from a wide variety of news sources.

The page also has links to selected Web sites about the death penalty.

Vital Stats:

Access method: WWW
To access: http://headlines.yahoo.com/Full_Coverage/US/
                   Death_Penalty

✓ Yahoo! News: Prison Issues

This page at Yahoo! (p. 17) provides access to news articles about various prison issues, either through links or articles archived at the site.

The primary links lead to dozens of selected articles printed or aired from mid-1998 to the present. The articles originated with the *Los Angeles Times, Miami Herald, Washington Post, Philadelphia Inquirer, New York Times, Christian Science Monitor, Irish Times (Ireland), Seattle Times,* Wired News, BBC, APB News Online, CBC, ABC, and other sources.

If you click on Yahoo! News Search on the left side of the page, you'll receive a comprehensive list of stories about prison topics around the world published in recent weeks. A typical search returns hundreds of articles.

The page also provides links to about a dozen related Web sites.

Vital Stats:

Access method: WWW
To access: http://headlines.yahoo.com/Full_Coverage/US/Prisons

---

Yahoo! Society and Culture: Death Penalty

Links to more than eighty Web sites about the death penalty are provided through this page at Yahoo! (p. 17). Each link has a brief annotation.

The main page provides links to about a dozen general sites, and the remainder of the links are available through four topic pages: death row inmates, opposing views, supporting views, and Web directories.

Vital Stats:

Access method: WWW
To access: http://dir.yahoo.com/Society_and_Culture/Crime/
                 Correction_and_Rehabilitation/Death_Penalty

DEFENSE POLICY

The Arms Control Association

Articles about a wide range of arms control and weapons issues are available at this site, which is operated by the Arms Control Association. Some of the topics covered include Iraq and the United Nations weapons inspections, specific nuclear weapons treaties, NATO expansion, South Asian nuclear tests, and tracking missile proliferation.

Other highlights include the full text of the magazine *Arms Control Today* and more than two dozen fact sheets about various aspects of strategic arms control, nuclear and ballistic missile nonproliferation, nuclear testing, chemical and biological arms control, and control of conventional arms.

Vital Stats:

Access method: WWW
To access: http://www.armscontrol.org

Center for Defense Information

At its Web site, the Center for Defense Information offers data, articles, and reports about a wide range of defense issues. The center is an independent research organization that studies military issues around the world.

The Issues Area section of the site contains most of the documents. Within the section the documents are divided by more than two dozen topics, including alternatives to military intervention, United States policy toward Cuba, arms control, nuclear weapons accidents, the arms trade, military spending in the United States and around the world, European security, biological and chemical warfare, naval power and strategy, space and ballistic missile defenses, and women in the military. The amount of information varies by topic, and some topics are updated more frequently than others.

One of the most interesting publications is the *Nuclear Weapons Database,* a huge document that offers detailed information about the various types of nuclear weapons developed by countries around the world.

The full text of the CDI magazine *Defense Monitor* also is available at the site, and you can sign up to receive two free newsletters by e-mail: *Weekly Defense Monitor* and *CDI Russia Weekly*.

Vital Stats:

Access method: WWW
To access: http://www.cdi.org

Council for a Livable World

Through hundreds of documents—legislative updates, articles, action alerts, detailed analyses of federal budget legislation, briefing books, official government texts, and more—this site provides a huge array of information about military and defense issues.

The site is jointly operated by the Council for a Livable World, Council for a Livable World Education Fund, and PeacePAC. All three groups support arms control and eliminating weapons of mass destruction, and the latter two also lobby and endorse political candidates.

Most of the documents are arranged into six categories: national security legislation, arms control treaties, military spending, ballistic missile defense, conventional arms trade, and UN peacekeeping.

However, a special section for the 2000 election provides an analysis of all U.S. Senate races in 2000, information about House and Senate candidates endorsed by the Council for a Livable World or PeacePAC, and voting records on selected national security and nuclear arms legislation for each member of Congress from 1995 to the present.

Vital Stats:

Access method: WWW
To access: http://www.clw.org

Defense Nuclear Facilities Safety Board

The Defense Nuclear Facilities Safety Board site has documents related to the oversight of nuclear weapons plants operated by the U.S. Department of Energy (DOE). The board reviews operations and accidents at DOE nuclear facilities and makes recommendations aimed at protecting public health and safety.

The site has board recommendations, annual reports to Congress, weekly reports by board representatives at major facilities such as Hanford and Rocky Flats, technical documents, reports about inspection trips to various nuclear facilities by staff members, testimony by board officials at meetings and hear-

ings, notices of public hearings, press releases, and links to other Energy
Department Web sites.

Vital Stats:

Access method: WWW
To access: http://www.dnfsb.gov

✓ DefenseLINK

DefenseLINK, the home page for the U.S. Department of Defense, is a gateway
into the huge amount of information that the department offers on the
Internet.

Some of the highlights include an introduction to the Defense Department
titled *DoD 101,* the *Defense Almanac,* fact sheets about equipment and
weapons, data about military personnel strength, a report to Congress titled
*Domestic Preparedness Program in the Defense Against Weapons of Mass
Destruction,* a list of Defense Department installations around the world, and
information about the anthrax vaccination program.

The site also has a virtual tour of the Pentagon, a report titled *Economic
Renewal: Community Reuse of Former Military Bases,* news articles and photos,
transcripts of news briefings, speeches, links to hundreds of other Defense
Department sites, and lots more.

Vital Stats:

Access method: WWW
To access: http://www.defenselink.mil

Department of Defense Legislative Affairs

This site's highlight is a schedule of upcoming congressional activities on
defense issues, including committee hearings and floor votes. The site, which is
operated by the Defense Department's Legislative Affairs office, also has transcripts of testimony by department officials at congressional hearings.

Vital Stats:

Access method: WWW
To access: http://www.la.osd.mil

DoD News by E-Mail

Visitors to this page at DefenseLINK can sign up to receive various Defense
Department documents by e-mail. Separate mailing lists distribute news arti-

cles, press releases, contract announcements, transcripts of news conferences and background briefings, Army press releases, and Marine Corps news stories, among other documents.

Vital Stats:

Access method: WWW
To access: http://www.defenselink.mil/news/subscribe.html

Federation of American Scientists

The Federation of American Scientists offers a huge amount of valuable information about defense policy at its site, although you may have to dig for awhile to find what you're seeking.

The defense documents are divided into seven categories: arms sales monitoring, biological and toxin weapons, intelligence resources, military analysis, nuclear resources, nuclear nonproliferation and disarmament, and space policy.

The types of documents provided in each category vary, but they commonly include official reports and other documents from the federal government, congressional bills, action alerts, news stories, articles and policy recommendations from the FAS, and links to related Web sites.

The most impressive documents at the site are the full texts of two books: *The Arms Trade Revealed: A Guide for Investigators and Activists* and *Bombs for Beginners: Introduction to Special Weapons.*

Vital Stats:

Access method: WWW
To access: http://www.fas.org

National League of POW/MIA Families

Regular updates and status reports about the POW/MIA issue highlight this site, which is operated by the National League of POW/MIA Families. The league seeks the release of any remaining prisoners of war, an accounting for U.S. soldiers and civilian staff missing in action, and repatriation of all recoverable remains of POWs and MIAs who died in the Vietnam War.

The site also provides the league's position about improving relations with Vietnam, lists for many states of POWs and MIAs still unaccounted for from Vietnam, data about supposed live sightings of American POWs in Southeast

Asia since the end of the Vietnam War, and information about National POW/MIA Recognition Day.

Vital Stats:

Access method: WWW
To access: http://www.pow-miafamilies.org

Open Directory Project: War, Weapons, and Defense

Links to hundreds of sites about war and defense are available through this page at the Open Directory Project (p. 11). Each link has a brief annotation.

The page provides links to a few general sites, and other pages available through it provide links in the following categories: antiwar, biological and chemical, current conflicts, disarmament, economic, electronic and information, environmental, helicopters, land mines, missiles, nuclear, psychological, Russian weapons, smuggling and black markets, 21st century issues, and war crimes.

Vital Stats:

Access method: WWW
To access: http://dmoz.org/Society/Issues/War,_Weapons_and_Defense

---

Project Vote Smart: Defense

This page at Project Vote Smart (p. 15) provides links to dozens of selected Web sites about defense issues. The sites are operated by the Army Environmental Policy Center, Business Executives for National Security, Center for Defense Information, Central Committee for Conscientious Objectors, Chemical and Biological Arms Control Institute, Military Spending Working Group, National Commission for Economic Conversion & Disarmament, NATO, PeacePAC, Physicians for Social Responsibility, and the U.S. Nuclear Weapons Cost Study Project, among others.

Each link is briefly annotated.

Vital Stats:

Access method: WWW
To access: http://www.vote-smart.org/issues/DEFENSE

Town Hall: Defense Budget and Readiness

Links to more than two dozen articles and reports about defense issues from a variety of conservative sources are provided through this page at Town Hall.

The documents date from January 1999 to the present, and were produced by such organizations as the Heritage Foundation, *Washington Times, National Review,* Claremont Institute, Concerned Women for America, Ashbrook Center, Media Research Center, Family Research Council, National Taxpayers Union, and Christian Coalition.

The page also has links to news articles about defense issues produced in the previous few weeks by the *Washington Post,* the *New York Times, USA Today,* Nando Times, ABC, Fox News, and the Conservative News Service, among other sources.

Vital Stats:

Access method: WWW
To access: http://www.townhall.com/issueslibrary/defense

Town Hall: Missile Defense

This page at Town Hall provides links to dozens of articles and reports about missile defense systems from a variety of conservative groups, organizations, and publications.

The documents, which date from late 1998 to the present, were published by organizations including the Heritage Foundation, Family Research Council, *National Review,* Ashbrook Center, and the Center for Security Policy.

The page also provides links to news articles about missile defense that were published or aired within the previous few weeks. Recent sources included the *Washington Post,* the *New York Times,* Nando Times, ABC, and the Conservative News Service.

Vital Stats:

Access method: WWW
To access: http://www.townhall.com/issueslibrary/missiledefense

---

Yahoo! News: Missile Defense System

Through links and articles archived at the site, this page at Yahoo! (p. 17) provides more than a dozen selected news articles about United States efforts to build a missile defense system and related issues.

The articles date from March 1999 to the present. Stories are provided from the *Christian Science Monitor, The Times (London),* Reuters, CNN, and the BBC, among other sources.

The page also has links to selected Web sites about missile defense systems.

Vital Stats:

Access method: WWW
To access: http://fullcoverage.yahoo.com/fc/US/
                   Missile_Defense_System

DISABILITIES

Consortium for Citizens with Disabilities

Regular updates about legislation affecting people with disabilities are provided at this site. It's operated by the Consortium for Citizens with Disabilities, a coalition of about 100 disability organizations involved in national public policy issues.

The site also has analyses of pending legislation and testimony before congressional committees by the consortium about topics such as child care, developmental disabilities, education, employment and training, fiscal policy, health, housing, long-term services and supports, prevention, rights, Social Security, technology, and transportation.

One especially handy document provides detailed contact information for all groups that belong to the consortium, including links to their Web sites.

Vital Stats:

Access method: WWW
To access: http://www.c-c-d.org

National Council on Disability

This site has more than three dozen reports published by the National Council on Disability, an independent federal agency that makes recommendations to the president and Congress about disability issues.

Some sample titles include *Enforcing the Civil Rights of Air Travelers with Disabilities: Recommendations for the Department of Transportation and Congress, National Disability Policy: A Progress Report, Grassroots Experiences with Government Programs and Disability Policy, Equality of Opportunity: The Making of the Americans with Disabilities Act, Assisted Suicide: A Disability Perspective Position Paper, Outreach to Minorities with Disabilities and People with Disabilities in Rural Communities, Achieving Independence: The Challenge for the 21st Century,* and *Access to the Information Superhighway and Emerging Information Technologies by People with Disabilities.*

The site also has *Federal Register* notices, articles about various disability issues, and press releases.

Vital Stats:

Access method: WWW
To access: http://www.ncd.gov

Open Directory Project: Disabilities

This page at the Open Directory Project (p. 11) provides links to more than 7,000 sites about disabilities. The top page has links to a few general sites, and it also leads to separate pages about abuse, accessibility, advocacy, assisted suicide and euthanasia, etiquette, laws, news, sexuality, and specific disabilities. Each link is briefly annotated.

Vital Stats:

Access method: WWW
To access: http://dmoz.org/Society/Issues/Disabilities/

Project Vote Smart: Disabilities

This page at Project Vote Smart (p. 15) offers links to just over a dozen selected Web sites about disabilities. Each link is briefly annotated.

Vital Stats:

Access method: WWW
To access: http://www.vote-smart.org/issues/DISABILITIES

TASH

This site provides advocacy information for people with various types of physical or mental disabilities, their loved ones, and professionals. It's operated by TASH, a group formerly known as the Association for Persons with Severe Handicaps.

Some of the site's highlights include news about challenges to the Americans with Disabilities Act, information about upcoming demonstrations and conferences, and more than thirty TASH resolutions on ethical issues such as deinstitutionalization, nutrition and hydration, integrated employment, the right to communicate, and physician-assisted suicide.

Vital Stats:

Access method: WWW
To access: http://www.tash.org

Yahoo! News: Disabilities and the Disabled

This page at Yahoo! (p. 17) provides links to dozens of selected news articles about disabilities from news sources around the world.

Articles are available from June 1999 to the present. Stories are provided from newspapers such as the *Los Angeles Times, Philadelphia Inquirer, The Times (United Kingdom), Dallas Morning News, Boston Globe, Cleveland Plain Dealer, San Francisco Examiner, Lincoln Journal Star, Irish Times (Ireland), Sunday Times (South Africa), Sydney Morning Herald (Australia),* and the *New York Times;* wire services such as the Associated Press; and TV networks such as the BBC, CNN, and MSNBC.

Vital Stats:

Access method: WWW
To access: http://headlines.yahoo.com/Full_Coverage/World/
                   Disabilities_and_the_Disabled

Yahoo! Society and Culture: Disabilities

This page at Yahoo! (p. 17) has hundreds of links to Web sites about various aspects of disabilities. The top page has links to a small group of general disability sites, and it also leads to more than two dozen separate pages where links are divided by specific disability topics. Topics covered by specific pages include abuse, children, education, employment, independent living, legal issues, organizations, specific disabilities, therapy and rehabilitation, universal design, and Web directories, among others.

Vital Stats:

Access method: WWW
To access: http://dir.yahoo.com/Society_and_Culture/Disabilities

DRUG POLICY

Drug Enforcement Administration

Intelligence reports about ecstasy, the supply of illicit drugs in the United States, the South American cocaine trade, and the availability of southwest Asian heroin in the United States highlight this site from the U.S. Drug Enforcement Administration, which is part of the Justice Department (p. 106).

The site also has a document outlining the medical myths of marijuana, a report titled *Speaking Out Against Drug Legalization,* congressional testimony by DEA officials, the full text of the Controlled Substances Act, and the *DEA Briefing Book,* which has sections about the current drug problem in the United States, DEA programs and accomplishments, drug legalization, and federal drug trafficking penalties, among other subjects.

Vital Stats:

Access method: WWW
To access: http://www.usdoj.gov/dea

The Drug Policy Foundation

The Drug Policy Foundation promotes alternatives to what it calls "the failing war on drugs." At its Web site, the group provides a monthly news report about legislative and regulatory drug policy proposals, action alerts, testimony by DPF officials before congressional committees, the journal *Drug Policy Letter,* press releases, and annotated links to dozens of related Web sites.

You also can sign up at the Web site to receive regular news updates by e-mail.

Vital Stats:

Access method: WWW
To access: http://www.dpf.org

Marijuana Policy Project

Through original documents and links, this site provides articles, reports, and other publications about the medical use of marijuana, marijuana-related legislation in Congress, and efforts to change federal sentencing guidelines for marijuana cultivation. It's operated by the Marijuana Policy Project, an advocacy organization.

Other highlights include news alerts for activists, the full text of the regular *Marijuana Policy Report,* and press releases.

The project also publishes the MPPupdates e-mail newsletter.

Vital Stats:

Access method: WWW
To access: http://www.mpp.org

MPPupdates

MPPupdates is a mailing list that provides periodic news updates and information about legislative efforts to change marijuana laws. The list is operated by the Marijuana Policy Project, an advocacy organization that also operates a Web site.

Vital Stats:

Access method: E-mail
To access: Send an e-mail message to majordomo@igc.org
Subject line:
Message: **subscribe MPPupdates**

National Institute on Drug Abuse

The National Institute on Drug Abuse site offers fact sheets about specific drugs, speeches and congressional testimony by NIDA officials, articles about research, a catalog of NIDA publications, a calendar of events, and press releases.

The site also has reports titled *Inhalant Abuse: Its Dangers Are Nothing to Sniff At* and *Anabolic Steroids: A Threat to Body and Mind,* materials for teachers, and links to other Internet sites about drug abuse.

Vital Stats:

Access method: WWW
To access: http://www.nida.nih.gov

NORML

This site presents extensive information about efforts by the National Organization for the Reform of Marijuana Laws (NORML) to decriminalize marijuana.

Some of the highlights include a weekly news bulletin, updates about marijuana bills pending before state legislatures, testimony by NORML officials before congressional committees, numerous articles and other documents about the medical use of marijuana, legal briefs from various marijuana cases, numerous publications about drug testing, details about marijuana penalties in each state, and links to related sites.

You also can sign up at the Web site to receive a free electronic newsletter.

Vital Stats:

Access method: WWW
To access: http://www.norml.org

Office of National Drug Control Policy

Original documents and links at this site provide extensive information about drug use, prevention, treatment, medicine, and enforcement efforts. The site is operated by the White House Office of National Drug Control Policy (ONDCP).

Some of the site's highlights include a report titled *National Drug Control Strategy,* an ONDCP statement on using marijuana for medical purposes, a special section of documents for parents, a map of High Intensity Drug Trafficking Areas throughout the country, facts and statistics about various types of drugs, and links to dozens of reports about drug policy from various governmental agencies.

The site also has information about the drug control budget, reports about international drug control efforts, details about types of treatment for drug abusers, speeches and congressional testimony, a calendar of conferences, press releases, and links to many related sites.

Vital Stats:

Access method: WWW
To access: http://www.whitehousedrugpolicy.gov

Open Directory Project: Drugs

Links to dozens of sites about drug policy are available through this page at the Open Directory Project (p. 11). Each link has a brief annotation.

The page has links to more than a dozen general sites, and other pages available through it provide links about AIDS and substance abuse, anti-legalization, heroin, pro-legalization, and the war on drugs.

Vital Stats:

Access method: WWW
To access: http://dmoz.org/Society/Issues/Drugs

Project Vote Smart: Illegal Drugs

This page at Project Vote Smart (p. 15) contains links to several dozen selected Web sites about drugs. The sites are operated by various groups, including Alcoholics Anonymous, the American Council for Drug Education, the Drug Policy Foundation, the Drug Reform Coordination Network, the Marijuana Policy Reform Activists, the National Center on Addiction and Substance Abuse, the National Clearinghouse for Alcohol and Drug Information, and the Partnership for a Drug Free America. Each link is briefly annotated.

Vital Stats:

Access method: WWW
To access: http://www.vote-smart.org/issues/DRUGS

Public Agenda Online: Alcohol Abuse

One of the highlights of the alcohol abuse section at the Public Agenda site is a page called the Fact File. This page leads to statistics from various sources about the cost of alcohol abuse, teen alcohol use, binge drinking, drinking during pregnancy, using cartoons to sell beer, drunk driving, and related topics.

The site also provides summaries of recent news articles and reports about alcohol abuse, links to recent studies, and contact information (including links to Web sites) for major groups and agencies that study alcohol abuse.

Vital Stats:

Access method: WWW
To access: http://www.publicagenda.org/issues/
                    frontdoor.cfm?issue_type=alcohol

Public Agenda Online: Illegal Drugs

This section of the Public Agenda site offers a wide variety of information about illegal drugs. Public Agenda is a nonprofit, nonpartisan organization that researches and reports on public policy.

Among other resources, the site presents digests of recent reports and news stories (with links to the full texts where available), links to recent studies, statistics on various drug topics, and contact information (including links to Web sites) for major organizations that study illegal drugs.

Vital Stats:

Access method: WWW
To access: http://www.publicagenda.org/issues/
                    frontdoor.cfm?issue_type=illegal_drugs

sci.med.cannabis

Legal and policy issues involving the medical use of marijuana are discussed in the newsgroup sci.med.cannabis.

Vital Stats:

Access method: Usenet newsgroup
To access: news:sci.med.cannabis

Yahoo! Health: Drug Policy

This page at Yahoo! (p. 17) contains links to dozens of Web sites about drug policy. The top page has links to more than a dozen general sites, and it also leads to separate pages with links to sites about harm reduction, marijuana, organizations, and the U.S. war on drugs.

Vital Stats:

Access method: WWW
To access: http://dir.yahoo.com/Health/Pharmacy/
                   Drugs_and_Medications/Drug_Policy

Yahoo! News: Medical Marijuana

Through links, this page at Yahoo! (p. 17) provides dozens of selected news articles about the medical use of marijuana from a variety of sources.

The articles date from March 1998 to the present. Stories are provided from the *Los Angeles Times, New York Times, Christian Science Monitor, San Francisco Examiner, Denver Post, Sacramento Bee, Electronic Telegraph (United Kingdom),* BBC, ABC, CNN, CBC, and SF Gate.com, among other sources.

The page also has links to two dozen Web sites about medical marijuana.

Vital Stats:

Access method: WWW
To access: http://headlines.yahoo.com/Full_Coverage/
                   US/Medical_Marijuana

ECONOMIC AND TAX POLICY

Board of Governors of the Federal Reserve System

This site from the Board of Governors of the Federal Reserve System specializes in technical economic data.

Some of the highlights include a searchable database of bank ratings under the Community Reinvestment Act, background information about the Federal Reserve System, biographies of members of the Board of Governors, information about the Federal Open Market Committee, congressional testimony and speeches by Federal Reserve officials, press releases, reports to Congress, a summary of Federal Reserve regulations, a few consumer pamphlets about topics such as vehicle leasing and home mortgages, articles from the *Federal Reserve Bulletin,* and links to Internet sites operated by Federal Reserve banks.

Vital Stats:

Access method: WWW
To access: http://www.bog.frb.fed.us

Center on Budget and Policy Priorities

The Center on Budget and Policy Priorities site offers dozens of reports and other documents about pension benefits, the minimum wage, Social Security, health insurance, welfare reform, Medicaid, income inequality, low-income housing, taxes, and related topics. Many of the documents analyze bills currently before Congress.

The center is a nonprofit organization that studies government policies and programs, with an emphasis on those affecting low- and moderate-income people.

Vital Stats:

Access method: WWW
To access: http://www.cbpp.org

The Concord Coalition

This site's highlight is an annual scorecard rating votes by each member of Congress on a range of federal budget bills. It's operated by The Concord Coalition, a nonpartisan group that favors eliminating federal budget deficits while ensuring the future of Social Security, Medicare, and Medicaid.

The site also provides numerous documents analyzing the federal government budget and budget bills before Congress, in addition to position papers and other documents about Social Security reform, Medicare reform, and other federal entitlement programs.

Vital Stats:

Access method: WWW
To access: http://www.concordcoalition.org

Congressional Budget Office

This site offers current federal budget and economic projections, historical budget data, congressional testimony, and a monthly budget review from the Congressional Budget Office, a nonpartisan agency that provides Congress with economic and budget information.

The site also has a large collection of full-text reports about various topics. The reports cover such subjects as financial institutions, the president's budget proposals, reducing the deficit, energy and natural resources, federal employees and pay, federalism and intergovernmental relations, health, pensions and Social Security, welfare and housing, defense budgets, strategic issues and arms control, computers and information sciences, tax analysis, trade, and transportation and infrastructure.

Vital Stats:

Access method: WWW
To access: http://www.cbo.gov

Economic Policy Institute

The Economic Policy Institute site offers a broad range of reports and policy papers about topics such as the federal budget, deregulation and privatization, monetary policy, health and education, public investment, global trade, manufacturing and industrial policy, employment and wages, labor and industrial relations, sustainable economics, and politics and public opinion. The institute is a nonprofit think tank that researches the economy.

At first glance, the Web site makes it appear that you must pay for the reports. You do have to pay if you want paper copies, but electronic versions of the documents are free.

Other highlights include weekly economic snapshots, opinion articles and speeches by EPI staff and associates, analyses of important government economic indicators, and a consumer's guide to public opinion data on the Web.

You also can sign up at the site to receive the monthly *EPI News* by e-mail.

Vital Stats:

Access method: WWW
To access: http://www.epinet.org

Economic Statistics Briefing Room

Links to a variety of federal economic statistics are available through this page at the White House Web site (p. 32).

Data are available about topics such as housing starts, durable goods orders, manufacturing and trade inventories and sales, industrial production, capacity utilization, gross domestic product, personal saving rate, corporate profits, U.S. expenditures for research and development, per capita income, farm sector income, poverty rate, unemployment rate, productivity, consumer price index, crude oil prices, interest rates, airline domestic operating revenues, and U.S. international trade in goods and services.

The data are provided by the Bureau of Economic Analysis, Bureau of Labor Statistics, Bureau of Transportation Statistics, Economic Research Service, Energy Information Administration, Federal Reserve Board, National Agricultural Statistics Service, National Science Foundation, and U.S. Census Bureau.

Vital Stats:

Access method: WWW
To access: http://www.whitehouse.gov/fsbr/esbr.html

Joint Economic Committee

Through logic known only to them, the House and Senate run separate sites for the Joint Economic Committee. This is especially strange because the content of the two sites is very similar.

They provide newly released economic indicators, videos from recent hearings, press releases, and committee reports. Some of the available report titles include *Entrepreneurial Dynamism and the Success of U.S. High-Tech, Cutting Capital Gains Tax Rates: The Right Policy for the 21st Century, Social Security*

Reform: Recent Legislative Proposals, and *The Citizen's Guide to the U.S. Economy.*

Vital Stats:

Access method: WWW
To access: http://www.senate.gov/~jec/ (Senate) or
                   http://www.house.gov/jec (House)

National Taxpayers Union and National Taxpayers Union Foundation

This site offers position papers and press releases about pending congressional tax and spending legislation, the federal budget, Internet taxes, congressional office spending limits, congressional pay raises, government antitrust suits, entitlement programs, term limits, Social Security reform, interest groups, and related topics. It's operated by the National Taxpayers Union, a nonprofit group that favors lowering taxes and reducing spending, bureaucracy, and regulation at all levels of government.

Other highlights at the site include a huge list of state and local taxpayer groups around the country and links to other Web sites about taxes and fiscal policy. You also can sign up to receive e-mail news updates from the NTU.

Vital Stats:

Access method: WWW
To access: http://www.ntu.org

The New York Times: U.S. Budget

This page at the *New York Times* site has dozens of stories about the federal budget published from 1997 to the present. The page also contains links to government sites related to the budget and a forum about tax cuts.

Vital Stats:

Access method: WWW
To access: http://www.nytimes.com/library/politics/index-budget.html

Office of Management and Budget

The full text of the federal government budget as proposed by the president is available at this site, which is operated by the Office of Management and Budget. The site provides budget documents from 1996 to the present.

You can read the budget documents online, download them in PDF format, or search many of them online. Many budget tables are available as spreadsheet files.

The site also has periodic budget updates, the full text of *A Citizen's Guide to the Federal Budget,* and the full text of the annual *Economic Report of the President.*

Vital Stats:

Access method: WWW
To access: http://www.gpo.gov/usbudget

OMB Watch

Reports and press releases at this site address issues related to the federal budget, regulatory policy, advocacy by nonprofit groups, access to government information, and activities at the federal Office of Management and Budget. Many of the documents report on or analyze pending legislative and regulatory proposals in Washington. The site is operated by OMB Watch, a nonprofit research and advocacy organization.

You also can subscribe at the site to electronic mailing lists about information policy, nonprofit advocacy, regulatory reform, and community right-to-know laws, among other subjects.

Vital Stats:

Access method: WWW
To access: http://www.ombwatch.org

Open Directory Project: Economic Issues

Links to more than 400 Web sites about various economic issues are available through this page at the Open Directory Project (p. 11).

The main page provides a handful of links to general sites. It also leads to separate pages where links are divided by the following topics: economic sanctions, environmental, foreign aid, international, minimum wage, money supply, national debt, privatization, regulations, Social Security reform, taxation, and trade policy. Each link is briefly annotated.

Vital Stats:

Access method: WWW
To access: http://dmoz.org/Society/Issues/Economic/

Project Vote Smart: Economy

Links to several dozen selected Web sites about economic policy are supplied by this page at Project Vote Smart (p. 15).

The sites are operated by the American Council for Capital Formation, the Center for Defense of Free Enterprise, Citizens for a Sound Economy, the Competitive Enterprise Institute, the Economic Security Project, the National Bureau of Economic Research, the National Commission for Economic Conversion and Disarmament, the National Taxpayers Union, and the U.S. Chamber of Commerce, among other groups. Each link is briefly annotated.

Vital Stats:

Access method: WWW
To access: http://www.vote-smart.org/issues/ECONOMIC

Public Agenda Online: Economy

This section of the Public Agenda site offers a wide range of information about economic issues. Public Agenda is a nonprofit, nonpartisan organization that researches and reports on public policy.

Among other resources, the site has summaries of recent reports and news stories (with links to the full texts where available), links to recent studies, statistics on various economic topics, results from public opinion polls, and contact information (including links to Web sites) for major organizations that study economic topics.

Vital Stats:

Access method: WWW
To access: http://www.publicagenda.org/issues/
                   frontdoor.cfm?issue_type=economy

Public Agenda Online: The Federal Budget

One of the highlights of the federal budget section at the Public Agenda site is a page called Sources and Resources. This page provides links to dozens of Web sites and reports about the federal budget.

The section also has summaries of recent news articles about the budget, a wide selection of budget data, and information about public opinion concerning the budget.

Vital Stats:

Access method: WWW

To access: http://www.publicagenda.org/issues/frontdoor.cfm?issue_type=federal_budget

---

Town Hall: Budget and Tax

This page at Town Hall provides links to dozens of articles and reports about federal budget and tax issues from various conservative groups and publications.

The documents, which date from mid-1999 to the present, were prepared by the National Taxpayers Union, the Institute for Policy Innovation, the Heritage Foundation, the *National Review*, Citizens Against Government Waste, the Ashbrook Center, the Family Research Council, and Americans for Tax Reform, among other groups.

The page also has a calendar of upcoming economic conferences and links to news articles about budget and tax issues that have been published or aired within the previous few weeks. Recent sources included the *New York Times*, *Washington Post*, *USA Today*, ABC News, and the Conservative News Service.

Vital Stats:

Access method: WWW

To access: http://www.townhall.com/issueslibrary/budgetandtax

---

U.S. House Budget Committee

Through original documents and links, this highly partisan site from the House Budget Committee presents views of the Republican and Democratic members about various federal budget and taxation issues.

It offers committee reports, transcripts of selected committee hearings, briefing papers, press releases, and speeches. The site also offers similar documents produced by the Social Security Task Force, which is part of the Budget Committee.

Vital Stats:

Access method: WWW

To access: http://www.house.gov/budget

Washingtonpost.com: Budget Special Report

Dozens of important stories about the federal budget from the *Washington Post* are available at this page. The page also has selected budget editorials and opinion articles, a glossary of budget terms, a budget game, links to other sites, and links to other special reports about tax policy, Social Security, and Medicare.

Vital Stats:

Access method: WWW

To access: http://www.washingtonpost.com/wp-srv/
                              politics/special/budget/budget.htm

---

Yahoo! News: U.S. Budget Debate

Through links and articles archived at the site, this page at Yahoo! (p. 17) provides access to hundreds of news stories about the U.S. federal budget.

The articles date from February 1998 to the present. Some of the sources include the *Christian Science Monitor, Washington Post, The Times (United Kingdom), Chicago Tribune, Los Angles Times, New York Times, Philadelphia Inquirer, Investor's Business Daily,* Associated Press, Reuters, CNN, ABC, and the BBC.

The page also contains links to a handful of Web sites about the U.S. budget.

Vital Stats:

Access method: WWW

To access: http://fullcoverage.yahoo.com/Full_Coverage/
                              US/U_S__Budget

EDUCATION

✓ AskERIC

AskERIC is an extraordinary resource for anyone interested in education issues. The site is operated by the ERIC Clearinghouse on Information and Technology, with funding from the Office of Educational Research and Improvement at the U.S. Department of Education.

The site's highlight is its collection of AskEric InfoGuides, each of which lists Internet, ERIC, and print resources about a particular topic. The dozens of InfoGuides cover such subjects as at-risk students, bilingual elementary education, child abuse, English as a second language, fairness in testing, gay and lesbian parents, gender and ethnic bias in instruction, learning disabilities, motivating students, school violence, teen pregnancy and parenting, and year-round education.

Another interesting feature is an online form that teachers, librarians, administrators, and others interested in education can use to submit requests to AskERIC for education information.

The site also has a calendar of hundreds of education-related conferences, links to other Internet sites that have education information, and lots of other resources.

Vital Stats:

Access method: WWW
To access: http://www.askeric.org

Center for Education Reform

This site has reports, articles, news alerts, answers to frequently asked questions, and other resources about topics such as school choice, tuition tax credits, charter schools, school financing, state and local school reform, standards, and teacher quality. It's operated by the Center for Education Reform, a nonprofit advocacy organization that focuses on school choice, charter schools, and related topics.

You also can sign up at the site to receive regular e-mail updates about education reform issues.

Vital Stats:

Access method: WWW
To access: http://www.edreform.com

EDInfo

Subscribers to the EDInfo mailing list receive reports and information from the U.S. Department of Education. EDInfo distributes findings from education research, statistics, highlights from new reports, news about department initiatives and programs, legislative updates, and information about updates to the department's Web site (p. 136). The list typically delivers two or three messages per week.

Vital Stats:

Access method: E-mail
To access: Send an e-mail message to listproc@inet.ed.gov
Subject line:
Message: **subscribe edinfo *firstname lastname***

Home School Legal Defense Association

At its Web site, the Home School Legal Defense Association provides statistics and reports about home schooling, news about home schooling court cases, and updates about current legislative proposals affecting home schooling.

The site also has information about home schooling laws in each state, listings of home schooling organizations around the country, legislative goals of the HSLDA, an events calendar, and press releases.

Vital Stats:

Access method: WWW
To access: http://www.hslda.org

✓ National Center for Education Statistics

This site offers a huge collection of technical data, publications, and databases about education. It's operated by the National Center for Education Statistics, which is part of the Department of Education.

Some of the major publications available include *Projections of Education Statistics to 2009, The Digest of Education Statistics, Writing: Report Card for the Nation and the States,* and an annual report to Congress titled *The Condition of Education.*

Other publications include *Indicators of School Crime and Safety, America's Children: Key National Indicators of Well-Being, Dropout Rates in the United States, State Comparisons of Education Statistics: 1969–70 to 1996–97, Violence and Discipline Problems in U.S. Public Schools, Education Indicators: An International Perspective, Participation of Kindergartners through Third-Graders in Before and After-School Care, Predicting the Need for Newly Hired Teachers in the United States to 2008–09, Measuring Teacher Qualifications, College Access and Affordability, Internet Access in Public Schools and Classrooms, Teacher Quality: A Report on Teacher Preparation and Qualifications of Public School Teachers, The Civic Development of 9th Through 12th Grade Students in the United States, Long-Term Trends in Student Mathematics Performance,* and *Federal Support for Education.*

You also can sign up at the site to receive e-mail notices about new NCES publications and data products.

Vital Stats:

Access method: WWW
To access: http://nces.ed.gov

National Education Association

The National Education Association site has articles, reports, and results of public opinion polls about topics such as school violence, school vouchers, racial diversity in schools, class size, education funding, corporate operation of public schools, modernization of school buildings, student assessment, charter schools, and bilingual education.

Some other highlights include a report card detailing the voting record of every member of Congress on important education-related bills, weekly updates about education bills before Congress, congressional testimony by NEA officials, and information about the NEA's congressional priorities.

The site also has news about education reports issued by various government agencies and private organizations, education statistics, news about groups that oppose the NEA, links to Web sites operated by education advocacy groups, and lots more.

Vital Stats:

Access method: WWW
To access: http://www.nea.org

National PTA

The Web site of the National Parent Teacher Association offers articles and other materials about issues such as before- and after-school care, charter schools, class size reduction, school facilities, school funding, school reform, tax subsidies, testing, violence prevention, and vouchers.

Other highlights include a weekly Washington legislative report, updates about education bills pending in Congress, articles and press releases about

PTA positions on proposed legislation, testimony at congressional hearings by PTA representatives, information about the PTA's legislative priorities, and links to Web sites operated by other PTA and child advocacy groups.

You also can sign up at the site to receive e-mail updates about pending legislation affecting children.

Vital Stats:

Access method: WWW
To access: http://www.pta.org

Open Directory Project: Education

The education page at the Open Directory Project (p. 11) offers hundreds of links to education sites on the Web. Each link is briefly annotated.

The main page provides links to a few dozen general sites, and it also leads to separate pages with links about bilingual education, development, education reform, home schooling, literacy, school choice, school finance, school violence, and sex education.

Vital Stats:

Access method: WWW
To access: http://dmoz.org/Society/Issues/Education

Project Vote Smart: Education

This page at Project Vote Smart (p. 15) provides links to several dozen selected Web sites about education. Each link is briefly annotated.

The sites are operated by the American Council on Education, American Federation of Teachers, Center for Education Reform, *Chronicle of Higher Education,* Citizens for Responsible Education Reform, Educational Excellence Network, Education Policy Institute, *Education Week,* Learning Disabilities Association, National Dropout Prevention Center, National Education Association, National Institute for Literacy, and the United States Student Association, among others.

Vital Stats:

Access method: WWW
To access: http://www.vote-smart.org/issues/EDUCATION

Public Agenda Online: Education

Among other highlights, the education section at Public Agenda Online offers a page called the Fact File. It provides statistics from various sources about high school dropouts, math proficiency, SAT scores, international reading scores, average teacher salaries, pupil-teacher ratios, and school crime rates, among other topics.

The site also has summaries of recent news articles about education, links to recent studies, results from public opinion polls, and contact information (including links to Web sites) for major education organizations.

Vital Stats:

Access method: WWW
To access: http://www.publicagenda.org/issues/
  frontdoor.cfm?issue_type=education

Town Hall: Education

Links to dozens of articles and reports about education policy issues from a variety of conservative sources are provided through this page at Town Hall.

The documents date from January 1999 to the present, and were produced by such organizations as the Family Research Council, Heritage Foundation, Claremont Institute, Traditional Values Coalition, *National Review,* Pacific Research Institute, Institute for Policy Innovation, Concerned Women for America, Fordham Foundation, Ashbrook Center, Federalist Society, and the Christian Coalition.

The page also provides links to a small number of recent news articles about education issues from the *New York Times, USA Today, Washington Post,* Conservative News Service, CNN, and ABC, among other sources.

Vital Stats:

Access method: WWW
To access: http://www.townhall.com/issueslibrary/education

✓✓ U.S. Department of Education

The U.S. Department of Education site offers thousands of documents about education—everything from extensive reports about education reform to details about the administration's education priorities and initiatives.

The site's highlight is its collection of full-text reports, studies, and other publications. Some of the available titles include *Safe and Smart: Making After-School Hours Work for Kids, Taking Responsibility for Ending Social Promotion: A*

Guide for Educators and State and Local Leaders, Tools for Schools: School Reform Models Supported by the National Institute on the Education of At-Risk Students, The Charter School Roadmap, Reducing Class Size: What Do We Know?, Catalog of School Reform Models, Turning Around Low-Performing Schools: A Guide for State and Local Leaders, A Compact for Learning: An Action Handbook for Family-School-Community Partnerships, Promising Practices: New Ways to Improve Teacher Quality, and *Creating Safe and Drug-Free Schools: An Action Guide.*

The site also provides an extensive group of statistical publications, an overview of U.S. Department of Education programs and services, a directory of more than 2,400 education-related organizations around the country, a searchable bibliographic database of more than 20,000 publications produced or funded by the department since 1980, the texts of various federal education laws, speeches by department officials, and links to other department Web sites.

The department also operates the EdInfo mailing list (p. 133).

Vital Stats:

Access method:	WWW
To access:	http://www.ed.gov

Yahoo! News: Education Curriculum and Policy

You can access dozens of news articles about educational policy issues through this page at Yahoo! (p. 17). The articles cover topics such as education ethics, pupil promotion, creationism, education standards, school reform, same-sex classes, and school discipline, among others.

The articles date from mid-1999 to the present. Some of the sources include the Associated Press, CNN, the *Dallas Morning News, Washington Post, Boston Globe, Baltimore Sun, New York Times, Los Angeles Times, Christian Science Monitor, Chicago Tribune,* and *Kansas City Star.*

The page also provides links to a small collection of related Web sites.

Vital Stats:

Access method:	WWW
To access:	http://fullcoverage.yahoo.com/fc/US/ Education_Curriculum_and_Policy

Yahoo! News: School Choice and Tuition Vouchers

Through links and articles archived at the site, this page at Yahoo! (p. 17) provides several dozen selected articles about charter schools and tuition vouchers dating from early 1999 to the present.

The news sources include the Associated Press, Reuters, CNN, *Boston Globe, Los Angeles Times, Washington Post, San Francisco Examiner, New York Times, Chicago Tribune, Cleveland Plain Dealer, Las Vegas Review-Journal, Florida Times-Union,* and *Albuquerque Tribune,* among others.

If you select Yahoo! News Search on the left side of the screen, stories about school vouchers published within the previous two weeks are displayed. The page also provides links to a handful of Web sites about vouchers and related issues.

Vital Stats:

Access method: WWW
To access: http://fullcoverage.yahoo.com/fc/US/
                            School_Choice_and_Tuition_Vouchers

ENVIRONMENT

About.com: The Environment

A collection of links to hundreds of Web sites highlights the Environment page at About.com.

The links are divided by dozens of topics, including acid rain, air pollution, alternative energy, biodiversity, coastal environmental issues, desertification, endangered species, environmental economics, environmental interest groups, forestry, global climate change, hazardous waste, marine pollution, nuclear waste, pesticides, sustainable development, trade and the environment, wetlands, and whales, among others.

Vital Stats:

Access method: WWW
To access: http://environment.about.com

✓ Envirofacts Data Warehouse and Applications

This amazing site provides access to many of the most important environmental databases maintained by the U.S. Environmental Protection Agency.

The databases provide detailed information about the status of Superfund sites, violations of drinking water regulations, activities of firms involved in hazardous waste generation and disposal, releases and transfers of more than 650 toxic chemicals to the environment by various facilities, discharges by wastewater treatment facilities, compliance with air pollution regulations, and other topics.

You can search a single database or all the databases simultaneously. The databases are updated monthly. The site also provides links to other environmental search engines and sources.

Vital Stats:

Access method: WWW
To access: http://www.epa.gov/enviro/index_java.html

Environment and Public Works

The Senate Environment and Public Works Committee operates this site. It provides a list of all bills referred to the committee (along with links to the full texts of the bills), notices about upcoming committee and subcommittee hearings, a link to transcripts of selected committee hearings, and a description of the committee's jurisdiction.

Vital Stats:

Access method: WWW
To access: http://www.senate.gov/~epw

House Committee on Resources

The House Committee on Resources, which is responsible for environmental legislation, operates this site. It has the texts of bills before the committee and its subcommittees, a schedule of upcoming committee and subcommittee hearings and other meetings, links to transcripts of committee hearings, background information about major issues before the committee, the texts of bills referred to the committee, and press releases.

The site also provides links to pages operated by the panel's subcommittees: National Parks and Public Lands; Water and Power; Energy and Mineral Resources; Forests and Forest Health; and Fisheries Conservation, Wildlife, and Oceans.

Vital Stats:

Access method: WWW
To access: http://www.house.gov/resources

League of Conservation Voters

This site's highlight is the *National Environmental Scorecard*, an annual document that rates the environmental voting records of every member of Congress. The online version also allows you to perform customized searches that compare voting records of various sub-groups in the House and Senate, such as members of a particular state's delegation. The site is operated by the League of Conservation Voters, which works to elect pro-environment candidates to Congress.

Other interesting features include lists of congressional candidates either endorsed or targeted for defeat by the league, LCV letters to members of Congress about environmental issues, and press releases.

You also can sign up at the site to receive information about environmental votes by e-mail.

Vital Stats:

Access method: WWW
To access: http://www.lcv.org

National Parks and Conservation Association

This site from the National Parks and Conservation Association has extensive information about protecting and enhancing the National Park System.

Among other highlights, the site provides news about pending federal legislation affecting national parks, alerts about current threats to individual parks, reports about topics such as the ten most endangered parks, selected articles from *National Parks* magazine, and *National Park Lines,* a weekly newsletter that provides news and calls to action regarding national park issues across the country. You also can sign up at the site to receive the newsletter by e-mail.

Vital Stats:

Access method: WWW
To access: http://www.npca.org

Office of Civilian Radioactive Waste Management

The Office of Civilian Radioactive Waste Management site contains information about efforts to build a permanent repository for high-level radioactive waste from nuclear power plants and other facilities. The office is part of the Department of Energy.

The site has background information about the office, abstracts of technical reports prepared by the office, the text of the Nuclear Waste Policy Act of 1982, budget information, congressional testimony and speeches by DOE officials, a calendar of events, a newsletter, *Federal Register* notices, information about nuclear waste disposal programs in other countries, links to other Internet sites related to civilian radioactive waste management, and fact sheets about radiation, storage and disposal of spent nuclear fuel, transportation of spent nuclear fuel, and related subjects.

Vital Stats:

Access method: WWW
To access: http://www.rw.doe.gov

Open Directory Project: Environment

Links to more than 800 Web sites about the environment are provided through this page at the Open Directory Project (p. 11). Each link has a brief description.

The top page provides links to general sites, and also leads to more than three dozen pages with links to sites about specific environmental topics. Some of the subjects covered include activism, antienvironmentalism, climate change, conservation and endangered species, directories and indexes, environmental justice, news, nuclear, organizations, population, sustainable development, and water.

Vital Stats:

Access method: WWW

To access: http://dmoz.org/Society/Issues/Environment

Project Vote Smart: Environment

This page at Project Vote Smart (p. 15) provides links to dozens of selected Web sites about the environment. Each link is briefly annotated.

The sites are operated by American Forests, American Rivers, Center for International Environmental Law, Citizens Clearinghouse for Hazardous Waste, Defenders of Wildlife, Earthwatch, Environmental Defense Fund, Environmental Health Center, Environmental Law Institute, Foundation for Research on Economics and the Environment, Friends of the Earth, Global Futures Foundation, Greenpeace, League of Conservation Voters, League of Private Property Voters, National Audubon Society, National Wildlife Federation, Natural Resources Defense Council, Nature Conservancy, Northwest Forestry Association, Ozone Action, Rainforest Action Network, Sierra Club, and the Wilderness Society, among others.

Vital Stats:

Access method: WWW

To access: http://www.vote-smart.org/issues/ENVIRONMENT

Public Agenda Online: Environment

A wide range of environmental information is available through this section of the Public Agenda site. Public Agenda is a nonprofit, nonpartisan organization that researches and reports on public issues.

The site has summaries of recent reports and news stories (with links to the full texts where available), statistics about various environmental issues, results from public opinion polls about the environment, and contact information (including links to Web sites) for major environmental organizations.

Vital Stats:

Access method: WWW

To access: http://www.publicagenda.org/issues/
                     frontdoor.cfm?issue_type=environment

✓ Scorecard

By simply typing your zip code in a box at Scorecard, you can get a huge range of environmental information for your community. The site is a superb example of what an activist group can do with government data and the Internet.

A single zip code search retrieves detailed data for your community about toxic chemical releases from manufacturing facilities, releases of hazardous air pollutants, air pollution emission levels, and agricultural pollution. Many of the data sets list which facilities are the biggest polluters in your area.

The site is operated by the Environmental Defense Fund and uses data from the U.S. Environmental Protection Agency (p. 144).

Vital Stats:

Access method: WWW
To access: http://www.scorecard.org

Sierra Club

The Congressional VoteWatch page is the highlight of this site from the Sierra Club. The page, which is frequently updated, lists how individual members of Congress voted on recent environment-related legislation.

The Sierra Club site also has articles and reports about topics such as sprawl, logging on federal lands, pollution by factory farms, wildlands, global warming, population, clean air, habitat and species, nuclear waste, toxic waste, and wetlands.

Vital Stats:

Access method: WWW
To access: http://www.sierraclub.org

Town Hall: Environment

Links to several dozen articles and reports about environmental issues from a variety of conservative sources are provided through this page at Town Hall.

The documents date from January 1999 to the present. Sources include the Greening Earth Society, National Wilderness Institute, *National Review*, Pacific Research Institute, Heritage Foundation, Capital Research Center, Small Business Survival Committee, and the National Taxpayers Union, among others.

The page also provides links to recent news articles about environmental issues from sources such as the *Washington Post, USA Today, New York Times,* CNN, Conservative News Service, and MSNBC.

Vital Stats:

Access method: WWW
To access: http://www.townhall.com/issueslibrary/environment

United States Environmental Protection Agency

The United States Environmental Protection Agency site offers an immense assortment of information about everything from acid rain to pollution prevention. It has thousands of documents and databases—some of them extremely valuable—but the site's poor design makes finding anything difficult.

Ignore the useless interface on the home page. There are two better options for accessing the site. If you know exactly what you're seeking, the best choice is to use the site's search engine. If your quest is more general, select Browse on the site's home page. Doing this arranges the site's information by subject.

One of the site's highlights is a selection of searchable databases. They provide information about Superfund sites, sites that produce hazardous waste, releases of toxic chemicals, releases of airborne contaminants, and other topics.

Another helpful feature is Search by Zip Code. By simply typing in your zip code, you can get a list of facilities in your county that release pollutants or handle hazardous materials, details about where Superfund sites are located and the status of their cleanup efforts, and much more.

The site also contains publications about pesticides, air quality, pollution prevention, hazardous waste, solid waste, water quality, wetlands, and other topics; *Federal Register* documents that deal with the environment or environment-related issues; technical reports and publications; and links to EPA laboratories and research centers.

Other notable offerings include statistics about environmental quality and trends, extensive details about Superfund sites, lists of EPA clearinghouses and hotlines, a catalog of more than 5,000 EPA documents that can be ordered for free, speeches by EPA officials, and guides and curricula for teachers.

Vital Stats:

Access method: WWW
To access: http://www.epa.gov

✓ U.S. Nuclear Regulatory Commission

This site has a huge amount of information about facilities—primarily nuclear power plants—that are regulated by the Nuclear Regulatory Commission. It offers a list of troubled nuclear plants on the NRC's special watchlist, daily reports about problems at nuclear plants, a map showing the location of commercial nuclear power plants in the United States, information about the disposal of low-level and high-level radioactive waste, and Systematic Assessment of Licensee Performance (SALP) reports, which are detailed performance reviews of individual nuclear plants.

One of the site's highlights is a collection of Plant Information Books for every operating nuclear reactor in the United States. The books have information about emergency response facilities, the plant site, evacuation routes, and the nuclear reactor and its various systems. There are even diagrams of some plant systems, such as the reactor coolant system, the emergency core cooling systems, and reactor containment.

Vital Stats:

Access method:	WWW
To access:	http://www.nrc.gov

✓ Yahoo! News: Environment and Nature News

Through links and articles archived at the site, this page at Yahoo! (p. 17) provides access to hundreds of news stories about a wide range of environment and nature issues.

The stories originated with sources such as the *Boston Globe, Dallas Morning News, Philadelphia Inquirer, The Times (United Kingdom), Chicago Tribune, Los Angeles Times, San Francisco Examiner, Washington Post, Seattle Times, Christian Science Monitor, New York Times,* Reuters, AP, Environmental News Network, Reuters, BBC, CBC, and the Panafrican News Agency.

The page also provides links to selected environmental news sources and related Web sites.

Vital Stats:

Access method:	WWW
To access:	http://fullcoverage.yahoo.com/Full_Coverage/Science/ Environment_and_Nature_News

✓ Yahoo! News: Global Warming

This page at Yahoo! (p. 17) provides access to more than 100 news stories about global warming. The stories date from October 1997 to the present.

Some of the sources include the *Miami Herald, The Times (United Kingdom), Irish Times (Ireland), Seattle Times, the New York Times, Boston Globe, Philadelphia Inquirer, Chicago Tribune, Time, Christian Science Monitor, San Francisco Examiner,* Reuters, AP, BBC, ABC, and Environmental News Network.

If you select Yahoo! News Search on the left side of the page, you'll receive a list of stories about global warming published in recent weeks. A search commonly returns a couple dozen articles.

The page also provides links to a selection of Web sites about global warming.

Vital Stats:

Access method: WWW
To access: http://headlines.yahoo.com/Full_Coverage/World/
                   Global_Warming

Yahoo! Society and Culture: Environment and Nature

Through this page, Yahoo! (p. 17) offers links to well over 1,000 Web sites about the environment and nature. Each link is briefly annotated.

The top page provides links to just over a dozen general sites. It also leads to dozens of pages about such subjects as climate change policy, environment and development policies, environmental justice, forests, global warming, mining issues, oil and gas issues, overpopulation, parks, pollution, recycling, sustainable development, waste management, water resources, Web directories, wilderness, and wildlife.

Vital Stats:

Access method: WWW
To access: http://dir.yahoo.com/society_and_culture/
                   environment_and_nature

GAY AND LESBIAN ISSUES

✓ About.com: Gay/Lesbian Issues

This superb page at the About.com site has a huge amount of information about gay and lesbian issues, including many political issues.

The site's highlight is the hundreds of annotated links. They're neatly arranged by topics such as activist organizations, campus life, enemies list, ex-gay movements, hate crimes, health and science, marriage, military, out and outing, politics, political organizations, work issues, and youth.

The page also offers a large selection of articles, bulletin boards, and regular chat sessions.

Vital Stats:

Access method: WWW
To access: http://gaylesissues.about.com

American Civil Liberties Union: Lesbian & Gay Rights

This page at the American Civil Liberties Union site (p. 97) has a wide range of materials about lesbian and gay rights.

It has information about congressional legislation affecting gay and lesbian rights, court cases involving gay and lesbian rights (including many cases where the ACLU is a party), laws banning discrimination based on sexual orientation, states and cities that offer domestic partnership registration, same-sex marriage laws, gays in the military, lesbian and gay adoption, and transgender rights, among other topics.

Vital Stats:

Access method: WWW
To access: http://www.aclu.org/issues/gay/hmgl.html

✓ Gay and Lesbian Politics: WWW and Internet Resources

An administrator and lecturer at Indiana University operates this site, which offers a huge collection of links to carefully selected Internet sites about gay, lesbian, bisexual, and transgender political issues.

The links are separated by topic: latest news reports, Usenet newsgroups, electronic mailing lists, organizations, federal government, in the states, policy

and political issues, law and legal resources, genetics and science, elected officials, transgender, media, academic, and other meta-sites.

The policy and political issues section is broken down further by subject:
AIDS; civil rights and nondiscrimination; hate crimes, antiviolence, and antiha-
rassment; marriage and domestic partnership; military; parenting, adoption,
and family; schools, youth, and Boy Scouts; and workplace and employment.

Vital Stats:

Access method: WWW
To access: http://www.indiana.edu/~glbtpol

GLAAD Online

This site focuses primarily on how the lesbian, gay, bisexual, and transgender
community is represented in film, television, print, radio, the Internet, and
other types of media. It's operated by the Gay and Lesbian Alliance Against
Defamation (GLAAD).

The site has information about the GLAAD Media Awards, news articles, and
lists of lesbian, gay, bisexual or transgender characters on primetime television
programs. You also can sign up at the site to receive biweekly alerts from
GLAAD by e-mail.

Vital Stats:

Access method: WWW
To access: http://www.glaad.org

Human Rights Campaign

Highlights at this site include alerts about pending congressional bills that
affect the rights of gays and lesbians and links to the texts of important bills
before Congress. The site is operated by the Human Rights Campaign, a group
that works on gay and lesbian rights issues.

The site also has news about the 2000 election, press releases, and background information about hate crimes, fighting HIV/AIDS, workplace discrimination, lesbian health issues, marriage, and transgender issues.

You also can sign up at the site to receive action alerts and news releases by
e-mail.

Vital Stats:

Access method: WWW
To access: http://www.hrcusa.org

Lambda Legal Defense and Education Fund

This site's highlight is its collection of memos, briefs, decisions, and other legal documents from cases involving the rights of lesbians and gays. It's operated by the Lambda Legal Defense and Education Fund, a legal organization that works for the civil rights of lesbians, gays, and people with HIV/AIDS.

Other important files provide detailed information divided by state about state and local laws affecting the rights of lesbians and gays, a status report about the progress of laws banning same-sex marriages, a chart listing the states and municipalities that have laws banning sexual orientation discrimination, and extensive background information about topics such as anti-gay initiatives, domestic partnerships, employment, housing, immigration and political asylum, marriage, reproductive rights, and youth.

Vital Stats:

Access method: WWW
To access: http://www.lambdalegal.org

Project Vote Smart: Gay, Lesbian, Bisexual, and Transgender Issues

This page at Project Vote Smart (p. 15) provides links to several dozen Web sites about gay, lesbian, bisexual, and transgender issues. Each link is briefly annotated.

The sites are operated by the American Civil Liberties Union, Dignity USA, Gay and Lesbian Alliance Against Defamation, Human Rights Campaign, Lambda Legal Defense and Education Fund, National Gay and Lesbian Task Force, and the Transgender Forum and Resource Center, among others.

Vital Stats:

Access method: WWW
To access: http://www.vote-smart.org/issues/GAY_LESBIAN_
                  BISEXUAL_AND_TRANSGENDER_ISSUES

Task Force Online

The full text of *Courting the Vote 2000,* a report that analyzes the stands of the 2000 presidential candidates on issues affecting gay, lesbian, bisexual, and transgender people, is available at this site. It's operated by the National Gay and Lesbian Task Force.

The full texts of several other reports also are available. Some of the available titles include *The Domestic Partnership Organizing Manual for Employee Benefits; Capital Gains and Losses: A State by State Review of Gay, Lesbian,*

Bisexual, Transgender, and HIV/AIDS-Related Legislation; Out and Voting: The Gay, Lesbian, and Bisexual Vote in Congressional House Elections 1990–1996; and *Gay, Lesbian, Bisexual and Transgender Civil Rights Laws in the U.S.*

The site also offers news about national and state legislative actions around the country affecting the rights of gays and lesbians, press releases, and the opportunity to sign up to receive press releases, media advisories, and related materials by e-mail.

Vital Stats:

Access method: WWW
To access: http://www.ngltf.org

Yahoo! News: Gay and Lesbian News

Through links and articles archived at the site, this page at Yahoo! (p. 17) provides access to more than 200 news articles about gay and lesbian issues. The articles date from July 1998 to the present.

Some of the news sources include the BBC, ABC, CNN, *U.S. News and World Report, The Times (England), San Francisco Examiner, Christian Science Monitor, USA Today, Sydney Morning Herald (Australia), Village Voice, Los Angeles Times, Seattle Times, Wired, Denver Post, New York Times, Irish Times (Ireland), New York Law Journal, Jerusalem Post (Israel), Philadelphia Inquirer, Time, Baltimore Sun, New York Daily News,* and *Chicago Tribune.*

The site also provides links to a selected group of Web sites about gay and lesbian issues.

Vital Stats:

Access method: WWW
To access: http://fullcoverage.yahoo.com/fc/World/
                   Gay_and_Lesbian_News

GENERAL GOVERNMENT POLICY AND REFORM

AEI-Brookings Joint Center for Regulatory Studies

The most important documents at this site are working papers that provide in-depth analyses of high profile regulatory issues. The AEI-Brookings Joint Center for Regulatory Studies is a project of the American Enterprise Institute and the Brookings Institution, two of the most prominent think tanks in Washington, D.C.

Working papers available at the site include *The Economics of Regulating Cellular Phones in Vehicles; Regulatory Reform: Assessing the Government's Numbers; The Impact of Economics on Environmental Policy; Balancing Costs and Benefits of New Privacy Mandates; Are Risk Regulators Rational? Evidence from Hazardous Waste Cleanup Decisions;* and *Managed Competition in U.S. Telecommunications.*

Three pamphlets at the site provide broad overviews of the center's research: *An Agenda for Regulatory Reform; Benefit-Cost Analysis in Environmental, Health, and Safety Regulation;* and *Improving Regulatory Accountability.*

The site also has congressional testimony by center scholars, papers analyzing proposed regulations and congressional legislation, and a page where you can sign up to receive news by e-mail about center publications and events.

Vital Stats:

Access method: WWW
To access: http://www.aei.brookings.org

American Conservative Union

The chief feature at the American Conservative Union site is the group's annual ratings for each member of Congress, dating from 1971 to the present. The site also has analyses of important issues currently before Congress, newspaper columns by various ACU officials, links to Web sites operated by other conservative organizations, and press releases.

You also can sign up at the site to automatically receive articles, news releases, and other documents by e-mail.

Vital Stats:

Access method: WWW
To access: http://www.conservative.org

American Enterprise Institute for Public Policy Research

Through reports, articles, and transcripts of speeches and congressional testimony, this site provides information about such policy issues as the Microsoft antitrust litigation, the United Nations, pharmaceutical price controls, Taiwan, the International Monetary Fund, NATO, Medicare, U.S. aid to North Korea, free trade, Social Security, welfare reform, and health care. The site is operated by the American Enterprise Institute, a major conservative think tank in Washington, D.C.

Other highlights at the site include the *AEI Newsletter,* descriptions of AEI books, and links to selected articles from *The American Enterprise* magazine.

Vital Stats:

Access method: WWW
To access: http://www.aei.org

Americans for Democratic Action and the Americans for Democratic Action Education Fund

Documents at this site provide news about bills currently before Congress on topics such as the minimum wage, campaign finance reform, Social Security, civil rights, federal budget priorities, health care, military spending, and foreign policy. The site is operated by Americans for Democratic Action and the Americans for Democratic Action Education Fund. The ADA bills itself as "the nation's oldest independent liberal political organization."

The site also provides ratings of the voting records for each member of Congress from 1989 to the present, details about the ADA's legislative priorities, and e-mail addresses and other contact information for each member of Congress,

You also can sign up at the site to receive legislative alerts automatically by e-mail.

Vital Stats:

Access method: WWW
To access: http://adaction.org

Brookings Institution

The Brookings Institution is generally regarded as the granddaddy of liberal think tanks in Washington, D.C. The highlight of its Web site is a collection of *Policy Briefs* about a wide range of public policy topics.

The briefs, which are written by Brookings scholars, tackle topics such as the working poor, greenhouse gas emissions, human rights in China, emerging financial markets, NATO, tax cuts, military readiness, Social Security taxes, telecommunications competition, environmental policy, urban education, economic sanctions, revitalizing cities, trade policy, and student performance.

Brookings scholars also express their views through op-ed articles, congressional testimony, and other documents available at the site.

You also can subscribe at the site to receive weekly e-mail notifications about events and publications at Brookings.

Vital Stats:

Access method: WWW
To access: http://www.brookings.org

The Center for Public Integrity

The Center for Public Integrity is a nonprofit, nonpartisan research organization in Washington that's best known for its investigative reports on various public policy issues.

A few of the center's reports are available for free at its Web site. The available titles are *Nothing Sacred: The Politics of Privacy; Unreasonable Risk: The Politics of Pesticides;* and *Fat Cat Hotel,* which helped break the story about campaign fundraisers and donors staying overnight at the White House. Other center reports about topics such as the influence of special interests in Congress, the politics of airline safety, and the politics of food-borne illnesses can be purchased through the Web site.

Vital Stats:

Access method: WWW
To access: http://www.publicintegrity.org

Citizens Against Government Waste

Jack Anderson is chairman of Citizens Against Government Waste, which documents what it considers wasteful spending practices by the federal government. Highlights at the group's Web site include the annual *Pig Book,* a report documenting pork-barrel spending by Congress, and the *Prime Cuts Catalog,* an annual report detailing proposed cuts throughout the federal budget.

The site also has investigative reports about government spending, ratings of the voting records for all member of Congress, legislative alerts, links to important spending bills moving through Congress, the monthly *Wastewatcher* newsletter, congressional testimony, and press releases.

Vital Stats:

Access method: WWW
To access: http://www.cagw.org

Committee on Government Reform

Documents about campaign finance reform, clemency for Puerto Rican terrorists, and activities of federal law enforcement agencies at Waco dominate this site from the House Committee on Government Reform. The documents include reports, hearing transcripts, transcripts of speeches, and news articles about committee activities from various publications.

Other documents address topics such as end-of-life care, defense vaccines, cancer, dietary supplements, federalism, complementary and alternative medicine, and waste and fraud in government programs.

Separate pages provide documents from the panel's subcommittees on the Census; the Civil Service; Criminal Justice, Drug Policy, and Human Resources; the District of Columbia; Government Management, Information, and Technology; National Economic Growth, Natural Resources, and Regulatory Affairs; National Security, Veterans' Affairs, and International Relations; and the Postal Service.

Vital Stats:

Access method: WWW
To access: http://www.house.gov/reform

Committee on Governmental Affairs

Documents about topics such as espionage by China at nuclear weapons laboratories, violations of campaign finance laws, the future of the Independent Counsel Act, and federalism highlight this site from the Senate Committee on Governmental Affairs.

Most of the documents are witness statements at hearings. The site also has videos of selected hearings, the texts of legislation being considered by the committee, and separate pages for the Subcommittee on International Security, Proliferation, and Federal Services; the Subcommittee on Oversight of

Government Management, Restructuring, and the District of Columbia; and the Permanent Subcommittee on Investigations.

Vital Stats:

Access method: WWW
To access: http://www.senate.gov/~gov_affairs

Common Cause

At its Web site, Common Cause offers a large collection of studies and other documents about campaign finance reform, ethics in government, open government, civil rights, and corporate welfare, among other subjects.

The site is divided into sections. Here are the three best:

- Campaign Finance Studies: A collection of reports about campaign finance and the influence of money in politics. Some of the available titles include *Banking on Congress: Special Interests, Not Consumers, are the Big Winners in Financial Services Agreement; Left at the Gate: How the Airlines Beat Back Congress on Passenger Rights; Paying to Play: How Masters of Washington's Big Money Game Won in the 1999 Tax Bill; Sale of the Century: Special Interests Contribute Record Amounts of Soft Money During First Six Months of 1999;* and *Wall Street Interests Pushing for Social Security Privatization Gave $53 Million in Political Contributions During Past Decade.*

- Soft Money Laundromat: Background information about soft money political contributions, lists of the top soft money donors in recent elections, profiles of the largest soft money donors, and a searchable database of special interest soft money contributions to the Democratic and Republican national party committees. You can search the database by donor name, donor location, or industry.

- Know Your Congress: A searchable database that provides basic information about members of Congress. For each member, the database provides contact information, summaries of campaign contributions from special interest groups, and details about recent votes on Common Cause issues. You can search the database by member name, state, or zip code.

You also can sign up at the Web site to receive news alerts by e-mail.

Vital Stats:

Access method: WWW
To access: http://www.commoncause.org

The Conservative Caucus

This site is operated by the Conservative Caucus, a group founded and chaired by the well-known conservative activist Howard Phillips. It has action alerts about congressional bills and hearings, e-mail addresses for all members of Congress, articles and reports about topics ranging from the Chemical Weapons Treaty to federal police power, and links to a large number of conservative Web sites.

You also can sign up at the Web site to receive legislative alerts and other news by e-mail.

Vital Stats:

Access method: WWW
To access: http://www.conservativeusa.org

Eagle Forum

This site's highlights are its alerts concerning congressional bills about issues ranging from consumer privacy to the Nuclear Test Ban Treaty. The site is operated by the Eagle Forum, whose president is Phyllis Schlafly.

The site also provides links to congressional voting records on selected issues, news about executive orders signed by the president, numerous articles about the power of the federal judiciary, a questionnaire for federal candidates prepared by the Eagle Forum, and newspaper columns and radio commentaries by Schlafly.

Vital Stats:

Access method: WWW
To access: http://www.eagleforum.org

✓ FAS Project on Government Secrecy

A huge collection of documents about government secrecy—most of them official documents from government agencies—highlights this site from the Federation of American Scientists.

The documents include reports from the State Department, Central Intelligence Agency, President's Foreign Intelligence Advisory Board, and other government agencies; Supreme Court decisions in secrecy cases; witness testimony at congressional hearings about secrecy; news articles about secrecy and security from a variety of sources; the texts of pending legislation about secrecy; and the full text of the *Secrecy & Government Bulletin,* which is published by the FAS.

The site also contains links to Freedom of Information Act sites operated by selected national security agencies and links to other government and non-government sites about secrecy.

Vital Stats:

Access method:	WWW
To access:	http://www.fas.org/sgp

The Heritage Foundation

The Heritage Foundation site offers hundreds of reports, articles, papers, and other documents about a huge range of public policy issues. The foundation is a major think tank in Washington, D.C., that focuses on "rolling back the liberal welfare state and building an America where freedom, opportunity, and civil society flourish," according to its Web site.

Documents at the site address such subjects as education, missile defense, Asia, Internet taxes, Social Security, the federal budget, Russia, labor, national security, federal regulations, tax reform, health care, affirmative action, church-state relations, environmental policy, lobbying reform, and trade, among many others.

Some of the available titles include *How "Emergency" Farm Spending Squanders the Surplus; Top Ten Ways to Avoid Wasting the Surplus; How Taxes Reduce Savings; Broadband Telecommunications for the 21st Century: A Legislative Report Card; Federal Litigation Against the Tobacco Industry: Elevating Politics Over Law; Rising Costs, Reduced Access: How Regulation Harms Health Consumers and the Uninsured; Tensions Across the Strait: China's Military Options Against Taiwan Short of War; Missile Defense Testing Needed to Meet North Korean Threat; Lessons from the War in Kosovo;* and *Why Congress Should Hold Firm on Reducing Foreign Aid.*

The site also has congressional testimony by Heritage scholars, links to House and Senate schedules, links to articles from *Policy Review,* online chats, links to other conservative policy sites, and a page where you can sign up to receive news updates by e-mail.

Vital Stats:

Access method:	WWW
To access:	http://www.heritage.org

Open Directory Project: Policy Institutes

This page at the Open Directory Project (p. 11) provides links to Web sites operated by dozens of public policy institutes and think tanks. Many of the larger institutions such as the Brookings Institution and Heritage Foundation are included, but the page also provides links to many lesser-known organizations.

Some of the latter include the Allegheny Institute for Public Policy, Beacon Hill Institute for Public Policy Research, Center for the Study of American Business, Century Foundation, Discovery Institute, Ethics and Public Policy Center, Free Congress Foundation, Hudson Institute, Pacific Research Institute, Regulatory Policy Center, and the Rockefeller Institute of Government.

Vital Stats:

Access method: WWW
To access: http://dmoz.org/Society/Issues/Policy_Institutes

People for the American Way

Documents about such hot button issues as school vouchers, Internet censorship, flag desecration, civil rights for gays and lesbians, and judicial nominations before Congress highlight this site from People for the American Way, a liberal organization in Washington, D.C.

Most of the documents are divided into six topical categories: education, about the religious right, free expression, religious liberty, equal rights, and building democracy. The types of documents available vary by category, but often include reports, articles, and legal filings.

The site also has legislative updates, information about court cases in which PFAW is involved, resources for progressive activists, press releases, and three newsletters: *Right Wing Watch Online, Attacks on the Freedom to Learn Online,* and *Education Activist Online.*

You also can sign up at the site to receive various types of publications by e-mail.

Vital Stats:

Access method: WWW
To access: http://www.pfaw.org

Project Vote Smart: General Public Policy

Links to just under twenty Web sites about general public policy issues are provided through this page at Project Vote Smart (p. 15). Each link carries a short description.

The sites are operated by the American Conservative Union, Americans for Democratic Action, Campaign for America's Future, Conservative Caucus,

Eagle Forum, Empower America, John Birch Society, and the Ripon Society, among other groups.

Vital Stats:

Access method: WWW
To access: http://www.vote-smart.org/issues/
                   GENERAL_PUBLIC_POLICY

Project Vote Smart: Government Reform

This page at Project Vote Smart (p. 15) offers links to just over a dozen selected Internet sites about government reform. Each link is briefly annotated.

The sites are operated by the Alliance for Redesigning Government, Center for Voting and Democracy, Citizens Against Government Waste, Congressional Accountability Project, Federation of American Scientists, Fund for Constitutional Government, Project on Government Oversight, and the Taxpayer Assets Project, among others.

Vital Stats:

Access method: WWW
To access: http://www.vote-smart.org/issues/
                   GOVERNMENT_REFORM

Project Vote Smart: Think Tanks and Research Institutes

This page at Project Vote Smart (p. 15) provides links to dozens of sites operated by think tanks and research institutes, most of which publish large numbers of studies and other documents about a broad range of government and public policy topics. Each link has a brief description of the organization that operates the site.

Some of the organizations represented include the American Enterprise Institute, Annenberg Public Policy Center, Brookings Institution, Carnegie Endowment for International Peace, Cato Institute, Center for Nonproliferation Studies, Center for Policy Alternatives, Council on Foreign Relations, Economic Policy Institute, Heritage Foundation, Hudson Institute, Media Institute, National Research Council, Progressive Policy Institute, and the Urban Institute.

Vital Stats:

Access method: WWW
To access: http://www.vote-smart.org/organizations/
                   THINK_TANKS_RESEARCH_INSTITUTES

Public Citizen

The Public Citizen site offers hundreds of reports, legal briefs, articles, and other documents about a huge range of political issues. Public Citizen is a consumer group founded by Ralph Nader.

The documents cover topics such as the Independent Counsel Act, medical malpractice litigation, no-fault insurance, the correlation between tobacco industry campaign contributions and congressional votes, failures by the Nuclear Regulatory Commission, utility holding companies, nuclear waste disposal, the North American Free Trade Agreement, the World Trade Organization, prescription and over-the-counter drugs, electronic government records, the Freedom of Information Act and government secrecy, open court proceedings, election laws, the First Amendment, health and safety regulations, labor unions, and corporate welfare.

Vital Stats:

Access method: WWW
To access: http://www.citizen.org

RAND

The highlight of the RAND site is its collection of reports about public policy topics ranging from health care to national defense. RAND is a private research and analysis organization that's supported by the federal government, foundations, private firms, and individuals.

Some of the reports available in full text include *Sending Your Government a Message: Email Communication Between Citizens and Government, The Army After Next: Exploring New Concepts and Technologies for the Light Battle Group, The United States and a Rising China: Strategic and Military Implications, A Review of the Scientific Literature As It Pertains to Gulf War Illnesses, Diverting Children from the Life of Crime: Measuring Costs and Benefits, Health Insurance Among Children of Unemployed Parents, Investing in Our Children: What We Know and Don't Know About the Costs and Benefits of Early Childhood Interventions, The Changing Role of the U.S. Military in Space,* and *Sources of Conflict in the 21st Century: Regional Futures and U.S. Strategy.*

The site also offers dozens of research briefs about prescription drugs and the elderly, drug use prevention, family support of the elderly, resources of retired couples, health insurance, youth violence, managed care, teenage alcohol misuse, drug policy, undergraduate education, nursing homes, military base closures, trends in civil jury verdicts, maternity-leave policy, test scores, contraception in developing countries, Russia's air force, the United States and Japan after the cold war, recruiting options for the military, women in the military, national missile defense programs, and war in cyberspace, among other topics.

Vital Stats:

Access method: WWW
To access: http://www.rand.org

Town Hall: Government Reform

This page at Town Hall provides links to dozens of articles and reports about various aspects of government reform from a variety of conservative sources. The documents address many topics, including campaign finance reform, welfare reform, term limits, federal regulations, government waste, and taxes.

The documents date from January 1999 to the present, and some of the sources include the American Conservative Union, Media Research Center, Concerned Women for America, Heritage Foundation, Capital Research Center, National Taxpayers Union, Citizens Against Government Waste, Pacific Research Institute, and Family Research Council.

The page also provides links to recent news articles about government reform from sources such as the Conservative News Service, the *Washington Post, USA Today,* the *New York Times,* and MSNBC.

Vital Stats:

Access method: WWW
To access: http://www.townhall.com/issueslibrary/governmentreform

GUN CONTROL

America Under the Gun

More than one hundred *New York Times* articles about guns and gun control are available through this page at the newspaper's Web site. Most of the articles date from January 1999 to the present, although selected articles dating back to December 1990 also are provided.

The site also has an interactive map with summaries of gun laws in each state, a forum about gun control, and a link to a page with articles and lesson plans about school violence.

Vital Stats:

Access method: WWW
To access: http://www.nytimes.com/library/national/index-guns.html

Bureau of Alcohol, Tobacco, and Firearms

The Bureau of Alcohol, Tobacco, and Firearms site has answers to frequently asked questions about guns and gun control, extensive information about federal firearms laws, a special section about the Brady handgun law, and the *Federal Firearms Regulation Reference Guide.* The bureau is part of the U.S. Treasury Department.

The site also has reports titled *Gun Crime in the Age Group 18–20* and *Gun Shows: Brady Checks and Crime Gun Traces,* documents about the youth crime gun interdiction initiative, and telephone numbers for toll-free ATF hotlines to report illegal firearms activities.

Vital Stats:

Access method: WWW
To access: http://www.atf.treas.gov

Firearms Litigation Clearinghouse

This site has information about lawsuits around the country against gun manufacturers and dealers. It's operated by the Firearms Litigation Clearinghouse, which is a project of the Educational Fund to End Handgun Violence.

Some of the site's highlights include summaries of suits that more than two dozen municipalities have filed against the gun industry, dozens of legal documents filed in suits against the gun industry, articles from the *Firearms Litigation Reporter,* and information about the legal rights of shooting victims.

Vital Stats:

Access method: WWW
To access: http://www.firearmslitigation.org

Gunfree

The Gunfree site has action alerts about gun bills before Congress, voting records for members of Congress on selected gun bills, and descriptions of gun bills introduced in state legislatures nationwide. It's operated by the Coalition to Stop Gun Violence and the Educational Fund to Stop Handgun Violence.

The site also offers state and federal firearms regulations, a map showing which states have laws regulating the carrying of concealed weapons, a list of recent multiple shootings, and fact sheets about topics such as the number of guns in the United States and the extent of gun violence.

Vital Stats:

Access method: WWW
To access: http://www.gunfree.org

Gun Laws, Gun Control & Gun Rights

This page at JURIST: The Law Professor's Network is an excellent guide to gun control information across the Internet. JURIST is operated by the University of Pittsburgh School of Law.

The page provides little original information. Instead, its value lies in the neatly arranged collection of links to gun control information at other Web sites. The links lead to press releases from pro- and anti-gun groups, information about current legal cases against gun manufacturers and dealers, gun-related legislation before Congress and state legislatures, the positions of presidential candidates on gun laws, major legal decisions in gun cases, selected state and federal firearms laws, and reports about guns and gun violence from federal agencies.

Other links lead to Web sites operated by groups on both sides of the gun control debate, Web sites operated by gun manufacturers, news articles about gun issues, and gun laws and regulations in other countries.

Vital Stats:

Access method: WWW
To access: http://jurist.law.pitt.edu/guns

Gun Owners of America

This site has alerts about gun bills before Congress and state legislatures, analyses and the full texts of many gun bills being considered by Congress, and voting records for every member of Congress on gun legislation. It's operated by Gun Owners of America, which bills itself as "the only no-compromise gun lobby in Washington."

The site also offers news about gun bills before Congress for which the GOA is seeking co-sponsors, letters that visitors can copy and send to Congress about various gun bills, briefs filed by the GOA's foundation in legal cases involving gun laws, a newsletter titled *The Gun Owners,* and fact sheets about gun control issues.

You also can sign up at the Web site to receive e-mail alerts about gun control efforts on the federal level and in specific states.

Vital Stats:

Access method: WWW
To access: http://www.gunowners.org

Handgun Control and the Center to Prevent Handgun Violence

This slightly chaotic site has news about pending gun legislation before Congress, links to voting records for each member of Congress on major gun bills, and an outline of Handgun Control's legislative agenda. It's operated by Handgun Control and the Center to Prevent Handgun Violence, which is Handgun Control's educational and research affiliate.

The site also has fact sheets and articles about lawsuits against the gun industry, safety locks, guns in the home, guns in schools, the Second Amendment, the Brady law, waiting periods, background checks, gun trafficking, and gun shows, among other topics.

Additional highlights include articles and legal documents from lawsuits against the gun industry, details about state and federal gun laws, answers to frequently asked questions about gun laws, press releases, and links to related Web sites.

Vital Stats:

Access method: WWW
To access: http://www.handguncontrol.org

National Rifle Association Institute for Legislative Action

This site provides legislative alerts and summaries of gun bills introduced in the current Congress. It's operated by the Institute for Legislative Action, which is the National Rifle Association's political and lobbying arm.

One of the site's highlights is a collection of fact sheets. They address issues such as age restrictions on the purchase and possession of firearms, court decisions overturning gun restrictions, gun turn-in programs, federal gun crime prosecutions, lawsuits against gun manufacturers, pro-gun groups, the gun lobby, the right to keep and bear arms, semi-automatic firearms, school safety, "smart" guns, the United Nations and gun control, and anti-gun organizations.

The site also has a report titled *Crimes Committed With Firearms: A Report for Parents, Prosecutors, and Policy Makers,* articles, congressional testimony by NRA officials, brochures about federal firearms laws and firearms laws in each state, and a page where you can sign up to receive legislative alerts by fax or e-mail.

Vital Stats:

Access method: WWW
To access: http://www.nraila.org

Open Directory Project: Gun Control

Links to more than 150 Web sites about gun control are provided through this page at the Open Directory Project (p. 11). Each link is briefly described.

The top page provides links to a few general sites. It also leads to separate pages with links to sites about the following subjects: anti-regulation, conferences and rally announcements, gun rights organizations, international, media, and pro-regulation.

Vital Stats:

Access method: WWW
To access: http://dmoz.org/Society/Issues/Gun_Control

Project Vote Smart: Gun Control/Ownership

This page at Project Vote Smart (p. 15) provides links to more than two dozen selected Web sites about gun control and ownership. Each link is briefly annotated.

The sites are operated by Cease Fire, Citizens Committee for the Right to Keep and Bear Arms, Gunfree, Gun Owners of America, Handgun Control, National Rifle Association, National Shooting Sports Foundation, Second

Amendment Foundation, and the Violence Policy Center, among other groups.

Vital Stats:

Access method: WWW
To access: http://www.vote-smart.org/issues/
                   GUN_CONTROL_OWNERSHIP

---

talk.politics.guns

Participants in the very active talk.politics.guns Usenet newsgroup discuss a variety of political issues related to gun ownership and control. The discussions are not for the faint of heart—many of the postings are quite strident.

Vital Stats:

Access method: Usenet newsgroup
To access: news:talk.politics.guns

Violence Policy Center

The full texts of numerous studies about guns and gun violence are available through this site, which is operated by the Violence Policy Center. The center is a nonprofit organization that works to reduce gun deaths and injuries by approaching firearms violence as a public health issue.

Some of the studies available include *Assault Weapons and Accessories in America; Where Did You Get That Statistic?—A Firearms and Firearms Violence Bibliography and Resource Guide for Advocates Working to Reduce Firearms Violence; Who Dies? A Look at Firearms Death and Injury in America; Start 'Em Young: Recruitment of Kids to the Gun Culture;* and *NRA Family Values: The Extremism, Racism, Sexism, Legal Woes, and Gun Industry Ties of the National Rifle Association's Board of Directors.*

Other highlights include fact sheets and press releases about topics such as assault weapons, concealed carry laws, federal legislation, the firearms industry, pro-gun groups, firearms marketing, firearms violence, gun shows, litigation, "smart" guns, state firearms policy, trigger locks, and youth and firearms violence.

The site also has analyses and the full texts of major gun legislation before Congress, background information about lawsuits filed against the gun industry and the texts of many of the legal complaints, and the texts of firearms laws in each state.

Vital Stats:

Access method: WWW
To access: http://www.vpc.org

✓ Yahoo! News: Gun Control Debate

Hundreds of news stories about gun control are available through this page at Yahoo! (p. 17). The articles date from June 1998 to the present.

Some of the sources include Reuters, Associated Press, CBS, BBC, CNN, *Denver Post, Los Angeles Times, Washington Post, New York Times, Time, Seattle Post-Intelligencer, Dallas Morning News, Boston Globe, Baltimore Sun, Hartford Courant, The Times (United Kingdom), Chicago Tribune, Cincinnati Post, San Francisco Chronicle, Christian Science Monitor, Detroit News, Irish Times (Ireland), St. Louis Post-Dispatch,* and *USA Today.*

If you select Yahoo! News Search on the left side of the page, you'll receive a list of stories about various aspects of guns—including gun control—published in recent weeks. A search commonly returns hundreds of news articles.

The page also provides links to more than two dozen Web sites and documents about gun control.

Vital Stats:

Access method: WWW
To access: http://headlines.yahoo.com/Full_Coverage/US/Gun_Issues

---

Yahoo! Society and Culture: Firearms Policy

This page at Yahoo! (p. 17) offers links to nearly 100 Web sites about gun policy. The top page provides links to a handful of general sites, but most of the links are located on separate pages about gun control and gun rights. Each link has a brief description.

Vital Stats:

Access method: WWW
To access: http://dir.yahoo.com/Society_and_Culture/Firearms/
                   Firearms_Policy

HEALTH CARE

American Medical Association

The Policy and Advocacy section of the American Medical Association site has legislative updates, speeches and congressional testimony by AMA officials, the AMA's legislative priorities, AMA letters to federal agencies about proposed regulations, and press releases.

Vital Stats:

Access method: WWW
To access: http://www.ama-assn.org

CSPINET

This site has articles, reports, congressional testimony, petitions to federal agencies, and press releases about a variety of health and nutrition issues. It's operated by the Center for Science in the Public Interest, a nutrition advocacy organization in Washington, D.C.

Some of the topics covered include food safety standards, food labeling, soft drinks, antibiotic resistance, irradiated food, regulation of the poultry industry, false and misleading advertisements, trans fats in foods, food additives, international food safety and labeling rules, food disparagement laws, diet and attention deficit disorder, and alcohol advertising.

Vital Stats:

Access method: WWW
To access: http://www.cspinet.org

Health Hippo

The goofy name aside, Health Hippo is a good directory of health policy and regulatory information available on the Internet. The site would deserve far greater praise if it were updated more frequently.

Health Hippo provides more than 5,000 links, which are divided by more than 30 topics. Some of the most important topics include advance directives, consumers, insurance, long-term care, Medicare and Medicaid, mental health, race and health, reform, and reproductive rights.

Vital Stats:

Access method: WWW
To access: http://hippo.findlaw.com

Henry J. Kaiser Family Foundation

Highlights at this site include news articles, fact sheets, policy briefs, and reports about such health care topics as AIDS/HIV, Medicaid, Medicare, minority health, reproductive and sexual health, the uninsured, and women's health policy. The Henry J. Kaiser Family Foundation operates the site.

You also can sign up at the site to receive various types of e-mail updates.

Vital Stats:

Access method: WWW
To access: http://www.kff.org

House of Representatives Prescription Drug Task Force

A wide range of information about the cost and availability of prescription drugs is available from this site, which is operated by the House of Representatives Prescription Drug Task Force. Three Democratic House members chair the panel.

The site provides the texts of bills about prescription drugs, links to news articles about prescription drug prices from various media sources, and a report from the minority staff of the House Committee on Government Reform titled *Prescription Drug Pricing in the United States: Drug Companies Profit at the Expense of Older Americans.*

Other highlights include links to reports about prescription drug prices from a variety of organizations, a fact book titled *Seniors Beware: The Need for Prescription Drug Coverage, How Drug Pricing Has Harmed Seniors, and Debunking the Myths of Drug Makers,* and links to prescription drug pages and sites operated by individual members of Congress, public interest groups, and trade associations.

Vital Stats:

Access method: WWW
To access: http://www.house.gov/berry/prescriptiondrugs

LIST.HEALTHPLAN

LIST.HEALTHPLAN is a one-way mailing list that distributes occasional news reports about developments in federal health care policy. The reports generally support Clinton administration initiatives. A private individual operates the list.

Vital Stats:

Access method: E-mail
To access: Send an e-mail message to list.healthplan-subscribe@
                     igc.topica.com
Subject line:
Message:

National Alliance for the Mentally Ill

The National Alliance for the Mentally Ill site contains alerts about congressional actions on mental health bills, links to the full texts of important bills before Congress, NAMI's public policy platform, and analyses of Supreme Court decisions affecting people with mental illness.

Other highlights include information about state mental illness insurance parity laws, news about NAMI initiatives in state legislatures, a page where you can sign up to receive legislative and policy alerts by e-mail, hundreds of articles about various types of mental disorders and treatments, and position papers about topics such as parity in insurance coverage, managed care, the criminalization of people with mental illness, and confidentiality and access to medical records.

Vital Stats:

Access method: WWW
To access: http://www.nami.org

National Coalition for Patient Rights

The National Coalition for Patient Rights focuses on protecting the medical privacy of patients. The group's Web site has news about state and federal bills that affect medical privacy, analyses of privacy bills introduced in Congress, articles about various medical privacy issues, a newsletter, and a form where you can sign up to receive e-mail alerts.

Vital Stats:

Access method: WWW
To access: http://www.nationalcpr.org

National Coalition on Health Care

The highlights of this site are reports about the rising number of uninsured workers, health care quality, health care spending, and Medicare reform, among other issues. It's operated by the National Coalition on Health Care, a nonpartisan coalition supported by foundations that seeks to secure health insurance for all and improve the quality of care.

The site also has the results of a poll about how Americans perceive the health care system and fact sheets about health care spending and health care coverage.

Vital Stats:

Access method: WWW
To access: http://www.nchc.org

The New York Times: Health Care

This page provides dozens of articles from the *New York Times* about issues such as Medicare, Medicaid, the drug industry, health insurance, managed care, patients' rights, health care legislation, and medical privacy. Most of the articles date from June 1999 to the present, although selected stories date back as far as January 1998.

The page also has descriptions of selected health care legislation, a forum about health care reform, and links to a handful of health care sites.

Vital Stats:

Access method: WWW
To access: http://www.nytimes.com/library/politics/
                   index-healthcare.html

Open Directory Project: Health Policy

Links to more than three dozen sites about health policy are provided by this page at the Open Directory Project (p. 11). Each link is briefly annotated.

The sites are operated by the Ad Hoc Committee to Defend Health Care, Americans for Free Choice in Medicine, Citizens for Better Medicare, Council for Affordable Health Insurance, Duke Center for Health Policy, Institute for Health Freedom, MedicareWatch, National Academy of Social Insurance, National Organization of Physicians Who Care, Physicians for a National

Health Program, and the Universal Health Care Action Network, among other organizations.

Vital Stats:

Access method: WWW
To access: http://dmoz.org/Society/Issues/Health/Health_Policy

Project Vote Smart: Health Care

Links to dozens of sites about health care are available through this page at Project Vote Smart (p. 15). Each link is briefly described.

The sites are operated by the Agency for Health Care Policy and Research, Alan Guttmacher Institute, American Council on Science and Health, American Health Care Association, American Public Health Association, Citizens for Health, Health Care Liability Alliance, Health Insurance Association of America, National Alliance for the Mentally Ill, National Coalition on Health Care, Physicians Committee for Responsible Medicine, and the Universal Health Care Action Network, among other groups.

Vital Stats:

Access method: WWW
To access: http://www.vote-smart.org/issues/HEALTH_CARE

Public Agenda Online: Health Care

Information about health care policy is available through this section of the Public Agenda site. Public Agenda is a nonprofit, nonpartisan organization that researches and reports on public issues.

The site has summaries of recent reports and news stories (with links to the full texts where available), statistics about various health care issues, results from public opinion polls about health care, and contact information (including links to Web sites) for major health care organizations.

Vital Stats:

Access method: WWW
To access: http://www.publicagenda.org/issues/
                   frontdoor.cfm?issue_type=healthcare

talk.politics.medicine

Participants in the talk.politics.medicine newsgroup discuss medical privacy, patients' rights, pharmaceutical costs, managed care, medical marijuana, health care costs, and other issues.

Vital Stats:

Access method: Usenet newsgroup
To access: news:talk.politics.medicine

Town Hall: Health Care

Links to dozens of articles and reports about a variety of health care issues from various conservative sources are provided through this page at Town Hall.

The documents date from January 1999 to the present. Sources include the Family Research Council, Claremont Institute, Heritage Foundation, Concerned Women for America, Traditional Values Coalition, *National Review,* Capital Research Center, Pacific Research Institute, National Taxpayers Union, Citizens Against Government Waste, Small Business Survival Committee, and Americans for Tax Reform, among others.

The page also provides links to more than two dozen news articles about health care produced in recent weeks by the *Washington Post, USA Today,* the *New York Times,* ABC News, Fox News, and other sources.

Vital Stats:

Access method: WWW
To access: http://www.townhall.com/issueslibrary/healthcare

U.S. Department of Health and Human Services

This site primarily serves as a gateway to Web sites operated by agencies of the U.S. Department of Health and Human Services. Some of the agencies include the Administration on Aging, Administration for Children and Families, Agency for Health Care Policy and Research, Centers for Disease Control and Prevention, Food and Drug Administration, Health Care Financing Administration, National Institutes of Health, and Substance Abuse and Mental Health Services Administration, among others.

The site also has congressional testimony and speeches by HHS officials.

Vital Stats:

Access method: WWW
To access: http://www.hhs.gov

Yahoo! Health: Health Care Policy

This page at Yahoo! (p. 17) provides links to dozens of sites about health care policy. The main page contains about two dozen links, and it also leads to separate pages with links related to articles and papers, journals, managed care, and Medicare.

Vital Stats:

Access method: WWW

To access: http://dir.yahoo.com/Health/Health_Care/Policy

Yahoo! News: Health Care Debate

More than one hundred news stories about various health care issues are available through this page at Yahoo! (p. 17). Most of the stories date from January 1999 to the present, although a few 1998 stories also are provided.

Some of the sources include Reuters, AP, ABC, CNN, MSNBC, the *Baltimore Sun, Boston Globe, Washington Post, USA Today, New York Times, Los Angeles Times, San Jose Mercury News, Dallas Morning News, San Francisco Chronicle, Chicago Tribune, Christian Science Monitor,* and *Seattle Times.*

The page also provides links to more than two dozen selected Web sites about health care.

Vital Stats:

Access method: WWW

To access: http://headlines.yahoo.com/Full_Coverage/US/
                   Health_Care_Debate

HUMAN RIGHTS

AAAS Science and Human Rights Program

This site offers documents about a variety of human rights topics, including refugee flow patterns in Kosovo, scientific freedom and national security, the right to travel to Cuba, economic and cultural rights, human rights in Honduras and Guatemala, cryptography and human rights, and human rights violations in South Africa's health sector, among others. The Human Rights Program at the American Association for the Advancement of Science operates the site.

Of special interest is the site's Directory of Human Rights Resources on the Internet. The directory offers hundreds of nicely annotated links to Web sites and electronic mailing lists.

The site also provides alerts about human rights cases around the world involving scientists (broadly defined to include political scientists, doctors, physicists, and others). You can sign up to automatically receive new alerts by e-mail.

Vital Stats:

Access method: WWW
To access: http://shr.aaas.org/program/index.htm

✓ About.com: Human Rights

The highlight of this site, which is part of the About.com network, is its collection of links to hundreds of sites and individual documents about human rights. Each link is briefly annotated.

There are links about human rights in individual countries, and also links about topics such as children, the death penalty, genocide, the international criminal court, international government agencies, labor rights, landmines, nongovernment organizations, political rights, refugees, the School of the Americas, sexual orientation, torture, U.S. government agencies, and women's rights.

The site also provides articles, a calendar of human rights events, a chat room, and a list of recommended books.

Vital Stats:

Access method: WWW
To access: http://humanrights.about.com

Amnesty International On-line

Amnesty International operates this site, which provides details about campaigns on behalf of human rights victims around the world.

The site also has a large collection of reports and press releases about topics such as the crisis in Kosovo, trade unions, human rights in the United States, China, the rights of women, the death penalty, the Universal Declaration of Human Rights, fair trials, and the human rights situation in countries around the world.

You also can subscribe at the site to receive any of Amnesty International's dozens of mailing lists that distribute press releases about specific regions or topics. List topics include Africa, the Americas, conscientious objectors, the death penalty, Europe, extrajudicial executions, freedom of speech, human rights developments, minorities, police abuse, prison conditions, refugees, religious intolerance, students, unfair trials, and women, among others.

Vital Stats:

Access method: WWW
To access: http://www.amnesty.org

Democracy, Human Rights, and Labor

This page at the State Department's Web site (p. 191) has information about human rights in countries around the world. It's operated by the State Department's Bureau of Democracy, Human Rights, and Labor Affairs.

The most noteworthy document provided is the annual *Country Reports on Human Rights Practices,* which analyzes human rights practices in every country in the world. The page also has a report titled *Erasing History: Ethnic Cleansing in Kosovo* and transcripts of speeches and press conferences by State Department officials.

Vital Stats:

Access method: WWW
To access: http://www.state.gov/www/global/human_rights

Human Rights and Humanitarian Aid

This page has links to more than 150 Web sites and mailing lists about human rights. It's operated by the Canadian Forces College, which is part of Canada's Department of National Defense.

Most of the links lead to Web sites operated by human rights groups in individual countries around the world. Other links lead to general sites, sites operated by human rights groups and programs, and mailing lists.

Vital Stats:

Access method: WWW
To access: http://www.cfcsc.dnd.ca/links/intrel/hum.html

✓ Human Rights Watch

The Human Rights Watch site provides news about human rights abuses around the world and reports about the human rights situation in every country.

The site's detailed reports about specific topics—ranging in length from dozens to hundreds of pages—are of special interest. Some of the titles available in full text include *Confessions at any Cost: Police Torture in Russia; No Minor Matter: Children in Maryland's Jails; Crime or Custom: Violence Against Women in Pakistan; When Tyrants Tremble: The Pinochet Case; Politics by Other Means: Attacks Against Christians in India; China and Tibet: Profiles of Tibetan Exiles; Federal Republic of Yugoslavia: Abuses Against Serbs and Roma in the New Kosovo; Persona Non Grata: The Expulsion of Civilians from Israeli-Occupied Lebanon; Cuba's Repressive Machinery: Human Rights Forty Years After the Revolution;* and *The Internet in the Middle East and North Africa: Free Expression and Censorship.*

Other documents at the site address such subjects as cruelty and neglect in Russian orphanages, the trafficking of women and children, child soldiers, corporations and human rights, landmines, war criminals in the former Yugoslavia, U.S. policy toward Cuba, human rights and democracy in Latin America and the Caribbean, the human rights situation in various world hotspots, prison conditions, and free expression, among others.

Human Rights Watch also operates six electronic mailing lists that distribute press releases and public letters written by the organization. One list distributes all materials released by Human Rights Watch; the others distribute materials about Africa, the Americas, Asia, Europe and Central Asia, and the Middle East.

Vital Stats:

Access method: WWW
To access: http://www.hrw.org

Open Directory Project: Human Rights

This page at the Open Directory Project (p. 11) offers links to more than 250 selected sites about human rights. Each site is briefly described.

The top page provides links to more than two dozen general sites. It also leads to separate pages on the following subjects: the death penalty, human rights organizations, indigenous people, political prisoners, press freedom, regional issues, slavery, women's rights, and workers rights.

Vital Stats:

Access method: WWW
To access: http://dmoz.org/Society/Issues/Human_Rights

United Nations Human Rights Website

The United Nations High Commissioner for Human Rights operates this site, which offers a wide range of documents about human rights issues around the world. The site is available in English, Spanish, and French.

Of special interest is the site's collection of more than two dozen lengthy fact sheets about various human rights issues. Some of the topics addressed include combating torture, enforced or involuntary disappearances, the rights of indigenous peoples, the rights of children, extrajudicial or summary executions, contemporary forms of slavery, minority rights, refugees, discrimination against women, the rights of migrant workers, and forced evictions and human rights.

Other highlights include special pages devoted to human rights issues in world hotspots (at the end of 1999 the site had pages about Kosovo and East Timor), transcripts of speeches by the high commissioner for human rights, reports from the World Conference on Human Rights, information about the Universal Declaration of Human Rights, a calendar of UN human rights meetings, and press releases.

Vital Stats:

Access method: WWW
To access: http://www.unhchr.ch

✓ University of Minnesota Human Rights Library

The University of Minnesota Human Rights Library provides an astounding collection of more than 6,000 documents about human rights issues. Most of the documents originated with international organizations such as the United Nations or with government bodies in various nations.

The documents are divided into seven categories: treaties and other international instruments, other United Nations documents, regional materials, bibliographies and research guides, human rights education, asylum and refugee materials, and U.S. human rights documents.

The site also has a search engine that lets you simultaneously query more than a dozen major human rights Web sites. Another important feature is a collection of links to over 1,000 other human rights sites, divided by more than two dozen topics.

Vital Stats:

Access method: WWW
To access: http://www1.umn.edu/humanrts

Yahoo! News: Human Rights

Dozens of news articles about human rights issues around the world are available through this page at Yahoo! (p. 17). The stories date from December 1998 to the present.

Some of the sources include the *Chicago Tribune, The Times (United Kingdom), Washington Post, Christian Science Monitor, Irish Times (Ireland), Sydney Morning Herald (Australia), New York Times, Philippine Daily Inquirer (Philippines), Times of India (India), Jerusalem Post (Israel),* Reuters, BBC, AP, BBC, Panafrican News Agency, CNN, and Radio Netherlands.

If you choose Yahoo! News Search on the left side of the page, you'll receive a list of stories about human rights published in recent weeks. A search commonly returns hundreds of articles.

The page also provides links to twenty selected Web sites about human rights.

Vital Stats:

Access method: WWW
To access: http://headlines.yahoo.com/Full_Coverage/
                      World/Human_Rights

Yahoo! Society and Culture: Human Rights

Through this page, Yahoo! (p. 17) provides links to more than 400 Web sites about various human rights issues. Each link is briefly annotated.

The top page provides links to several dozen general sites. It also leads to separate pages with links to sites about books, campaigns, child labor, countries and regions, the death penalty, genocide, government agencies, institutes, journals, mining issues, oil and gas issues, organizations, police brutality, refugees, reports, treaties and pacts, Web directories, and Usenet.

Vital Stats:

Access method: WWW
To access: http://dir.yahoo.com/Society_and_Culture/
                              Issues_and_Causes/Human_Rights

IMMIGRATION

✓ About.com: Immigration Issues

This excellent page at the About.com site contains a huge amount of information about immigration issues, including many political issues.

The site's highlight is its collection of hundreds of annotated links. They're arranged by topics such as advocacy/alien support, asylum/refugees, cultural adaptation, immigration law, languages and translation, opponents of immigration, and racial and ethnic tensions.

The page also provides numerous articles, forums, a bulletin board, and a newsletter to which you can subscribe.

Vital Stats:

Access method: WWW
To access: http://immigration.about.com

The Federation for American Immigration Reform (FAIR)

This site's highlight is its extensive collection of information about immigration-related legislation before Congress. The Federation for American Immigration Reform, a nonprofit group that seeks to reduce immigration levels, operates the site.

The site contains legislative alerts about immigration bills before Congress, updates about the status of important bills, summaries of immigration bills, summaries of recent congressional hearings about immigration issues, and congressional testimony by FAIR officials.

Other highlights include news updates and articles about a variety of immigration issues, current and historical data about immigration, newsletters titled *Fair Warning* and *Immigration Report,* executive summaries of various FAIR reports, and links to other immigration sites.

Vital Stats:

Access method: WWW
To access: http://www.fairus.org

Hearing Testimony Presented to Subcommittee on Immigration and Claims

Testimony from hearings about various immigration issues is available at this site. It's operated by the Subcommittee on Immigration and Claims, which is part of the House Committee on the Judiciary.

Full transcripts are available for some hearings, while written statements by individual witnesses are available for others. Some of the topics covered include operations of the Immigration and Naturalization Service, immigration reform, specific immigration bills, temporary visas for professional workers, counterfeiting of identity documents, illegal immigration, visa fraud, and the impact of immigration on low-skilled American workers and on American minority communities, among others.

Vital Stats:

Access method: WWW
To access: http://www.house.gov/judiciary/6.htm

Immigration and Naturalization Service

This site provides statistics about immigration to the United States, the number of illegal aliens, and the number of legal permanent residents and aliens eligible to apply for naturalization in each state. It's operated by the U.S. Immigration and Naturalization Service, which is part of the Department of Justice.

Other highlights include testimony by INS officials at congressional hearings, information about immigration laws and regulations, immigration forms, links to Census Bureau reports about the foreign-born population, and press releases.

Vital Stats:

Access method: WWW
To access: http://www.ins.usdoj.gov

The National Clearinghouse for Bilingual Education

The History, Legislation & Policy section of this site offers links to federal bills related to bilingual education pending before the House and the Senate. The site is operated by the National Clearinghouse for Bilingual Education, which is funded by the U.S. Department of Education's Office of Bilingual Education and Minority Languages Affairs.

The site also provides links to enacted legislation about bilingual education, links to Supreme Court decisions about bilingual education and English-only laws, articles and reports about various issues related to bilingual education, links to other sites about language policy, and a page where you can sign up to receive a biweekly news bulletin by e-mail.

Vital Stats:

Access method: WWW
To access: http://www.ncbe.gwu.edu/library/policy/index.htm

Open Directory Project: Immigration

Through this page, the Open Directory Project (p. 11) provides links to about three dozen sites concerning immigration issues. Each link has a brief description.

The sites are operated by the Association of Professionals for Spousal Reunification, Center for Immigration Studies, Central American Refugee Center, Federation for American Immigration Reform, Haitian-American Grassroots Coalition, National Immigration Forum, National Network for Immigration and Refugee Rights, Numbers USA, United States' Lesbian and Gay Immigration Rights Task Force, U.S. Border Control, and the U.S. Commission on Immigration Reform, among others.

Vital Stats:

Access method: WWW
To access: http://dmoz.org/Society/Issues/Immigration

Project Vote Smart: Language

This page at Project Vote Smart (p. 15) provides a small collection of links to sites about language issues. Each link is briefly annotated.

The sites are operated by the Center for Applied Linguistics, English First, English for the Children, National Association for Bilingual Education, National Clearinghouse for Bilingual Education, Office of Bilingual Education and Minority Languages, and U.S. English, among others.

Vital Stats:

Access method: WWW
To access: http://www.vote-smart.org/issues/LANGUAGE

Public Agenda Online: Immigration

A variety of resources about immigration are available through this section of the Public Agenda site. Public Agenda is a nonprofit, nonpartisan organization that researches and reports on public issues.

Highlights include summaries of recent reports and news stories, with links to the full texts where available; statistics about various immigration issues; results from public opinion polls about immigration; and contact information, including links to Web sites, for major organizations involved in immigration.

Vital Stats:

Access method: WWW
To access: http://www.publicagenda.org/issues/
        frontdoor.cfm?issue_type=immigration

U.S. English

This site features articles, statistics, and results of state and national surveys about making English the official language of government in the United States. It's operated by U.S. English, a nonprofit group that promotes English-only laws and encourages immigrants to learn English.

The site provides information about official language legislation pending before Congress, details about efforts to pass official English legislation in various states, a list of states that have official English laws, news about court challenges to official English laws, publications about bilingual education, lists of groups that support or oppose official English legislation, and answers to frequently asked questions.

Vital Stats:

Access method: WWW
To access: http://www.us-english.org

Yahoo! News: Immigration News

Dozens of news stories about various immigration issues are available through this page at Yahoo! (p. 17). The articles date from January 1998 to the present.

Some of the sources include the Associated Press, Reuters, CNN, *Boston Globe, Seattle Times, Dallas Morning News, Australian Financial Review (Australia), Miami Herald, Washington Post, Christian Science Monitor, San Francisco Chronicle, New York Times, San Jose Mercury News, Sydney Morning Herald (Australia),* and the *Jerusalem Post (Israel).*

CHAPTER 5

The page also provides links to a small collection of Web sites about immigration.

Vital Stats:

Access method: WWW
To access: http://fullcoverage.yahoo.com/fc/US/Immigration

INTERNATIONAL AFFAIRS

CIA Electronic Document Release Center

This site offers numerous collections of previously secret documents that are frequently requested from the Central Intelligence Agency under the Freedom of Information Act.

The site contains document collections about Francis Gary Powers, the U-2 spy pilot who was shot down by the Soviet Union; UFOs; atomic spies Ethel and Julius Rosenberg; Lt. Col. Oleg Penkovsky, a Soviet military intelligence officer who spied for the United States and the United Kingdom; Guatemala; human rights in Latin America; the Bay of Pigs invasion; and American soldiers who were prisoners of war or missing in action during the Vietnam war.

The site also provides extensive information about how to request records from the CIA under the Freedom of Information Act; links to other sources of CIA documents; news items about public access to government information; and important court decisions involving the CIA's administration of the Privacy Act, the Freedom of Information Act, and related laws.

Vital Stats:

Access method: WWW
To access: http://www.foia.ucia.gov

Contemporary Conflicts

This useful site from the Canadian Department of National Defense contains links to Web sites about conflicts between countries around the world. The links are separated by country.

Some of the links lead to sites about hot conflicts, such as the war in Chechnya, while others lead to sites about cold conflicts, such as the long-running hostilities between the United States and Cuba.

Vital Stats:

Access method: WWW
To access: http://www.cfcsc.dnd.ca/links/wars/index.html

Country Studies

The full texts of one hundred books about countries around the world are available through this site from the Library of Congress. The books, which commonly run hundreds of pages, are prepared under the auspices of the Country Studies/Area Handbook Program sponsored by the U.S. Army.

Books are available about such countries as Albania, Cambodia, China, Colombia, Germany, Haiti, India, Indonesia, Iran, Iraq, Israel, Kuwait, Libya, Mexico, Nigeria, North Korea, Pakistan, Peru, Russia, Saudi Arabia, South Africa, South Korea, Sudan, Turkey, Vietnam, and the former Yugoslavia.

Each book provides detailed information about a country's history, geography, society, economy, transportation and telecommunications systems, government and politics, and national security, among other topics.

Vital Stats:

Access method: WWW
To access: http://lcweb2.loc.gov/frd/cs/cshome.html

European Union Internet Resources

The library at the University of California at Berkeley operates this directory of Internet sites related to the European Union.

The links lead to a variety of sites, including general and topical sites about the European Union, European Union documents such as bibliographic tools and treaties, sites in European Union countries, and sites operated by newspapers and journals.

Vital Stats:

Access method: WWW
To access: http://www.lib.berkeley.edu/GSSI/eu.html

Foreign Agents Registration Act

Who lobbies or otherwise acts on behalf of various foreign governments and companies in the United States? You can find out through this section of the U.S. Department of Justice site (p. 106).

The highlight is a semi-annual report about foreign agents who are registered with the Justice Department. If you browse both the country and registrant listings, you can find the name and address of each agent, a brief description of the agent's activities on behalf of each client, the amount of money the agent received in the last six months from each client, and the client list for each agent, along with other information.

Vital Stats:

Access method: WWW
To access: http://www.usdoj.gov/criminal/fara

House Committee on International Relations

The House Committee on International Relations provides links to hearing transcripts at this Web site. However, as of December 1999 the most recent transcript was for a hearing in September 1998.

The site also provides links to selected reports released by the committee, a special report by the committee's North Korea Advisory Group, a schedule of committee and subcommittee hearings, a weekly newsletter, and press releases.

The site also contains separate pages for the Subcommittee on International Operations and Human Rights, Subcommittee on International Economic Policy and Trade, Subcommittee on Africa, Subcommittee on the Western Hemisphere, and Subcommittee on Asia and the Pacific.

Vital Stats:

Access method: WWW
To access: http://www.house.gov/international_relations

Intelligence Resource Program

The Intelligence Resource Program site offers a huge assortment of government documents related to intelligence agencies and activities. The Federation of American Scientists operates the site.

The site provides transcripts of congressional hearings on intelligence reform, presidential directives and executive orders on intelligence, the texts of intelligence laws and regulations, General Accounting Office reports on intelligence, directives from the Central Intelligence Agency and the Defense Department, statements at hearings of the Commission on the Roles and Capabilities of the U.S. Intelligence Community, speeches by CIA officials and others on intelligence threat assessments, statements at congressional hearings on security in cyberspace, and much more.

Vital Stats:

Access method: WWW
To access: http://www.fas.org/irp

Political Science Resources: International Relations

Through this site, the University of Michigan Documents Center provides links to dozens of Web sites about international relations. The annotated links are divided into twelve categories: comprehensive listings, foreign news, human rights, intelligence, international organizations, peace and conflict, periodicals, simulations, terrorism, think tanks, treaties, and United States foreign policy.

Vital Stats:

Access method: WWW
To access: http://www.lib.umich.edu/libhome/
                  Documents.center/psintl.html

Project Vote Smart: Foreign Policy

This page at Project Vote Smart (p. 15) provides links to an eclectic collection of Web sites about foreign policy. Each link is briefly described.

The sites are operated by organizations such as the American Foreign Policy Council, Center for Security Policy, European Union, Foreign Policy Association, Friends Committee on National Legislation, Islamic Association for Palestine, Middle East Policy Council, North Atlantic Treaty Organization, Organization for Economic Cooperation and Development, United Nations, and the World Bank Group.

Vital Stats:

Access method: WWW
To access: http://www.vote-smart.org/issues/FOREIGN_POLICY

Public Agenda Online: America's Global Role

A variety of information about the role of the United States in world affairs is available through this section of the Public Agenda site. Public Agenda is a nonprofit, nonpartisan organization that researches and reports on public issues.

The site contains summaries of recent reports and news stories, with links to the full texts where available; statistics about various foreign affairs subjects; results from public opinion polls; and contact information (including links to Web sites) for major foreign policy organizations.

Vital Stats:

Access method: WWW
To access: http://www.publicagenda.org/issues/
                  frontdoor.cfm?issue_type=americas_global_role

✓ REFWORLD

REFWORLD is a one-stop source for information about refugee issues around the world. The Office of the United Nations High Commissioner for Refugees operates the site.

Among other highlights, the site offers a report titled *The State of the World's Refugees,* a daily digest of refugee news from media around the world, transcripts of press briefings, profiles of the refugee situation in countries around the world, and background papers about refugees and asylum seekers in particular countries.

The site also contains speeches by the high commissioner for refugees, articles from the quarterly *Refugees* magazine, links to publications by the United Nations Commission on Human Rights, a database containing information about more than 250 organizations performing research about refugees, lesson plans for teachers, and links to other sites about refugees.

Vital Stats:

Access method: WWW
To access: http://www.unhcr.ch/refworld

Senate Foreign Relations Committee

This site from the Senate Foreign Relations Committee is of limited use because it's infrequently updated. That problem aside, it offers prepared witness statements from selected hearings and links to transcripts of committee hearings.

Vital Stats:

Access method: WWW
To access: http://www.senate.gov/~foreign

Town Hall: Foreign Policy

This page at Town Hall provides links to dozens of articles and reports about U.S. foreign policy from a variety of conservative sources. The documents date from May 1999 to the present.

Some of the sources include the Family Research Council, *Washington Times Weekly, National Review, Weekly Standard,* American Conservative Union, Heritage Foundation, Claremont Institute, and the Media Research Center.

The page also provides links to recent news articles about U.S. foreign policy from sources such as the Conservative News Service, ABC, Fox News, the *Washington Post,* the *New York Times,* and *USA Today.*

Vital Stats:

Access method: WWW
To access: http://www.townhall.com/issueslibrary/foreignpolicy

✓ U.S. State Department

The U.S. State Department site offers an amazing collection of documents about U.S. foreign policy and countries of the world.

The site offers the State Department's annual human rights report, transcripts of speeches and briefings by State Department officials, details about the size of the U.S. foreign affairs budget, the State Department magazine *Dispatch,* an annual report titled *Patterns of Global Terrorism,* lists of contacts at American embassies and consulates around the world, books based on declassified State Department documents, and a directory of foreign embassies in the United States.

The site also provides background documents about every country in the world, guides to the commercial environment in various foreign countries, the names of foreign diplomats and their spouses in the United States, a list of phone numbers for State Department country desk officers for every country in the world, a directory of State Department employees, and much more.

Vital Stats:

Access method: WWW
To access: http://www.state.gov

The World Factbook

This site provides the full text of *The World Factbook,* an annual Central Intelligence Agency publication that provides detailed information about every country in the world.

For each country, the book provides details about the geography, climate, terrain, natural resources, environment, population, ethnic divisions, religions, languages, labor force, government, legal system, political parties and leaders, international disputes, embassies and consulates, economy, communications, and defense forces, among many other topics.

Vital Stats:

Access method: WWW
To access: http://www.odci.gov/cia/publications/factbook

✓ The WWW Virtual Library: International Affairs Resources

This section of the WWW Virtual Library provides annotated links to more than 1,400 sites about a wide range of international affairs topics. The section was created and is maintained by a professor of international studies at Elizabethtown College in Pennsylvania.

The links are divided into five broad categories: getting started, media sources, organizations, regions and countries, and topics. Each broad category is further divided. For example, the topics category contains separate pages for links about international business and economics, international communications, global environment, international and foreign law, international and comparative education, international development, world religions, conflict resolution and international security, human rights and humanitarian affairs, health, study and work abroad, general foreign languages, French language, Spanish language, and German language.

Vital Stats:

Access method: WWW
To access: http://www.etown.edu/vl

Yahoo! Government: Foreign Policy

Through this page, Yahoo! (p. 17) offers links to dozens of Web sites related to U.S. foreign policy. Each link is briefly annotated.

The main page provides links to just over a dozen general sites. It also leads to separate pages with links devoted to the following topics: economic sanctions, international relations, organizations, U.S.-Africa relations, U.S.-Canada relations, U.S.-China relations, U.S.-Cuba relations, U.S.-Iran relations, U.S.-Israel relations, and U.S.-Japan relations.

Vital Stats:

Access method: WWW
To access: http://dir.yahoo.com/government/u_s__government/
                    politics/foreign_policy

✓ Yahoo! News: Middle East Peace Process

Thousands of news stories about the Middle East peace process are available through this page at Yahoo! (p. 17). Most of the articles date from January 1997 to the present, although a few earlier stories also are provided.

Articles are available from sources such as the Associated Press, Reuters, ArabicNews, BBC, CNN, CBC, the *Jerusalem Post (Israel), Irish Times (Ireland),*

Christian Science Monitor, Washington Post, The Times (United Kingdom), Time, Los Angeles Times, Sydney Morning Herald (Australia), New York Times, and the *Chicago Tribune.*

The page also provides links to dozens of Web sites, documents, and news sources about the Middle East peace process.

Vital Stats:

Access method: WWW
To access: http://fullcoverage.yahoo.com/fc/World/
                    Israeli___Palestinian_Conflict

✓ Yahoo! News: United Nations

Dozens of selected news stories about the United Nations are available through this page at Yahoo! (p. 17). The articles date from September 1999 to the present.

Some of the sources include the BBC, Reuters, ABC News, Panafrican News Agency, Associated Press, CNN, the *Chicago Tribune, New York Times, Christian Science Monitor, The Independent (United Kingdom), Washington Post, Baltimore Sun, The Times (United Kingdom), Sydney Morning Herald (Australia), Boston Globe, The News Pakistan (Pakistan),* and the *Irish Times (Ireland).*

If you choose Yahoo! News Search on the left side of the page, you'll receive a list of stories about the United Nations published in recent weeks. A search typically returns hundreds of news articles.

The page also provides links to a small collection of Web sites and documents about the United Nations.

Vital Stats:

Access method: WWW
To access: http://fullcoverage.yahoo.com/fc/World/United_Nations

INTERNET AND TELECOMMUNICATIONS POLICY

American Civil Liberties Union: Cyber-Liberties

This page at the American Civil Liberties Union site (p. 97) offers a variety of information about cyber-liberties issues such as censorship, privacy, encryption, software filtering, and wiretapping.

Among other highlights, the site contains updates about numerous cyber-liberties lawsuits in which the ACLU is a plaintiff; news about recent congressional and administration actions; letters to Congress about proposals to regulate the Internet; ACLU comments in response to proposed regulations; congressional testimony by ACLU officials; and pamphlets about electronic monitoring, workplace drug testing, Social Security numbers, computers, phones, and
privacy.

Vital Stats:

Access method: WWW
To access: http://www.aclu.org/issues/cyber/hmcl.html

✓ The Center for Democracy and Technology

This site is a treasure trove of information about issues such as free speech online, health privacy, wiretapping, cryptography, encryption, Internet filtering, terrorism and infrastructure protection, digital authentication, junk e-mail, bandwidth, access to government information, and restrictions on Internet content. The site is operated by the Center for Democracy and Technology, a group that's a frequent plaintiff in cyber-liberties lawsuits.

The site provides news about bills before Congress and actions by federal agencies, congressional testimony by CDT officials, updates about lawsuits in which the CDT is challenging government regulations, and articles. It also offers the full text of a number of reports. Some of the available titles include

- *Square Pegs and Round Holes: Applying the Campaign Finance Law to the Internet—Risks to Free Expression and Democratic Values*

- *The Risks of Key Recovery, Key Escrow, & Trusted Third Party Encryption*

- *Regardless of Frontiers: Protecting the Human Right to Freedom of Expression on the Global Internet*

- *Report to the Federal Trade Commission of the Ad-Hoc Working Group on Unsolicited Commercial Email.*

Vital Stats:

Access method: WWW
To access: http://www.cdt.org

Coalition Against Unsolicited Commercial Email (CAUCE)

This site is operated by the Coalition Against Unsolicited Commercial Email (CAUCE), a group that seeks legislation barring junk e-mail, otherwise known as spam.

The site offers news about pending congressional bills about spam, congressional testimony by CAUSE officials, updates about state efforts to regulate spam, background information about the spam problem, and links to other Web sites about spam.

Vital Stats:

Access method: WWW
To access: http://www.cauce.org

Communications Policy & Practice

This Benton Foundation site features articles, reports, and summaries of news stories about various digital communications issues, including public service media, the digital divide, the e-rate for education, television, libraries, and non-profit organizations.

Several reports are available in full text. They include *Native Networking: Telecommunications and Information Technology in Indian Country, Networking for Better Health: Health Care in the Information Age, The Future's in the Balance: A Toolkit for Libraries and Communities in the Digital Age,* and *Losing Ground Bit by Bit: Low-Income Communities in the Information Age.*

The Benton Foundation also publishes the electronic newsletter *Communications-Related Headlines* (p. 196).

Vital Stats:

Access method: WWW
To access: http://www.benton.org/cpphome.html

Communications-Related Headlines

Communications-Related Headlines is a daily electronic newsletter that summarizes important news stories about communications issues from a variety of media sources and advocacy groups. Each summary includes a link to the full text of the story. The newsletter is operated by the Benton Foundation, which also operates the Communications Policy & Practice Web site (p. 195).

Each issue of the newsletter typically summarizes a dozen or so articles about telephony, broadband communications, the Internet, and media and society from sources such as the *Wall Street Journal, New York Times, Washington Post, Broadcasting & Cable,* OMB Watch, and the Center for Democracy and Technology.

Vital Stats:

Access method:	E-mail
To access:	Send an e-mail message to listserv@cdinet.com
Subject line:	
Message:	**subscribe benton-compolicy *firstname lastname***

✓ Electronic Frontier Foundation

This site offers a huge quantity of materials about Internet and cyberspace policy issues. The site would warrant two check marks if it were better organized. The Electronic Frontier Foundation, one of the premier cyber-liberties organizations, operates the site.

The site offers documents about topics such as encryption, electronic privacy, digital wiretapping, Internet content filtering, hyperlinking law, Internet governance, free speech online, the Freedom of Information Act, protecting children online, electronic surveillance, computers and academic freedom, intellectual property online, and Internet culture.

The types of documents provided include news alerts, updates about lawsuits in which the EFF is a plaintiff, congressional testimony, the texts of proposed legislation, articles, and reports. The site also provides links to related sites and a page where you can sign up to receive the *EFFector* newsletter by e-mail.

Vital Stats:

Access method:	WWW
To access:	http://www.eff.org

Media Access Project

This site offers a wide range of documents about media law and telecommunications policy. It's operated by the Media Access Project, a nonprofit public interest telecommunications law firm in Washington, D.C.

The site provides articles, press releases, and legal filings by MAP before the Federal Communications Commission and various courts, among other items. These materials address issues such as low-power radio, digital TV, free air time for political candidates, universal service, Internet access charges, identifying sponsors of issue advertisements, minority ownership of telecommunications companies, and the Communications Decency Act.

Vital Stats:

Access method: WWW
To access: http://www.mediaaccess.org

Open Directory Project: Internet Issues

This page at the Open Directory Project (p. 11) provides links to hundreds of sites about Internet issues. Each link is briefly described.

The top page contains links to just a few general sites. However, it also leads to separate pages with links to sites about mailing lists, organizations, censorship, the digital divide, encryption, plagiarism in education, spam, Internet abuse, cyberspace law, and Internet policy.

Vital Stats:

Access method: WWW
To access: http://dmoz.org/Society/Issues/Science_and_Technology/
        Computers/Internet

politech

The politech mailing list distributes articles, announcements, and other items about the politics of technology and the Internet. Some of the subjects covered include privacy, censorship, copyright, domain names, encryption, anonymity, antitrust, Internet governance, and activities by the White House, Congress, and other government agencies.

Declan McCullagh, a well-known writer about Internet issues, moderates the list.

Vital Stats:

Access method: E-mail
To access: Send an e-mail message to majordomo@vorlon.mit.edu
Subject line:
Message: **subscribe politech**

Public Agenda Online: Internet Speech and Privacy

This section of the Public Agenda site offers a variety of information about free speech and privacy issues in the online world. Public Agenda is a nonprofit, nonpartisan organization that researches and reports on public issues.

The site contains summaries of recent reports and news stories, with links to the full texts where available; statistics about various speech and privacy issues; results from public opinion polls; and contact information (including links to Web sites) for major organizations involved in Internet speech and privacy issues.

Vital Stats:

Access method: WWW
To access: http://www.publicagenda.org/issues/
                   frontdoor.cfm?issue_type=internet

Yahoo! Computers and Internet: Internet Policy

Through this page, Yahoo! (p. 17) provides links to hundreds of sites about various aspects of Internet policy. Each link is briefly annotated.

The top page contains links to a dozen general sites. It also leads to pages with links to sites about abuse, censorship, law, the National Information Infrastructure, privacy, ratings, ribbons, trade and copyright controversies, and use-tax issues.

Vital Stats:

Access method: WWW
To access: http://dir.yahoo.com/Computers_and_Internet/
                   Internet/Policy

✓ Yahoo! News: Internet Decency Debate

Through links and articles archived at the site, this page at Yahoo! (p. 17) provides access to more than 100 articles about topics such as Internet filtering, pornography on the Internet, and protecting children online. The stories date from January 1998 to the present.

The stories originate with a variety of sources, including MSNBC, Wired News, ABC, CNET, BBC, CNN, the *New York Times, Village Voice, The Times (United Kingdom), The Industry Standard, The Age (Australia), USA Today, Detroit Free Press, Christian Science Monitor, Denver Post, New York Post, Sydney Morning Herald (Australia), PC World, Irish Times (Ireland), San Francisco Chronicle*, and the *New York Law Journal*.

The page also provides links to more than two dozen Web sites and documents about Internet decency.

Vital Stats:

Access method: WWW
To access: http://fullcoverage.yahoo.com/fc/Tech/
                         Internet_Decency_Debate

✓ Yahoo! News: Internet Privacy

Hundreds of news stories about electronic privacy are available through this page at Yahoo! (p. 17). Most of the articles date from January 1999 to the present, although the site also provides a few earlier stories.

Some of the sources include Wired News, Reuters, Associated Press, CNET, BBC, MSNBC, CNN, *The Industry Standard, Boston Globe, Denver Post, San Jose Mercury News, New York Times, Washington Post, PC World, Time, Village Voice, Los Angeles Times, USA Today, Chicago Tribune*, and the *Seattle Times*.

If you select Yahoo! News Search on the left side of the page, the site will return stories about Internet privacy from the last few weeks. A search commonly returns about 100 articles.

The page also contains links to more than two dozen Web sites and documents about Internet privacy.

Vital Stats:

Access method: WWW
To access: http://fullcoverage.yahoo.com/fc/Tech/Internet_Privacy

LABOR AND EMPLOYMENT

AFL-CIO

This site contains articles, press releases, and transcripts of speeches and congressional testimony by AFL-CIO officials about a wide range of issues relevant to union members.

Some of the topics covered include job safety and health, working women, the World Trade Organization, ergonomics, the minimum wage, campaign spending by business, child care, workplace justice, the rights of immigrant workers, enforcement of civil rights laws, Medicare, Social Security, and education.

Vital Stats:

Access method: WWW
To access: http://www.aflcio.org

---

alt.society.labor-unions

Participants in the Usenet newsgroup alt.society.labor-unions discuss a wide range of labor topics. Some recent subjects include the right to strike, sweatshops, union organizing victories, the World Trade Organization, and labor campaigns.

Vital Stats:

Access method: Usenet newsgroup
To access: news:alt.society.labor-unions

Bureau of Labor Statistics

This site's highlight is its collection of national and regional economic and labor statistics. It's operated by the Bureau of Labor Statistics, which is part of the U.S. Department of Labor.

The site contains statistics regarding the Consumer Price Index, Producer Price Index, employment cost trends, worker safety and health, the labor force, local area unemployment, labor productivity, foreign labor, international price indexes, and many other subjects.

The site also contains the *Monthly Labor Review*, employment outlooks, press releases, and the full text of the *Occupational Outlook Handbook*.

Vital Stats:

Access method: WWW
To access: http://stats.bls.gov

✓ Labor Unions and the Internet

Librarians at Cornell University's Catherwood Library developed this directory, which offers nicely annotated links to dozens of Web sites and mailing lists for and about labor unions.

The links are divided into more than two dozen categories. Some of the categories include starting points, union directories, collective bargaining, wages, benefits, arbitration, safety and health, labor and employment law, international labor, organizing, strikes, and labor studies and labor libraries.

Vital Stats:

Access method: WWW
To access: http://www.ilr.cornell.edu/library/reference/
                   Guides/LUI.html

LabourStart

The highlight of this British site is its collection of links to news stories about labor unions around the world—from Antigua to Zimbabwe. New links are posted weekly and each new group in the collection typically contains dozens of links.

The site also offers a calendar of labor events worldwide, a list of labor Web sites of the week, discussion forums, articles about labor use of the Internet, annotated links to directories of labor-oriented Web sites, and more.

Vital Stats:

Access method: WWW
To access: http://www.labourstart.org

National Labor Relations Board

This site provides useful background information about the National Labor Relations Board and the National Labor Relations Act, which the NLRB enforces. Under the law, the NLRB conducts elections to determine whether employees want union representation and investigates unfair labor practices by employers and unions.

One of the site's highlights is the *Weekly Summary of NLRB Cases,* which summarizes all published NLRB decisions in unfair labor practice and representation election cases. The newsletter provides links to the full texts of the decisions.

The site also contains NLRB orders, decisions of NLRB administrative law judges, searchable versions of the board's Rules and Regulations, and *Federal Register* notices.

Vital Stats:

Access method: WWW
To access: http://www.nlrb.gov

Open Directory Project: Labor

This page at the Open Directory Project (p. 11) provides links to hundreds of sites about labor issues. Each link is briefly described.

The top page contains links to about two dozen general sites. It also leads to separate pages with links to sites about the following subjects: child labor, the minimum wage, slavery, labor activism, workers' rights, labor law, labor organizations, and work.

Vital Stats:

Access method: WWW
To access: http://dmoz.org/Society/Issues/Labor

Project Vote Smart: Labor/Employment

This page at Project Vote Smart (p. 15) provides links to several dozen selected sites about labor and employment issues. Each link is briefly annotated.

The sites are operated by numerous organizations, including the AFL-CIO, American Federation of Government Employees, Bureau of Labor Statistics, Campaign for Labor Rights, Employment Benefits Research Institute, Institute of Industrial Relations, Labor Policy Association, National Labor Relations Board, National Right to Work Legal Defense Foundation, Teamsters, United Auto Workers, and the U.S. Equal Employment Opportunity Commission.

Vital Stats:

Access method: WWW
To access: http://www.vote-smart.org/issues/LABOR_EMPLOYMENT

Sweatshop Watch

This site provides background information about sweatshops, documents analyzing alleged flaws in the White House–sponsored agreement to end sweatshops, and details about new sweatshop laws. It's operated by Sweatshop Watch, a coalition of labor, community, civil rights, immigrant rights, women's, and political organizations that seeks to eliminate sweatshop conditions in the garment industry worldwide.

The site also offers news about agreements to end sweatshops, information about the campaign on university campuses to end sweatshops, a list of other anti-sweatshop organizations, and a superb set of links to related sites.

Vital Stats:

Access method: WWW
To access: http://www.sweatshopwatch.org

United States Department of Labor

The United States Department of Labor site contains hundreds of documents about the workplace, including information about the minimum wage law, extensive details about the Family and Medical Leave Act, tips for avoiding clothes made in sweatshops, the text of proposed ergonomics rules, several reports about the use of child labor around the world, and documents about corporate citizenship.

The site also contains publications about the rights of women in the workplace, *Federal Register* notices, summaries of laws and regulations enforced by the Labor Department, the sections of the *Code of Federal Regulations* that apply to the Labor Department, compliance materials for employers, and reports titled *Futurework: Trends and Challenges for Work in the 21st Century, Genetic Information and the Workplace, A Look at Employers' Costs of Providing Health Benefits, Working Together for Public Service, Care Around the Clock: Developing Child Care Resources Before Nine and After Five,* and *Making Work Pay: The Case for Raising the Minimum Wage.*

In addition, it offers speeches and congressional testimony by Labor Department officials, press releases, and links to Internet sites operated by Labor Department agencies such as the Mine Safety and Health Administration and the Occupational Safety and Health Administration.

Vital Stats:

Access method: WWW
To access: http://www.dol.gov

Yahoo! Business and Economy: Labor

Through this page, Yahoo! (p. 17) provides links to more than 500 Web sites about labor. Each link includes a brief description.

The page is actually a gateway to more than a dozen pages with links to sites about the following topics: child labor, employment, government agencies, history, institutes, labor interest, news and media, occupational safety and health, organizations, statistics, sweatshops, unions, and Usenet.

Vital Stats:

Access method: WWW
To access: http://dir.yahoo.com/business_and_economy/labor

Yahoo! News: Downsizing and Layoffs

Through links and articles archived at the site, this page at Yahoo! (p. 17) provides access to dozens of new stories about downsizing and layoffs around the world. The stories date from June 1999 to the present.

The stories originate from a variety of news sources, including the CBC, CBS, BBC, Associated Press, Agence France-Presse, Reuters, CNNfn, *Boston Globe, New York Times, Sydney Morning Herald (Australia), San Francisco Chronicle, Financial Times (United Kingdom), The Times (United Kingdom), Christian Science Monitor, Washington Post,* and the *Cincinnati Post.*

Clicking on Yahoo! News Search on the left side of the page automatically launches a search for articles about downsizing and layoffs published in recent weeks. A search typically returns several hundred articles.

The page also contains links to a small group of Web sites and documents about downsizing and layoffs.

Vital Stats:

Access method: WWW
To access: http://fullcoverage.yahoo.com/fc/Business/
                   Downsizing_and_Layoffs

✓ Yahoo! News: Labor and Union News

More than 100 news stories about labor and unions are available through this page at Yahoo! (p. 17). The stories date from April 1999 to the present.

Some of the sources include the Associated Press, Reuters, Agence France-Presse, CBC, BBC, CNN, *Washington Post, Los Angeles Times, New York Times, Financial Times (United Kingdom), Christian Science Monitor, Boston Globe, Chicago Tribune, Detroit News, Detroit Free Press, Seattle Times, Sunday Times*

(South Africa), Irish Times (Ireland), The Times (United Kingdom), and the *San Francisco Chronicle.*

If you choose Yahoo! News Search on the left side of the page, the site will return links to stories about labor published in recent weeks. A search commonly returns more than 200 articles.

The page also contains links to a small collection of Web sites and documents about labor and unions.

Vital Stats:

Access method:	WWW
To access:	http://fullcoverage.yahoo.com/fc/Business/ Labor_and_Union_News

MEDIA AND COMMUNICATIONS POLICY

Fairness & Accuracy in Reporting (FAIR)

This site features dozens of articles and reports about such topics as corporate ownership of the media, the narrow range of debate in the media, advertiser influence, pressure groups, the public relations industry, and sexism, racism, and homophobia in the media. It's operated by Fairness & Accuracy in Reporting, a national group that believes the mainstream media "are increasingly cozy with the economic and political powers they should be watchdogging," according to the Web site.

The site also contains action alerts, a media activism kit, selected articles from the bimonthly media criticism magazine *Extra!,* weekly analyses of the economic reporting in the *New York Times* and *Washington Post,* and information about FAIR's weekly radio show CounterSpin.

You can sign up at the site to automatically receive news and action alerts by e-mail.

Vital Stats:

Access method:	WWW
To access:	http://www.fair.org

Online Journalism Review

The Online Journalism Review provides articles about news reporting on the Internet and the use of electronic tools by traditional journalists. The Web-based journal is produced at the Annenberg School for Communication at the University of Southern California.

Recent articles have examined how the Internet is changing communications and business in China's western provinces, growing coverage of the gay community, college newspapers online, the use of portable organizers by journalists, hate groups on the Web, hacking, and journalists basing stories on chat-room gossip.

Vital Stats:

Access method:	WWW
To access:	http://ojr.usc.edu

✓ Open Directory Project: Media and Free Speech

This page at the Open Directory Project (p. 11) provides links to hundreds of Web sites about the media. Each link is briefly annotated.

The top page offers an excellent group of links to about two dozen general sites about the media. It also leads to pages with links to sites about the following topics: access to airwaves, alternative media, bias and balance, consolidation and monopoly, crisis at Pacifica Radio, culture jamming, free speech, Internet issues, journalism, media industry news, opinions and analysis, organizations, public interest, regulation and policy, resources, and violence in media.

Vital Stats:

Access method: WWW
To access: http://dmoz.org/News/Current_Events/
                   Media_and_Free_Speech

Project for Excellence in Journalism

This site's highlight is the Daily Briefing, which provides links to stories about the media from newspapers, wire services, and other sources around the country. Dozens of new links are posted each week. The site is operated by the Project for Excellence in Journalism, which is affiliated with the Columbia University Graduate School of Journalism and funded by the Pew Charitable Trusts.

The Daily Briefing stories originate with such sources as the Associated Press, Reuters, *San Francisco Chronicle, New York Daily News, Boston Globe, New Times Los Angeles, San Francisco Examiner, New York Times, Washington Post, Los Angeles Times,* and the *Chicago Tribune.*

The site also offers reports about the quality of local TV news, numerous articles about the state of American newspapers, a study of newspaper coverage of state governments, and links to important media sites.

Vital Stats:

Access method: WWW
To access: http://www.journalism.org

Project Vote Smart: Media & Communication

This page at Project Vote Smart (p. 15) provides links to several dozen selected sites about the media. Each link is briefly described.

The sites are operated by Accuracy in Media, AdBusters, the Association of Alternative Newsweeklies, Center for Media and Public Affairs, Center for

Media Literacy, Committee to Protect Journalists, Fairness & Accuracy in Reporting, Freedom Forum, Media Research Center, National Association of Broadcasters, Pew Center for Civic Journalism, and Project Censored, among other groups.

Vital Stats:

Access method: WWW
To access: http://www.vote-smart.org/issues/
MEDIA_COMMUNICATION

The Reporters Committee for Freedom of the Press

Detailed reports about the rights of reporters highlight this site, which is operated by the Reporters Committee for Freedom of the Press. The group is a nonprofit organization that provides free legal help to reporters and news organizations.

The reports cover such topics as media law under the First Amendment, access to juvenile courts, reporters' use of confidential sources and information, open meetings and open records statutes and cases in all 50 states and the District of Columbia, and the legality of tape-recording telephone calls.

Vital Stats:

Access method: WWW
To access: http://www.rcfp.org

Yahoo! News: Media Watch

This page at Yahoo! (p. 17) provides access to hundreds of news stories about media issues around the world ranging from censorship to consolidation. The stories date back to early 1999.

Some of the sources include the Associated Press, Reuters, Agence France-Presse, CNN, Panafrican News Agency, BBC, CNET, Radio Netherlands, CBC, *San Francisco Examiner, Sydney Morning Herald (Australia), The Times (United Kingdom), Boston Globe, Financial Times (United Kingdom), Washington Post, Chicago Tribune, Forbes, San Francisco Examiner, Christian Science Monitor, Honolulu Star-Bulletin,* and the *American Journalism Review.*

The page also contains links to dozens of other sites and documents about the media.

Vital Stats:

Access method: WWW
To access: http://fullcoverage.yahoo.com/fc/World/Media_Watch

Yahoo! News: Violence in the Media

Several dozen news stories about violence in the media are available through this page at Yahoo! (p. 17). The stories date from June 1999 to the present.

The articles are from sources such as ABC, CBC, BBC, CNN, Reuters, the *Chicago Tribune, San Jose Mercury News, Christian Science Monitor, San Francisco Chronicle, New York Times, Denver Post, Financial Times (United Kingdom)*, and the *Dallas Morning News.*

The page also contains links to a small group of documents and Web sites about violence in the media.

Vital Stats:

Access method: WWW
To access: http://fullcoverage.yahoo.com/Full_Coverage/US/
                  Violence_in_the_Media

POVERTY AND WELFARE

ETA Welfare to Work

Exhaustive information about welfare-to-work programs is available from this site operated by the Employment and Training Administration, which is part of the U.S. Department of Labor.

The site provides fact sheets about various aspects of welfare to work, answers to frequently asked questions, information about applicable legislation, the texts of regulations, *Federal Register* notices, press releases, details about welfare-to-work tax credits for employers, links to related Web sites, and more.

Vital Stats:

Access method: WWW
To access: http://wtw.doleta.gov

National Coalition for the Homeless

The Legislation and Policy section of the National Coalition for the Homeless site contains legislative alerts, the coalition's federal legislative agenda, information about appropriations for federal homeless programs, and information about federal laws affecting the homeless.

Other sections of the site contain information about the civil rights of people who are homeless, fact sheets about topics such as mental illness and homelessness and addiction disorders and homelessness, abstracts of hundreds of reports about homelessness and poverty, directories of organizations working on homeless and housing issues around the country, a calendar of anti-poverty events, and more.

Vital Stats:

Access method: WWW
To access: http://nch.ari.net

The New York Times: Welfare

This page at the *New York Times* site provides several dozen articles about welfare and welfare reform published in the newspaper between September 1998 and the present. The page also offers an interactive map that shows the drop in the welfare rolls in each state since January 1993 and a forum about the U.S. welfare system.

Vital Stats:

Access method: WWW
To access: http://www.nytimes.com/library/politics/index-welfare.html

Open Directory Project: Poverty

This page at the Open Directory Project (p. 11) provides nicely annotated links to more than 100 Web sites about various aspects of poverty.

The top page contains links to just over a dozen general sites. It also leads to separate pages that have links listed under the following topics: homelessness, hunger, minimum wage, regional, and welfare and workfare.

Vital Stats:

Access method: WWW
To access: http://dmoz.org/Society/Issues/Poverty

PovertyNet

The World Bank operates this site, which offers extensive information about poverty issues around the world. Highlights include a report titled *Poverty Trends and Voices of the Poor,* data about poverty trends, estimates of income inequality, reports about efforts to reduce poverty, abstracts of nearly 200 documents about inequality and poverty, a newsletter, and links to many related Web sites.

Vital Stats:

Access method: WWW
To access: http://www.worldbank.org/poverty

Project Vote Smart: Welfare, Poverty, & Homelessness

This page at Project Vote Smart (p. 15) supplies links to several dozen selected Web sites about welfare, poverty, and homelessness.

The sites are operated by the Administration for Children and Families, American Public Welfare Association, Bread for the World, Commission on Homelessness & Poverty, Food Research and Action Center, Habitat for Humanity, Institute for Food and Development Policy, Low Income Housing

Coalition, National Coalition for the Homeless, National Neighborhood Coalition, and the Welfare Information Network, among other organizations.

Vital Stats:

Access method: WWW
To access: http://www.vote-smart.org/issues/
                WELFARE_POVERTY_HOMELESSNESS

Public Agenda Online: Welfare

This section of the Public Agenda site offers a wide range of information about welfare. Public Agenda is a nonprofit, nonpartisan organization that researches and reports on public issues.

The site contains summaries of recent reports and news stories, with links to the full texts where available; statistics about various welfare issues; results from public opinion polls; and contact information (including links to Web sites) for major organizations that work on welfare issues.

Vital Stats:

Access method: WWW
To access: http://www.publicagenda.org/issues/
                frontdoor.cfm?issue_type=welfare

Welfare Information Network (WIN)

The Welfare Information Network is a clearinghouse for information about welfare reform. It provides links to more than 9,000 documents at hundreds of Web sites about topics such as policy choices, promising practices, federal and state legislation and plans, and program and financial data.

The links are divided into dozens of categories, including adult education and literacy, child support, community-based strategies, domestic violence, economic and community development, employer involvement, health care and Medicaid, homelessness, immigrants, job readiness and searching, pregnancy prevention, privatization, rural issues, subsidized employment, teen parents, transportation, and vocational education training.

Vital Stats:

Access method: WWW
To access: http://www.welfareinfo.org

Welfare Law Center

This site contains extensive updates about welfare-related lawsuits around the United States, including contact information for plaintiffs' attorneys in each case. The site, which is operated by the Welfare Law Center, also provides articles about welfare law and links to related Web sites.

Vital Stats:

Access method: WWW
To access: http://www.welfarelaw.org

Yahoo! News: Poverty

This page at Yahoo! (p. 17) provides access to dozens of news articles about poverty around the world. The stories date from July 1999 to the present.

Sources include the Panafrican News Agency, Africa News Online, Associated Press, Reuters, ABC, BBC, Agence France-Presse, CNN, *The Times (United Kingdom), Irish Times (Ireland), New York Times, Sydney Morning Herald (Australia), Christian Science Monitor, San Francisco Examiner, San Jose Mercury News,* and the *Chicago Tribune.*

If you select Yahoo! News Search on the left side of the page, the site will return links to stories about poverty published in recent weeks. A search commonly returns more than 100 articles.

The page also contains links to a small collection of Web sites and documents about poverty.

Vital Stats:

Access method: WWW
To access: http://fullcoverage.yahoo.com/fc/World/Poverty

Yahoo! News: Welfare Reform

A small collection of news stories about welfare reform is available through this page at Yahoo! (p. 17). The stories date back to July 1999.

The articles originate from a variety of sources, including the Associated Press, Reuters, the *New York Times, Philadelphia Inquirer, Christian Science Monitor, Time, Chicago Tribune,* and the *Miami Herald.*

Clicking on Yahoo! News Search on the left side of the page automatically launches a separate search for news stories about welfare reform published in recent weeks. A search typically returns a couple dozen stories.

The page also contains links to a small group of sites and documents about welfare reform.

Vital Stats:

Access method: WWW

To access: http://fullcoverage.yahoo.com/fc/US/
                   Welfare_Reform/index.html

Yahoo! Society and Culture: Poverty

This page at Yahoo! (p. 17) provides links to more than 200 Web sites related to poverty. Each link is briefly annotated.

The top page contains links to a few general sites about poverty. However, it also leads to pages that link to sites about the following topics: homelessness, hunger, institutes that study homelessness, international development, news and media, organizations, panhandling, statistics, and welfare.

Vital Stats:

Access method: WWW

To access: http://dir.yahoo.com/Society_and_Culture/
                   Issues_and_Causes/Poverty

RACE AND ETHNICITY

Civil Rights Division

The Civil Rights Division of the U.S. Department of Justice (p. 106) operates this eclectic site, which presents a variety of materials about enforcement of civil rights laws.

The site's highlight is the ADA Home Page, which provides extensive information about the Americans with Disabilities Act. It has reports about ADA enforcement activities, settlement agreements and other court documents, details about a toll-free telephone number you can call to get answers to ADA questions, ADA regulations, technical assistance materials, and new or proposed regulations, among other items.

The site also provides detailed descriptions of the Civil Rights Division's sections and programs, a publication titled *Protecting the Civil Rights of American Indians and Alaska Natives,* two reports by the National Church Arson Task Force, several booklets for employers and employees about employment of immigrants, speeches and congressional testimony by division leaders, and selected complaints, briefs, consent decrees, and judgments.

Vital Stats:

Access method: WWW
To access: http://www.usdoj.gov/crt

---

civilrights.org

This site contains voting records for individual members of Congress on civil rights legislation, congressional schedules, and action alerts. It's operated by the Leadership Conference on Civil Rights, a coalition of more than 180 organizations that work to protect civil rights.

One of the site's highlights is a collection of documents about hate crimes. The collection includes a report about hate crimes in the United States, hate crime statistics, and information about state anti-hate efforts.

You also can sign up at the site to automatically receive action alerts by e-mail.

Vital Stats:

Access method: WWW
To access: http://www.civilrights.org

National Association for the Advancement of Colored People

The NAACP site provides articles and press releases about topics such as the lack of diversity in network TV, the lack of minority law clerks at the U.S. Supreme Court, and suits against restaurants and hotels over racial discrimination.

The site also provides issue alerts, information about NAACP programs, and speeches and columns by the NAACP president.

Vital Stats:

Access method: WWW
To access: http://www.naacp.org

National Council of La Raza

This site offers articles, action alerts, and press releases about topics such as the United States Census, civil rights, economic mobility, education, farmworkers, foreign policy, health, housing and economic development, immigration, and leadership development. The National Council of La Raza, a Hispanic organization, operates the site.

The site also provides a legislative forecast outlining the NCLR's positions on various issues, a list of publications that can be ordered from the council, links to other Web sites about Hispanic issues, and a page where you can sign up to automatically receive news by e-mail.

Vital Stats:

Access method: WWW
To access: http://www.nclr.org

Native American Rights Fund

This site offers news about legal cases and congressional actions that affect the rights of Native Americans. It's operated by the Native American Rights Fund.

The site also provides action alerts, a compilation of state Indian education laws, background information about the fund, a newsletter, and a page where you can sign up to receive e-mail updates about major developments in legal cases and legislation affecting Native Americans.

Vital Stats:

Access method: WWW
To access: http://www.narf.org

Project Vote Smart: Affirmative Action

This page at Project Vote Smart (p. 15) provides links to about twenty Web sites concerning affirmative action. Each link is briefly annotated.

The sites are operated by the Affirmative Action Information Center, American Association of University Professors, American Civil Rights Coalition, Americans Against Discrimination and Preferences, Americans United for Affirmative Action, Chinese for Affirmative Action, and the National Center for Policy Analysis, among other organizations.

Vital Stats:

Access method: WWW

To access: http://www.vote-smart.org/issues/AFFIRMATIVE_ACTION

Project Vote Smart: Civil Rights/Human Rights

This page at Project Vote Smart (p. 15) provides links to a diverse collection of Web sites about civil rights and human rights issues.

The sites are operated by various organizations, among them the American-Arab Anti-Discrimination Committee, Amnesty International, Anti-Defamation League, Human Rights Watch, Japanese American Citizens League, League of United Latin American Citizens, National Association for the Advancement of Colored People, Southern Poverty Law Center, and the U.S. Commission on Civil Rights. Each link is briefly annotated.

Vital Stats:

Access method: WWW

To access: http://www.vote-smart.org/issues/
        CIVIL_RIGHTS_HUMAN_RIGHTS

Project Vote Smart: Race & Ethnicity

Through this page, Project Vote Smart (p. 15) offers links to dozens of sites about race and ethnicity. Each link has a brief description.

The sites are operated by various groups, among them Americans for Indian Opportunity, American Jewish Committee, Cherokee Nation, Ethnic Heritage Council, Hispanic Association on Corporate Responsibility, LatinoLink, League of United Latin American Citizens, National Association of Latino Elected and

Appointed Officials, National Congress of American Indians, and the National Council of La Raza.

Vital Stats:

Access method: WWW
To access: http://www.vote-smart.org/issues/RACE_ETHNICITY

Public Agenda Online: Race

A variety of documents about race issues are provided at this section of the Public Agenda site. Public Agenda is a nonprofit, nonpartisan organization that researches and reports on public issues.

Some of the highlights include summaries of recent reports and news stories, with links to the full texts where available; statistics about various race issues; results from public opinion polls about race; and contact information (including links to Web sites) of major organizations involved in racial and ethnic issues.

Vital Stats:

Access method: WWW
To access: http://www.publicagenda.org/issues/
                  frontdoor.cfm?issue_type=race

United States Commission on Civil Rights

The United States Commission on Civil Rights examines complaints of discrimination based on a person's race, color, religion, sex, age, disability, or national origin. Its Web site provides a publication titled *Getting Uncle Sam to Enforce Your Civil Rights,* telephone numbers to call to file discrimination complaints, a directory of civil rights agencies and offices, a publications catalog, a list of regional offices, a calendar of meetings of the commission and state advisory committees, background information about the commission, and press releases.

Vital Stats:

Access method: WWW
To access: http://www.usccr.gov

U.S. Equal Employment Opportunity Commission

This site from the U.S. Equal Employment Opportunity Commission provides information about employment discrimination for both employees and employers.

One of the site's most useful features is a collection of fact sheets that describe what constitutes sexual harassment, racial discrimination, age discrimination, national origin discrimination, pregnancy discrimination, religious discrimination, and discrimination against people with disabilities. A special section offers information about the Americans with Disabilities Act, including publications titled *Your Responsibilities as an Employer, Your Employment Rights as an Individual With a Disability,* and *Small Employers and Reasonable Accommodation.*

The site also contains the texts of laws enforced by the EEOC, including Title VII of the Civil Rights Act of 1964, the Equal Pay Act of 1963, the Age Discrimination Employment Act of 1967, Sections 501 and 505 of the Rehabilitation Act of 1973, Titles I and V of the Americans with Disabilities Act of 1990, and the Civil Rights Act of 1991.

Other highlights include guidance for small businesses about how to comply with equal employment opportunity laws, new and proposed regulations, enforcement statistics, press releases about EEOC suits and settlements, contact information for EEOC field offices around the country, background information about the commission, and links to related sites.

Vital Stats:

Access method: WWW
To access: http://www.eeoc.gov

Yahoo! News: Affirmative Action

Dozens of selected news stories about affirmative action are available through this page at Yahoo! (p. 17). The articles date from November 1996 to the present.

Sources for the articles include the *Washington Post, Boston Globe, Christian Science Monitor, New York Times, Chicago Tribune, San Francisco Examiner, Atlanta Journal-Constitution, San Francisco Chronicle, Seattle Times, Detroit News,* and CNN, among others.

If you select Yahoo! News Search on the left side of the page, you'll automatically launch a search for news stories about affirmative action published in recent weeks. A search typically returns a handful of articles.

The page also provides links to a small collection of documents and Web sites about affirmative action.

Vital Stats:

Access method: WWW

To access: http://fullcoverage.yahoo.com/fc/US/Affirmative_Action

---

Yahoo! News: African American News

This page at Yahoo! (p. 17) provides access to more than 100 news stories about topics such as boycotts by the NAACP, racial bias lawsuits, racial disparities in school discipline, racial profiling, Confederate flag disputes, and racial disparities in health care, among others. The stories date from October 1998 to the present.

The stories originate with a variety of news organizations, including the *Village Voice, Christian Science Monitor, San Francisco Chronicle, The Economist (United Kingdom), Chicago Tribune, The Times (United Kingdom), Seattle Times, Detroit News, Detroit Free Press, Dallas Morning News, Philadelphia Daily News, Philadelphia Inquirer, New York Daily News, New York Times, Washington Post,* CNN, ABC, Panafrican News Agency, and Reuters.

The page also has links to a variety of news sources, documents, and Web sites about African American issues.

Vital Stats:

Access method: WWW

To access: http://fullcoverage.yahoo.com/fc/US/
                           African_American_News

Yahoo! News: Racial Profiling

More than two dozen news stories about racial profiling by police are available through this page at Yahoo! (p. 17). The stories date from February 1999 to the present.

Stories are available from the *Los Angeles Times, The Times (United Kingdom), Detroit Free Press, Seattle Times, San Francisco Chronicle, Time, Dallas Morning News, Christian Science Monitor, San Francisco Examiner, Newark Star-Ledger, Philadelphia Inquirer,* CNN, Reuters, Associated Press, Court TV, and APBnews.com, among other sources.

Choosing Yahoo! News Search on the left side of the page launches a search for stories about racial profiling published in recent weeks. A search typically returns about a dozen stories.

The page also has links to a small selection of documents and Web sites about racial profiling.

Vital Stats:

Access method: WWW
To access: http://fullcoverage.yahoo.com/fc/US/Racial_Profiling

RELIGION

American Civil Liberties Union: Religious Liberty

This page at the American Civil Liberties Union site (p. 97) contains a large collection of articles, press releases, and other documents about religious liberty. Some of the topics covered include posting of the Ten Commandments in schools and courthouses, the Religious Liberties Protection Act, school vouchers, taxpayer subsidies of religious schools, school prayer, and the separation of church and state.

   The page also provides links to a small collection of other sites about religious liberty.

Vital Stats:

Access method: WWW
To access: http://www.aclu.org/issues/religion/hmrf.html

Americans United for Separation of Church and State

Updates about legislative actions in Washington and state capitals regarding church-state issues highlight this site, which is operated by Americans United for Separation of Church and State. The group seeks to preserve religious freedom by opposing mandatory school prayer, tax money for parochial schools, government involvement in religion, and involvement by religious groups in partisan politics.

   The site also provides analyses of church-state bills currently before Congress, descriptions of major cases currently before the courts, brochures about various church-state issues, articles from the magazine *Church & State*, and a form where visitors can sign up to receive e-mail alerts.

Vital Stats:

Access method: WWW
To access: http://www.au.org

Anti-Defamation League

The Anti-Defamation League offers a variety of reports, articles, and press releases at its Web site. Some of the topics covered include hate groups, racist groups in U.S. prisons, school vouchers, Israel, anti-Semitic myths, religious freedom, separation of church and state, terrorism, and the Nation of Islam. The ADL is a Jewish organization.

Numerous reports are available online in full text. Some of the available titles are *Security for Community Institutions, Explosion of Hate: The Growing Danger of the National Alliance, Schooled in Hate: Anti-Semitism on Campus,* and *Y2K Paranoia: Extremists Confront the Millennium.*

The site also provides information about bills that the ADL is tracking in Congress, details about the ADL's HateFilter software program for filtering Internet sites, and much more.

Vital Stats:

Access method: WWW
To access: http://www.adl.org

Christian Coalition

The Christian Coalition site has a weekly roundup of news about abortion, the arts, campaign finance reform, education, gambling, religious freedom, and other issues. Pat Robertson is the group's president.

Other highlights include calendars of daily activities in the U.S. House and Senate, weekly lists of congressional committee hearings, contact information for members of Congress, contact information for newspapers and television stations around the country, and information about state and international Christian Coalition affiliates.

You also can sign up at the site to automatically receive a free weekly newsletter by e-mail.

Vital Stats:

Access method: WWW
To access: http://www.cc.org

free! The Freedom Forum Online: Religion

A strong collection of news stories about religious freedom issues around the country highlights this page at the Freedom Forum site (p. 100).

The page also provides links to several reports about religion issues. Some of the available titles include *A Teacher's Guide to Religion in the Public Schools, The Bible & Public Schools, Finding Common Ground: First Amendment Guide to Religion and Public Education,* and *Dieties & Deadlines.*

Vital Stats:

Access method: WWW
To access: http://www.freedomforum.org/religion/welcome.asp

Interfaith Working Group Online

The hundreds of links at this site are divided by political topic. Some of the subjects covered include homosexuality and religion, religion and sexual orientation, equal treatment for sexual minorities, reproductive freedom, the separation of church and state, religious diversity, and the radical religious right.

The site is operated by the Interfaith Working Group, a Philadelphia organization that supports gay rights, reproductive freedom, and the separation of church and state.

Vital Stats:

Access method: WWW
To access: http://www.iwgonline.org/links

National Conference of Catholic Bishops/United States Catholic Conference

This site outlines the United States Catholic Conference legislative program and provides reports about the status of legislation of interest to the conference.

The site also contains congressional testimony, fact sheets, and press releases about topics such as abortion, arms control and disarmament, cloning, the death penalty, environmental issues, euthanasia, the federal budget, health care, immigration, international debt relief, landmines, the minimum wage, refugees, regional conflicts, religious liberty, school vouchers, Social Security, and welfare.

Vital Stats:

Access method: WWW
To access: http://www.nccbuscc.org

National Council of Churches

The National Council of Churches site features congressional testimony, legislative analyses, and other resources about religious freedom and persecution around the world. It also has resolutions and other materials about antipersonnel landmines, affirmative action, organ and tissue donations, health care, global debt forgiveness, and other issues.

Vital Stats:

Access method: WWW
To access: http://www.ncccusa.org

Open Directory Project: Church-State Relations

More than 100 links to Web sites about church-state relations are provided through this page at the Open Directory Project (p. 11). Each link is briefly annotated.

The main page provides links to about twenty general sites. The remaining links are divided into pages by the following subjects: anti-separation, pro-separation, public schools, and regional.

Vital Stats:

Access method: WWW
To access: http://dmoz.org/Society/Issues/Church-State_Relations

---

Religion News Links

Zondervan Publishing House provides this directory of news sources about religion. The directory has more than 200 links that lead to news pages operated by religious organizations, religion pages at newspaper sites, sites operated by Christian newspapers, and articles about religion reporting.

Vital Stats:

Access method: WWW
To access: http://www.zondervan.com/newslink.htm

Worldwide Faith News

A database at this site provides a searchable archive of more than 12,000 official press releases and other documents issued by religious organizations around the world. Users also can browse the headlines of all releases posted in the last thirty days and subscribe to a mailing list to receive all documents as they're posted.

The Worldwide Faith News is a project of the National Council of Churches.

Vital Stats:

Access method: WWW
To access: http://www.wfn.org

✓ Yahoo! News: Religion

Through this page, Yahoo! (p. 17) provides access to hundreds of news stories about religious issues around the world. The stories date from March 1999 to the present.

Some of the sources include the *New York Times, Irish Times (Ireland), Christian Science Monitor, The Times (United Kingdom), Sydney Morning Herald (Australia), Dallas Morning News, Chicago Tribune, Baltimore Sun, Rocky Mountain News, Philadelphia Daily News, USA Today, Jerusalem Post (Israel), Detroit News, Washington Post,* BBC, CNN, Christian Broadcasting Network, Radio Netherlands, and ABC News.

If you click on Yahoo! News Search on the left side of the page, you'll automatically launch a search for religion news stories published in recent weeks. A search typically returns dozens of articles.

The page also has links to a small collection of documents and Web sites about religion.

Vital Stats:

Access method:	WWW
To access:	http://fullcoverage.yahoo.com/fc/World/Religion_News

---

Yahoo! Society and Culture: Church-State Issues

Links to dozens of Web sites about church-state issues are available through this Yahoo! (p. 17) page.

The top page has links to about twenty general sites. It also leads to pages of links about the following topics: freedom of religion, journals, religion in public schools, and religious right.

Vital Stats:

Access method:	WWW
To access:	http://dir.yahoo.com/Society_and_Culture/ Religion_and_Spirituality/Church_State_Issues

RIGHT TO DIE

Death and Dying: Euthanasia

This page at About.com's Death and Dying site provides links to more than two dozen documents and Web sites about euthanasia and assisted suicide. The documents include government reports, news articles, and position papers, and the Web sites are operated by such groups as Citizens United Resisting Euthanasia, the Euthanasia Research and Guidance Organization, and the International Anti-Euthanasia Task Force.

Vital Stats:

Access method: WWW
To access: http://dying.about.com/health/dying/msub18.htm

Doctor-Assisted Suicide: A Guide to Web Sites and the Literature

A librarian at the Longwood College Library created this page, which has an excellent set of links to sites that offer materials related to doctor-assisted suicide. There are links to whole sites about suicide, death, and related issues, as well as links to journal and newspaper articles, transcripts of radio and television programs, court decisions in assisted-suicide cases, the text of the Oregon Death with Dignity Act, and more.

Vital Stats:

Access method: WWW
To access: http://web.lwc.edu/administrative/library/suic.htm

---

The Hemlock Society

News about state and national legislation concerning euthanasia and doctor-assisted suicide highlights this site. It's operated by the Hemlock Society, a non-profit group that supports the right to die.

The site also has guidelines for right-to-die legislation, information about court decisions regarding assisted suicide, statements about Dr. Jack Kevorkian, documents about the rights of patients, a chronology of the right-to-die movement, and a list of publications that can be ordered from the society.

Vital Stats:

Access method: WWW
To access: http://www.hemlock.org

International Anti-Euthanasia Task Force

Articles, court decisions, proposed legislation, and news updates about euthanasia, physician-assisted suicide, the right to die, disability rights, and pain control highlight this site. It's operated by the International Anti-Euthanasia Task Force, a group that opposes euthanasia and physician-assisted suicide.

Vital Stats:

Access method: WWW
To access: http://www.iaetf.org

Open Directory Project: End-of-Life

This page at the Open Directory Project (p. 11) has links to more than fifty sites about various end-of-life issues. Most of the sites are about euthanasia and physician-assisted suicide.

Vital Stats:

Access method: WWW
To access: http://dmoz.org/Society/Issues/End-of-Life

Public Agenda Online: Right to Die

A variety of information about the right to die and assisted suicide is available through this section of the Public Agenda site. Public Agenda is a nonprofit, nonpartisan organization that researches and reports on public issues.

The site provides summaries of recent reports and news stories (with links to the full texts where available), statistics about various right-to-die issues, results from public opinion polls, and contact information (including links to Web sites) of major organizations involved in the right-to-die debate.

Vital Stats:

Access method: WWW
To access: http://www.publicagenda.org/issues/
                   frontdoor.cfm?issue_type=right2die

talk.euthanasia

Participants in the talk.euthanasia Usenet newsgroup discuss political policy and other issues associated with euthanasia and assisted suicide.

Vital Stats:

Access method: Usenet newsgroup
To access: news:talk.euthanasia

Yahoo! News: Assisted Suicide

This page at Yahoo! (p. 17) provides access to dozens of news stories about assisted suicide. The stories date from October 1997 to the present.

Some of the sources include the *Detroit Free Press, Detroit News, Christian Science Monitor, Sydney Morning Herald (Australia), San Francisco Chronicle, The Times (United Kingdom), Chicago Tribune, Washington Post, New York Times, Irish Times (Ireland), Seattle Post-Intelligencer, Time, Los Angeles Times,* CNN, ABC, BBC, Court TV, and Radio Netherlands.

The page also offers links to selected documents and Web sites about assisted suicide.

Vital Stats:

Access method: WWW
To access: http://fullcoverage.yahoo.com/fc/US/Assisted_Suicide

---

Yahoo! Society and Culture: Euthanasia

This page at Yahoo! (p. 17) provides links to dozens of sites about euthanasia and other end-of-life issues. The top page offers links to a few general sites and leads to pages about the following topics: advance directives, opposing views, physician-assisted suicide, and pro-euthanasia.

Vital Stats:

Access method: WWW
To access: http://dir.yahoo.com/Society_and_Culture/
                    Death_and_Dying/Euthanasia

SENIOR ISSUES

AARP Webplace

This slightly chaotic site provides reports, articles, and position papers about many issues, among them Social Security solvency, Medicare reform, patient protections under managed care, long-term care, Medicare, and electric utility restructuring. It's operated by the AARP, which used to be known as the American Association of Retired Persons but now just uses the initials.

The site also presents the AARP's public policy agenda, congressional testimony by AARP officials, press releases about the 2000 presidential campaign, questions to ask candidates, a report that profiles Americans age 65 and older, and links to Internet sites related to aging.

Vital Stats:

Access method: WWW
To access: http://www.aarp.org

Administration on Aging

The Administration on Aging site offers information about the Older Americans Act, reports from White House conferences on aging, and extensive demographic information about older Americans. The Administration on Aging is part of the U.S. Department of Health and Human Services.

The site also has consumer brochures, a database that provides information about assistance available for the elderly in cities around the country, links to Web sites operated by state agencies on aging, directories of area agencies on aging and state long-term care ombudsmen, press releases, links to numerous Internet sites that provide information for older Americans, and more.

Vital Stats:

Access method: WWW
To access: http://www.aoa.dhhs.gov

Medicare

This site has a wealth of information about Medicare, a federal program that provides health insurance to people age 65 and over, among others. It's operated by the Health Care Financing Administration, which is part of the U.S. Department of Health and Human Services.

Among other highlights, the site has documents about Medicare coverage of various diseases and medical procedures, answers to commonly asked questions about Medicare and Medicaid, numerous consumer pamphlets, and a program that provides information about costs, premiums, and types of services provided by managed care plans around the country.

Vital Stats:

Access method: WWW
To access: http://www.medicare.gov

The New York Times: Social Security

Selected articles about Social Security from the *New York Times* are provided through this page. The articles date from December 1998 to the present.

The page also has background information about Social Security, specifics of three major proposals for Social Security reform, and a forum about Social Security.

Vital Stats:

Access method: WWW
To access: http://www.nytimes.com/library/politics/index-socsec.html

---

Project Vote Smart: Seniors/Social Security

This page at Project Vote Smart (p. 15) provides links to two dozen Web sites about Social Security and other political issues of concern to seniors. Each link is briefly annotated.

The sites are operated by various groups, among them the AARP (formerly the American Association of Retired Persons), American Society on Aging, Citizens for REAL Retirement Security, National Caucus and Center on Black Aged, National Committee to Preserve Social Security and Medicare, National Council of Senior Citizens, National Senior Citizens Law Center, 60 Plus Association, Social Security Education Center, and the United Seniors Association.

Vital Stats:

Access method: WWW
To access: http://www.vote-smart.org/issues/
                       SENIORS_SOCIAL_SECURITY

Public Agenda Online: Medicare

A variety of information about Medicare is available through this section of the site operated by Public Agenda, a nonprofit, nonpartisan organization that researches and reports on public issues.

The site provides summaries of recent reports and news stories (with links to the full texts where available), facts and trends presented in graphs, results from public opinion polls about Medicare, and contact information (including links to Web sites) for major organizations interested in Medicare.

Vital Stats:

Access method: WWW
To access: http://www.publicagenda.org/issues/
                             frontdoor.cfm?issue_type=medicare

---

Public Agenda Online: Social Security

Results of public opinion polls about various Social Security policy options highlight this section of the Public Agenda Web site.

The site also presents summaries of selected news stories and reports, with links to the full texts where available; charts that graph facts and trends; and information about major organizations involved in the Social Security debate, including links to their Web sites.

Vital Stats:

Access method: WWW
To access: http://www.publicagenda.org/issues/
                             frontdoor.cfm?issue_type=ss

Social Security Online

This official site from the Social Security Administration has the full texts of Social Security laws and regulations, recent legislation, congressional testimony by SSA officials, and reports about the potential effects of policy changes to Social Security programs.

The site also presents the Social Security Administration's budget and its annual report to Congress; *Social Security Programs Throughout the World,* a publication that summarizes social security legislation in 165 countries; the

Social Security Handbook, which has detailed information about Social Security Administration programs; numerous Social Security forms; and much more.

Vital Stats:

Access method: WWW
To access: http://www.ssa.gov

Social Security Privatization

This site provides extensive information about proposals to privatize Social Security. It's operated by the Social Security Privatization Project at the Cato Institute, a Washington think tank.

The site offers a weekly roundup of news in the *Social Security This Week* newsletter, speeches and congressional testimony by Cato representatives, answers to frequently asked questions about Social Security, summaries of the presidential candidates' positions on Social Security, reports, articles, and a list of books about Social Security published by Cato.

You also can sign up at the site to receive the *Social Security This Week* newsletter by e-mail.

Vital Stats:

Access method: WWW
To access: http://www.socialsecurity.org

Town Hall: Social Security

This page at Town Hall provides links to dozens of articles and reports about Social Security from a variety of conservative sources. Most of the documents date from January 1999 to the present, although a few documents from 1998 also are available.

The sources include the Heritage Foundation, National Taxpayers Union, Institute for Policy Innovation, Capital Research Center, Citizens Against Government Waste, Society Security Reform Center, Pacific Research Institute, Christian Coalition, and the National Center for Policy Analysis, among other organizations.

The page also provides links to recent news articles about Social Security from sources such as the Conservative News Service, the *Washington Post,* and *USA Today.*

Vital Stats:

Access method: WWW
To access: http://www.townhall.com/issueslibrary/socialsecurity

U.S. Senate Special Committee on Aging

At its Web site, the U.S. Senate Special Committee on Aging offers links to the full texts of bills referred to the committee, a schedule of committee hearings, and press releases.

A highlight is a list of free hearing transcripts that you can order through the committee's Web site. The hearings address topics such as Social Security reform, complaint investigation and enforcement at nursing homes, long-term care, Medicare, shopping for assisted living, and battling disability among seniors.

Vital Stats:

Access method: WWW
To access: http://www.senate.gov/~aging

Washingtonpost.com: Medicare Special Report

This page archives major stories from the *Washington Post* about Medicare. More than three dozen stories are provided dating from June 1997 to the present.

The page also provides background information about Medicare, Associated Press stories about Medicare from the previous two weeks, and links to selected documents and Web sites about Medicare.

Vital Stats:

Access method: WWW
To access: http://www.washingtonpost.com/wp-srv/politics/
                   special/medicare/keystories.htm

Washingtonpost.com: Social Security Special Report

Several dozen selected stories about Social Security from the *Washington Post* are available through this page. Most of the stories date from January 1998 to the present, although a few earlier articles also are provided.

The page also offers background information about Social Security, Associated Press stories about Social Security from the previous two weeks, *Washington Post* editorials and opinion articles about Social Security, and links to selected documents and Web sites.

Vital Stats:

Access method: WWW
To access: http://www.washingtonpost.com/wp-srv/politics/
                   special/security/security.htm

Yahoo! News: Social Security Debate

Dozens of news stories about Social Security are available through this Yahoo! (p. 17) page. The stories date from April 1998 to the present.

Some of the sources include the *New York Times, USA Today, Christian Science Monitor, Chicago Tribune, Time, San Francisco Chronicle, Philadelphia Inquirer,* Associated Press, CNN, and ABC News.

Clicking on Yahoo! News Search on the left side of the page automatically launches a search for stories about Social Security published in recent weeks. A search typically returns several dozen stories.

The page also provides links to selected documents and Web sites about Social Security.

Vital Stats:

Access method: WWW
To access: http://fullcoverage.yahoo.com/fc/US/Social_Security

TOBACCO

Action on Smoking and Health

This site offers breaking news about smoking, previously secret tobacco company documents, and court decisions in various tobacco suits. Action on Smoking and Health, an advocacy organization, operates the site.

The site also presents the full texts of Food and Drug Administration rules regulating smoking, links to other Web sites about smoking, press releases, articles about a variety of smoking issues, and much more.

Vital Stats:

Access method: WWW
To access: http://ash.org

alt.smokers

Flame wars are common in the newsgroup alt.smokers, where passionate pro- and anti-smoking forces do battle.

Vital Stats:

Access method: Usenet newsgroup
To access: news:alt.smokers

The New York Times: The Tobacco Debate

This page provides an archive of selected *New York Times* articles about tobacco. The stories date from March 1997 to the present.

The page also provides links to other sites about tobacco and a discussion forum.

Vital Stats:

Access method: WWW
To access: http://www.nytimes.com/library/politics/tobacco-index.html

Open Directory Project: Tobacco

Links to more than 700 documents and Web sites about tobacco are provided through this page at the Open Directory Project (p. 11). Each link has a brief description.

The top page provides links to more than 200 sites. It also leads to separate pages with links about the following subjects: activism, effects, industry, quitting, resources, secondhand smoke, spit tobacco, teen smoking, and women.

Vital Stats:

Access method: WWW
To access: http://dmoz.org/Health/Substance_Abuse/Tobacco

Project Vote Smart: Tobacco

This page at Project Vote Smart (p. 15) provides links to about two dozen Web sites concerning tobacco. Each link is briefly annotated.

The sites are operated by Action on Smoking and Health, the American Heart Association, Americans for Nonsmokers' Rights, the Centers for Disease Control and Prevention, the National Center for Tobacco Free Kids, R.J. Reynolds Tobacco Company, and the State Tobacco Information Center, among others.

Vital Stats:

Access method: WWW
To access: http://www.vote-smart.org/issues/TOBACCO

TobaccoArchives.com

This site is a gateway to millions of pages of documents that the tobacco industry has produced in various civil suits. It leads to individual document databases operated by Philip Morris, R.J. Reynolds Tobacco Company, Brown & Williamson Tobacco Corporation, Lorillard Tobacco Company, The Tobacco Institute, and The Council for Tobacco Research.

Together, the databases contain images of more than 26 million pages of documents relating to cigarette research, manufacturing, marketing, advertising, and sales, among other subjects.

Vital Stats:

Access method: WWW
To access: http://www.tobaccoarchive.com

Tobacco Control Resource Center & The Tobacco Products Liability Project

Extensive information about lawsuits against the tobacco industry is available through this site. It has a list of current and upcoming trials, complaints from various suits, depositions, transcripts of testimony, and legal decisions. The site is operated by the Tobacco Control Resource Center and The Tobacco Products Liability Project, both of which are located at Northeastern University School of Law.

Vital Stats:

Access method: WWW
To access: http://tobacco.neu.edu

Yahoo! News: Tobacco

This Yahoo! (p. 17) page provides hundreds of news stories about tobacco issues around the world. The stories date from April 1997 to the present.

The stories are from dozens of sources, including the *Christian Science Monitor, New York Times, The Times (United Kingdom), Miami Herald, Washington Post, Boston Globe, Sydney Morning Herald (Australia), Baltimore Sun, Chicago Tribune, USA Today, Irish Times (Ireland), Time, San Francisco Chronicle, Dallas Morning News, New York Law Journal, Seattle Times,* Reuters, Associated Press, Agence France-Presse, BBC, CNN, ABC News, and Court TV.

Clicking on Yahoo! News Search on the left side of the page automatically launches a search for stories about tobacco published in recent weeks. A search commonly returns more than 100 articles.

The page also has links to a strong collection of documents and Web sites about tobacco.

Vital Stats:

Access method: WWW
To access: http://fullcoverage.yahoo.com/Full_Coverage/
      US/Tobacco_News

WOMEN

Center for American Women and Politics

One of the most interesting documents at this site is a regularly updated list of actual and potential women candidates for U.S. Senate, U.S. House, or gubernatorial races on major party tickets in the 2000 election. The Center for American Women and Politics at Rutgers University operates the site.

The site also has numerous articles and fact sheets about women in elected office, women candidates, women in the federal cabinet, women's political action committees, the effect of term limits on representation of women, voting patterns of young women and men, and related topics.

Vital Stats:

Access method: WWW
To access: http://www.rci.rutgers.edu/~cawp

Feminist Majority Foundation Online

News about court decisions and legislative proposals that affect women, action alerts, and a calendar of feminist events highlight this site from the Feminist Majority Foundation.

The site also presents numerous articles and press releases about abortion and reproductive rights, an annual survey of violence at abortion clinics, the *Feminist Majority Report* newsletter, listings of jobs and internships available at a variety of progressive organizations, and annotated links to numerous Web sites for women.

Vital Stats:

Access method: WWW
To access: http://www.feminist.org

National Organization for Women

Articles about topics such as abortion and reproductive rights, economic equity, lesbian rights, racial and ethnic diversity, violence against women, and women in the military highlight this site from the National Organization for Women. NOW also operates a separate site for its political action committees.

The main NOW site also offers periodic updates about legislation moving through Congress, articles from the *National NOW Times,* and a page where you can sign up to automatically receive action alerts and announcements by e-mail.

Vital Stats:

Access method: WWW
To access: http://www.now.org

National Organization for Women Political Action Committees

Lists of feminist candidates endorsed for federal, state, and local offices highlight this site. It's operated by the National Organization for Women's two political action committees: the NOW Political Action Committee, which supports candidates for federal office, and the NOW Equality PAC, which supports candidates for state and local offices. The site also provides articles analyzing gains by women in previous elections.

NOW also operates a separate organizational site.

Vital Stats:

Access method: WWW
To access: http://www.nowpacs.org

Open Directory Project: Women and Politics

Just over two dozen links to selected Web sites about women and politics are available through this page at the Open Directory Project (p. 11). Each link is briefly annotated.

The sites are operated by a variety of organizations, among them the Global Fund for Women, the Institute for Women's Policy Research, the League of Women Voters, the National Organization for Women Political Action Committees, the National Partnership for Women & Families, and the National Women's Party.

Vital Stats:

Access method: WWW
To access: http://dmoz.org/Society/People/Women/Politics

Project Vote Smart: Gender

This page at Project Vote Smart (p. 15) provides links to several dozen Web sites about gender issues. Each link has a brief description.

The sites are operated by the American Association of University Women, Concerned Women for America, the Feminist Majority Foundation, the National Coalition of Free Men, the National Organization for Women, the National Women's Political Caucus, and the United Nations Division for the Advancement of Women, among others.

Vital Stats:

Access method: WWW
To access: http://www.vote-smart.org/issues/GENDER

6

Political News

C-SPAN: Campaign Video Search

This page offers video clips from C-SPAN's coverage of the 2000 presidential campaign. The clips, which come from campaign speeches, interviews, debates, and other events, date from May 1997 to the present.

You can search the clips by keyword, and you can limit your search to clips from a particular candidate, party, or state. For each clip, the site returns an unedited transcript as well as the video.

Vital Stats:

Access method: WWW
To access: http://www.c-span.org/campaign2000/search

CNN/AllPolitics

CNN and *Time* magazine operate this site, which offers thousands of news stories and video clips about elections and politics from January 1996 to the present.

Clicking on Election 2000 takes you to a special page with articles and videos about the 2000 campaign. The page also has videos from the latest political ads, a calendar of primary and caucus dates, results from political opinion polls, and extensive background information about the election.

Vital Stats:

Access method: WWW
To access: http://cnn.com/ALLPOLITICS

Cox News: Campaign 2000

This page offers recent news stories and commentary about the 2000 campaign from Cox News Service and newspapers in the Cox Newspapers chain. It also has special reports about the impact of the Internet on the 2000 campaign, reviews of political books, profiles of the 2000 presidential candidates, and links to dozens of political Web sites.

Vital Stats:

Access method: WWW
To access: http://www.coxnews.com/2000

Election Notes

This site's highlight is its annotated links to current election news stories from around the world. It also has the full text of a book titled *Atlas of United States Presidential Elections*, links to worldwide election calendars, and links to election results from a variety of countries. It's operated by Klipsan Press.

Vital Stats:

Access method: WWW
To access: http://www.klipsan.com/elecnews.htm

EPN News

Each weekly issue of the EPN News mailing list contains information about new reports, research, and events announced by progressive policy organizations, most of which are located in Washington, D.C. In the case of reports and research, the mailing usually contains a link to the full text of the document.

Some of the organizations represented in a typical issue are the Brookings Institution, Campaign for America's Future, Center on Budget and Policy Priorities, Center for Law and Social Policy, and the Financial Markets Center. EPN News is operated by the Electronic Policy Network, which is a project of the *American Prospect* magazine.

Vital Stats:

Access method: E-mail
To access: Send an e-mail message to majordomo@epn.org
Subject:
Message: **subscribe epnnews**

Los Angeles Times: Campaign 2000

This page offers stories about the 2000 campaign from the *Los Angeles Times* and other sources. It has breaking political news from the Associated Press, selected stories from the *Times* about the presidential campaign dating from January 1999 to the present, *Times* interviews with several major presidential candidates, *Times* stories about state and local politics in California, and more.

One particularly nice feature lets you browse articles about the presidential campaign by candidate.

Vital Stats:

Access method: WWW
To access: http://www.latimes.com/news/politics/elect2000/pres

MSNBC News: Politics

This page from MSNBC offers dozens of news stories about a variety of political topics. The presidential and congressional elections dominate the coverage, although there also are stories about administration proposals, congressional actions, and current topics such as gun control.

Vital Stats:

Access method: WWW
To access: http://www.msnbc.com/news/politics_front.asp

The New York Times: Politics

A wealth of news and information about politics and the 2000 campaign is available through this page from the *New York Times.* Navigating the page is a trick, though, because it and related pages loop back and forth in a seemingly endless circle.

The page has political stories from the current day's issue of the *Times,* breaking political news from the Associated Press, political columns from the newspaper, an archive of campaign news stories dating from 1998 to the present, articles and background information about each of the presidential candidates in 2000, and videos of ads from the presidential campaign.

It also provides results from political polls, an archive of articles about the Internet and political campaigns, articles summarizing House and Senate campaigns in each state in 2000, a list of seats in the House and Senate that are open or considered vulnerable, articles about each of the gubernatorial races in 2000, and more.

Vital Stats:

Access method: WWW
To access: http://www.nytimes.com/yr/mo/day/national/
                   index-politics.html

Open Directory Project: Politics News

This page at the Open Directory Project (p. 11) has links to more than 200 Internet sites that offer political news. Each link is briefly annotated.

The top page has links to several dozen general political news sites. It also leads to separate pages that list sites in the following categories: humor, interntional elections, international politics, magazines, regional, television programs, and U.S. election 2000.

Vital Stats:

Access method: WWW
To access: http://dmoz.org/news/politics

✓ The Political Insider

Each day the Newswires section at this site provides links to hundreds of political news stories from media outlets around the United States. The links are divided into seven top-level categories: politics and election 2000 news, public policy news, media news, international relations and world news, business and finance news, Internet and technology news, and culture news. Each top-level category is divided into sub-categories.

The site also has links to major newspapers, newswires, magazines, political news sites, articles about specific presidential candidates, columns by dozens of political pundits, editorial and op-ed pages at major newspapers, political poll results, and sites about selected political issues.

Vital Stats:

Access method: WWW
To access: http://www.politicalinsider.com

Politics News from Wired News

Wired News provides its recent political stories through this page. Most are about cyberspace topics such as cryptography, Internet fraud, electronic privacy, campaign Web sites, and free speech online.

Vital Stats:

Access method: WWW
To access: http://www.wired.com/news/politics/index.html

Politics1: Today's Top Political News Stories

Links to several dozen political news stories are posted each day at this page from Politics1 (p. 14). The links are not archived.

Some of the news sources are the *Boston Phoenix, Washington Post, New York Times, New York Post,* CNN, Reuters, and Capitol Hill Blue.

Vital Stats:

Access method: WWW
To access: http://www.politics1.com/news1.htm

Town Hall: Conservative Columnists

Links to articles by dozens of conservative columnists are available through this page at Town Hall. The links are arranged by columnist, and for most columnists they provide access to the current column and an archive of past articles.

Some of the featured columnists are Michael Barone, Brent Bozell, William F. Buckley, Linda Chavez, Suzanne Fields, Rich Galen, Paul Greenberg, Arianna Huffington, Jeff Jacoby, Michael Kelly, Alan Keyes, James J. Kilpatrick, Charles Krauthammer, Dick Morris, Oliver North, Robert Novak, Wesley Pruden, William Safire, Phyllis Schlafly, Laura Schlesinger, Tony Snow, Cal Thomas, R. Emmett Tyrrell Jr., Ben Wattenberg, and George Will.

Vital Stats:

Access method: WWW
To access: http://www.townhall.com/columnists

Town Hall: Electronic Newsletters

This page at Town Hall provides links to the subscription pages of dozens of newsletters published by conservative organizations and publications. Each newsletter is briefly described.

The newsletters are published by Town Hall, the Heritage Foundation, the Media Research Center, the *National Review,* Americans for Tax Reform, the Traditional Values Coalition, the American Conservative Union, the Capital Research Center, the Claremont Institute, the Family Research Council, National Right to Work, and the Pacific Research Institute, among others.

Vital Stats:

Access method: WWW
To access: http://www.townhall.com/newsletters

U.S. Department of State: Washington File

Official U.S. government documents, policy statements, and articles are provided through this site, which is operated by the International Information Programs office at the U.S. State Department.

The files include press releases from federal agencies and the White House, transcripts of speeches by the president, transcripts of briefings by the Pentagon spokesman, and transcripts of briefings by United Nations officials, among many other types of documents.

There are three ways to browse the documents. You can browse items released within the previous forty-eight hours; items released within the previous two weeks organized by the topics of international security issues, economic issues, democracy and human rights, U.S. society and politics, and global issues and communication; or items released within the previous two weeks organized by the regions of the Americas, Europe and Russia, the Middle East and North Africa, South Asia, Africa, and East Asia and the Pacific.

You also can search a database that contains documents released within the past several years.

Vital Stats:

Access method: WWW
To access: http://www.usia.gov/products/washfile.htm

USA Today: Politics

The latest news from *USA Today* about a variety of political issues is presented through this page. Many of the stories are about the 2000 election campaign, but others cover such topics as proposals by the president, congressional actions, and Supreme Court decisions.

The page also has extensive archives of stories about each major presidential candidate, a state-by-state guide to the 2000 election, poll results, hundreds of stories about campaign finance dating from July 1997 to the present, and an archive of stories about Supreme Court rulings from 1997 to the present.

Vital Stats:

Access method: WWW
To access: http://www.usatoday.com/news/politics/polifront.htm

---

The Washington Times: Daybook

Each weekday this page from the *Washington Times* provides a calendar of major events scheduled for that day in and around Washington, D.C.

The calendar lists the schedules of the president and vice president, economic reports that will be released, major meetings at federal agencies, oral arguments at the Supreme Court, congressional floor and committee schedules, and major meetings, conferences, press conferences, and speeches in the Washington area.

You can sign up at the site to receive the Daybook automatically by e-mail.

Vital Stats:

Access method:	WWW
To access:	http://www.washtimes.com/national
Note:	After you reach the National page, scroll down and click on Daybook

Washingtonpost.com: On Politics

The latest political news from the *Washington Post* and the Associated Press highlights this page. It also has *Post* series that profile major presidential candidates, archived stories about dozens of political issues such as gun control and health care, a searchable database of results from polls conducted by the *Post* since 1998, a calendar of presidential primary and caucus dates, and more.

Vital Stats:

Access method:	WWW
To access:	http://www.washingtonpost.com/wp-dyn/politics

Yahoo! News: Politics Headlines

Current political news from Reuters, the Associated Press, and ABC News is featured on this Yahoo! (p. 17) page.

In deciding which stories to include, the page's editors use a broad definition of political news. The page often has stories about speeches by the president, administration actions in Washington, bills before Congress, studies by advocacy groups, and political activities in foreign countries, among other subjects.

The top page features stories from Reuters, and it leads to separate pages with articles from the Associated Press and ABC News. About twenty stories each from Reuters and the AP are posted each day, while a smaller number of articles are provided from ABC.

Political stories from each of the three news sources posted over the previous ten days also are available. The stories are available at the bottom of each source's page, where you can browse them by date.

The top page also links to a separate page containing election news. All the stories are from the Associated Press, and about twenty stories are posted each day.

Vital Stats:

Access method: WWW
To access: http://dailynews.yahoo.com/headlines/pl

Yahoo! News: U.S. Elections

Several dozen selected news stories about U.S. elections are available through this Yahoo! (p. 17) page. Most of the stories report on election trends, and they date from September 1999 to the present.

Some of the sources are the *Los Angeles Times, Wired, Washington Post, New York Times, San Francisco Examiner, Chicago Tribune, Time, USA Today, Christian Science Monitor,* Associated Press, CNN, and ABC News.

Vital Stats:

Access method: WWW
To access: http://fullcoverage.yahoo.com/fc/US/US_Elections

✓ Yahoo! News: U.S. Presidential Election

Each day, links to a dozen or more news stories about the 2000 presidential election from media outlets around the country are posted on this Yahoo! (p. 17) page. The page has links to well over 1,000 stories dating from January 1999 to the present.

Stories are available from such sources as the *New York Times, Washington Post, San Francisco Chronicle, Wired, Miami Herald, USA Today, Dallas Morning News, Boston Globe, Los Angeles Times, The Times (United Kingdom), Baltimore Sun, Business Week, Christian Science Monitor, Salon, Concord Monitor, International Herald Tribune, Time, Arizona Republic, San Jose Mercury News, Miami Herald, PC Week, Chicago Tribune,* Associated Press, Reuters, ABC News, CNN, and MSNBC.

The page also has links to selected sites about the 2000 campaign, political news sites, and presidential candidate sites.

Vital Stats:

Access method: WWW
To access: http://fullcoverage.yahoo.com/fc/US/
                           Presidential_Election_2000

7

Political Opinion

ABCNEWS.com: Poll Vault

Articles on this page summarize the results of polls conducted for the ABC-NEWS.com Web site. Results are available for dozens of polls dating from January 1999 to the present.

The polls measure public opinion about such topics as consumer confidence, terrorism, tobacco companies, racial discrimination, campaign finance reform, presidential candidates, gun control, and the war in Kosovo.

Vital Stats:

Access method: WWW

To access: http://abcnews.go.com/sections/politics/
                  PollVault/PollVault.html

CNN/AllPolitics: Presidential Polls

This page at the CNN/AllPolitics site (p. 244) has the results of public opinion polls about the 2000 presidential election conducted from January 1999 to the present. The polls were conducted by various combinations of CNN, *USA Today*, Gallup, *Time* magazine, and WMUR Radio.

Vital Stats:

Access method: WWW

To access: http://cnn.com/ELECTION/2000/resources/polls.html

Forage for Data

An excellent collection of annotated links to Web sites that offer polling data is available through this page from the Economic Policy Institute. The sites are operated by the *Washington Post, Los Angeles Times*, Public Agenda Online, Gallup, Harris, *USA Today, New York Times*, CNN, and Wirthlin Worldwide, among others.

Vital Stats:

Access method: WWW

To access: http://www.epinet.org/pulse/forage.html

Gallup Poll

Articles detailing the results from hundreds of Gallup Polls from 1997 to the present highlight this site from the Gallup Organization. You can search for a poll about a particular topic, or you can browse the articles by date or subject.

The polls are divided into five top-level subjects: politics and elections, business and the economy, social issues and policy, managing, and lifestyle.

Each of the top-level subjects is subdivided. For example, the Politics and Elections topic is split into nine sub-categories: elections, Clinton impeachment, Congress, Supreme Court, government and election reform, the presidency, special interest groups, political personalities, and political parties and ideology.

Similarly, the Social Issues and Policy topic is split into nine sub-categories: social issues, government, state of the nation, ethics and values, domestic policy, international affairs, the news media, societal institutions, and science, computers, and technology.

Special articles explore polling trends about such topics as the president's job approval rating and the public's mood regarding the economy.

You also can sign up at the site to receive automatic weekly updates about Gallup Polls by e-mail.

Vital Stats:

Access method: WWW
To access: http://www.gallup.com/poll

The Harris Poll

Results from an ongoing series of Harris Polls that track political trends on such issues as the president's job performance highlight this site. Other articles summarize the results of polls conducted from August 1999 to the present about the 2000 presidential candidates, health issues, the U.S. role in Asia, Medicare, and Waco, among other topics.

You must have Adobe Acrobat Reader software installed on your computer to read the articles.

Vital Stats:

Access method: WWW
To access: http://www.louisharris.com/harris_poll

Los Angeles Times Poll

This page at the *Los Angeles Times* site (p. 245) has results of polls conducted by the newspaper from 1992 to the present. There are results from national, state, and local polls. The national polls address such subjects as Iraq, the president's performance, and Medicare.

Vital Stats:

Access method: WWW
To access: http://www.latimes.com/news/timespoll

National Election Studies

This site, which is operated by the University of Michigan's Institute for Social Research, provides a wealth of polling data regarding voting, public opinion, and political participation from 1948 to the present.

Data are available about social and religious characteristics of the electorate, ideological self-identification, public opinion on public policy issues, support for the political system, evaluation of the presidential candidates, and evaluation of congressional candidates, among other subjects.

Vital Stats:

Access method: WWW
To access: http://www.umich.edu/~nes

The New York Times: Polls

Stories about public opinion polls conducted by the *New York Times* highlight this page. It provides poll results from March 1999 to the present.

The page also has an archive of weekly columns about polls conducted by other organizations, a special section with poll results from various sources about the 2000 presidential campaign, results of the latest polls in the New York Senate race between Hillary Rodham Clinton and Rudolph W. Giuliani, and links to a small collection of Internet sites about polling.

Vital Stats:

Access method: WWW
To access: http://www.nytimes.com/library/national/index-polls.html

The Pew Research Center for the People & the Press

This site presents the results of national public opinion polls regarding the press, politics, and public policy issues. The polls are conducted by the Pew Research Center for the People & the Press, which is sponsored by the Pew Charitable Trusts.

Results are available from dozens of polls conducted from 1995 to the present. The polls measure public attitudes about such topics as the 2000 presidential campaign, the Senate vote on the Test Ban Treaty, Kosovo, the most popular news stories, China policy, news on the Internet, social beliefs, and Congress.

Vital Stats:

Access method: WWW
To access: http://www.people-press.org

PollingReport.com

Summaries of results from a wide range of polls conducted by the major polling organizations are featured at this site. It's operated by *The Polling Report* newsletter, which covers polls.

Results from polls on a wide range of topics are provided. Some of the subjects covered are the 2000 presidential election, national priorities, abortion, the federal budget, the death penalty, education, the environment, America's role in world affairs, relations with Cuba, Internet voting, gun control, assisted suicide, Social Security reform, individual political figures, Congress, and major political institutions.

Vital Stats:

Access method: WWW
To access: http://www.pollingreport.com

USA Today: Polls/Surveys

Results from USA Today/CNN/Gallup Polls are presented on this page at the *USA Today* site (p. 249). Results of polls from October 1998 to the present are available.

The polls measure public opinion about the 2000 presidential election, Congress, the president's job performance, tax cuts, school integration, Hillary Rodham Clinton's Senate race, gun control, the war in Kosovo, the Colorado school shootings, the Senate impeachment trial of the president, Social Security, and Iraq, among other subjects.

Vital Stats:

Access method: WWW
To access: http://www.usatoday.com/news/poll001.htm

The Vanishing Voter

Results from weekly polls that measure Americans' involvement in the 2000 campaign are the prime attraction at this site. It's operated by the Joan Shorenstein Center on the Press, Politics and Public Policy at Harvard University's John F. Kennedy School of Government.

Poll results are available from November 1999 to the present. You also can sign up at the site to receive a weekly digest of new poll results by e-mail.

Vital Stats:

Access method: WWW
To access: http://www.vanishingvoter.org

Washingtonpost.com: Poll Vault

Results from dozens of national public opinion polls conducted by the *Washington Post* are available on this page at the newspaper's Web site. The polls date from January 1997 to the present.

The polls measure public opinion about the 2000 presidential election, gun control, ground troops in Kosovo, violence in schools, the president's performance, the Clinton impeachment trial, acceptance of gays, school vouchers, and race relations, among other topics.

Vital Stats:

Access method: WWW
To access: http://www.washingtonpost.com/
                            wp-srv/politics/polls/vault/vault.htm

8

Political Parties
and Organizations

FOREIGN AND U.S. PARTIES

Democratic Congressional Campaign Committee

The Democratic Congressional Campaign Committee assists Democratic candidates for the U.S. House of Representatives. In late January 2000 the site had press releases and information about how to join the DCCC, but much of the rest of the information (such as a political calendar) was outdated.

You also can sign up at the site to receive a biweekly DCCC newsletter by e-mail.

Vital Stats:

Access method: WWW
To access: http://www.dccc.org

The Democratic National Committee

This official Democratic National Committee site has press releases about Democratic and Republican stands on issues and the parties' respective candidates, articles about how Republican George W. Bush's record compares with his campaign speeches, analyses of television ads run by Republican candidates, and campaign finance reports that the DNC has filed with the Federal Election Commission.

The site also offers a calendar of Democratic events around the country, voter registration information for each state, papers explaining the Democratic Party's position on dozens of issues such as affirmative action and the minimum wage, a list of accomplishments of the Clinton–Gore administration, background information about the DNC and the Democratic Party, and links to national, state, and local Democratic Party Web sites.

You also can sign up at the site to receive DNC briefings and press releases by e-mail.

Vital Stats:

Access method: WWW
To access: http://www.democrats.org

Democratic Senatorial Campaign Committee

This site has updates about the 2000 races for the U.S. Senate in individual states, links to news stories about the 2000 Senate campaign from various newspapers, and a list of Democratic and Republican senators whose terms will expire in 2000 or 2002. The site is operated by the Democratic Senatorial Campaign Committee, which helps Democratic Senate candidates.

The site also offers a weekly newsletter, links to Web sites operated by Democratic Senate candidates, and press releases.

Vital Stats:

Access method: WWW
To access: http://www.dscc.org

✓ Directory of U.S. Political Parties

The richly detailed descriptions of each party—major and obscure alike—make this page at Politics1 (p. 14) the best directory of American political party Web sites on the Internet. It has links to Web sites operated by almost fifty national parties.

Each party description tracks the party's history, lists party leaders and major candidates the group has fielded, and provides other valuable background information. Many party descriptions also have links to related information.

The page begins with links to major Democratic and Republican party sites. It then lists links to Web sites of third parties such as the American Independent Party, American Reform Party, Communist Party USA, Constitution Party, Democratic Socialists of America, Green Party, Labor Party, Libertarian Party, Natural Law Party, Peace and Freedom Party, Reform Party, Socialist Workers Party, Southern Party, and Workers World Party, among others.

The next section—Other Parties—may make for the most interesting reading. It provides links to parties that have Web sites but that have not yet fielded or endorsed candidates for office. Most of them can most charitably be described as extremely obscure. They include the Confederate Party, Constitutional Action Party, Libertarian National Socialist Green Party, Nazi Party USA, Progressive Labor Party, Puritan Party, and the World Socialist Party of the USA.

Vital Stats:

Access method: WWW
To access: http://www.politics1.com/parties.htm

✓ Governments on the WWW: Political Parties

Links to well over 3,000 Web sites operated by political parties around the world are available through this page at the Governments on the WWW site (p. 46).

The links are arranged alphabetically by country. Some countries have only one or two links, but most have at least a half-dozen links and some have dozens.

Vital Stats:

Access method: WWW
To access: http://www.gksoft.com/govt/en/parties.html

Libertarian Party

Background information about the Libertarian Party, its philosophy, and its positions highlights this official party site.

The site also provides a list of possible Libertarian Party presidential and vice presidential candidates in 2000, the full text of the *Libertarian Party News* newspaper, an article criticizing the Commission on Presidential Debates for adopting rules that will likely exclude third-party candidates from presidential debates, a map showing states where the Libertarian Party will be on the 2000 presidential ballot, and lists of Libertarian Party candidates in 2000 on the federal, state, and local levels.

Other features include a calendar of upcoming party events, contact information for Libertarian Party affiliates in each state and links to the affiliates' Web sites, results for Libertarian presidential candidates in past elections, articles about ballot access issues, press releases, past party platforms, historical information about the party, and details about the party's national convention in 2000, which will be held June 30–July 4 in Anaheim, California.

The party also distributes announcements by e-mail to anyone who signs up at the site.

Vital Stats:

Access method: WWW
To access: http://www.lp.org

National Republican Congressional Committee

A monthly newsletter with articles about Republican congressional campaigns and Republican activities in Congress highlights this site. It's operated by the National Republican Congressional Committee, which helps Republican candidates for the U.S. House of Representatives.

The site also provides information about programs for major NRCC contributors, a brief outline of the Republican congressional agenda, a list of Republican achievements, and press releases.

You can sign up at the site to receive news and announcements from the NRCC by e-mail.

Vital Stats:

Access method: WWW
To access: http://www.nrcc.org

National Republican Senatorial Committee

Background information about campaigns in each state that will elect a U.S. senator in 2000 is the chief attraction at this site from the National Republican Senatorial Committee. The NRSC helps elect Republicans to the U.S. Senate.

The site also offers a weekly update about Republican senatorial campaigns around the country, excerpts from recent newspaper articles about Republicans and Democrats, information about special programs for major NRSC contributors, press releases, links to Web sites operated by national and state Republican organizations, and information about the Republican National Convention in 2000, which will be held July 30–August 4 in Philadelphia.

The NRSC also provides regular news updates by e-mail to users who sign up at the site.

Vital Stats:

Access method: WWW
To access: http://www.nrsc.org

Open Directory Project: Parties USA

More than 1,000 links to Web sites operated by political parties in the United States are available through this page at the Open Directory Project (p. 11). The links lead to sites run by national, state, and local parties.

The top page has links to a few general sites. It also leads to separate pages that have links arranged by party.

Vital Stats:

Access method: WWW
To access: http://dmoz.org/Society/Politics/Parties/USA

Political Parties of the Hemisphere

This page has links to Web sites operated by more than 100 political parties in countries throughout the Western Hemisphere. The links are arranged by country. The National Democratic Institute for International Affairs in Washington, D.C., operates the page.

Vital Stats:

Access method: WWW
To access: http://www.ndi.org/partidos/Parties.html

Project Vote Smart: Parties, Affiliated Groups, and Individuals

Links to hundreds of Web sites operated by state political parties around the United States are available through this page at Project Vote Smart (p. 15). The links are arranged by state, and most states have about a half-dozen links.

Vital Stats:

Access method: WWW
To access: http://www.vote-smart.org/state/Topics/multiplelink9.phtml

---

Reform Party

The official Reform Party site provides stories about the party and its candidates from various newspapers and wire services, lists of party candidates in the 2000 election, and a list of candidates who are seeking the party's presidential nomination in 2000.

The site also offers the party's platform and founding principles, a list of Reform Party candidates who have been elected, a calendar of events around the country, links to state Reform Party sites, information about party lawsuits over campaign finances and ballot access, and a history of the party.

You can subscribe at the site to two lists that distribute news and announcements by e-mail and to two other mailing lists where subscribers discuss party issues.

Vital Stats:

Access method: WWW
To access: http://www.reformparty.org

Republican National Committee

Highlights of the Republican National Committee site include articles criticizing Democratic presidential candidates Al Gore and Bill Bradley, videos from GOPTV, and links to Web sites operated by other national Republican organizations.

The RNC site also has articles about issues ranging from Social Security to the environment, information about registering to vote in each state, links to Web sites operated by state Republican party affiliates around the country, the 1996 Republican platform, a history of the Republican Party, online postcards, and press releases.

The site also has a page where you can sign up to receive activist alerts and updates by e-mail.

Vital Stats:

Access method: WWW
To access: http://www.rnc.org

3rd Party Central

Your answers to a set of questions at this site help determine which major parties and third parties you're compatible with. The purpose is to make users aware of political parties they might like. The site is operated by Keynetic Systems LLC.

The site also has links to Web sites operated by third parties throughout the United States, essays about third parties, and links to other political sites.

Vital Stats:

Access method: WWW
To access: http://www.3pc.net

The 2000 Democratic National Convention

This is the official site for the 2000 Democratic National Convention, which will be held August 14–17 in Los Angeles. It has extensive information about how convention delegates are selected, information about volunteering at the convention and obtaining press credentials, press releases, the platform adopted at the 1996 Democratic National Convention, and a list of presidential and vice presidential candidates chosen at Democratic conventions from 1832 to the present.

Vital Stats:

Access method: WWW
To access: http://www.dems2000.com

Yahoo! News: Democratic Party

Through this page, Yahoo! (p. 17) provides access to dozens of news stories about the Democratic Party and the party's leaders and candidates. The articles date from March 1999 to the present.

The stories are from a variety of news sources, including the *Washington Post, Time, Wired, New York Times, San Francisco Chronicle, Chicago Tribune, Industry Standard, USA Today, Las Vegas Review-Journal, Christian Science Monitor, Slate, San Jose Mercury News, Business Week, Seattle Post-Intelligencer, Dallas Morning News, Sacramento Bee,* Associated Press, FOX News, CNN, Reuters, and the BBC, among others.

Clicking on Yahoo! News Search on the left side of the page automatically launches a search for stories about the Democratic Party published in recent days. A search typically returns a couple hundred stories.

The page also has links to official party Web sites and to other sites and documents about the Democratic Party.

Vital Stats:

Access method: WWW
To access: http://fullcoverage.yahoo.com/fc/US/Democratic_Party

Yahoo! News: Reform Party

Dozens of news stories about the Reform Party and major party figures such as Patrick Buchanan, Jesse Ventura, and Donald Trump are available through this Yahoo! (p. 17) page. The stories date from July 1999 to the present.

Some of the sources are the *Chicago Tribune, Washington Post, New York Times, San Francisco Chronicle, Salon, Dallas Morning News, Christian Science Monitor, Los Angeles Times, Time, The Times (United Kingdom), Village Voice,* Associated Press, CNN, FOX News, MSNBC, ABC News, and the BBC.

The page also has links to the official party site and to other sites and documents about the Reform Party.

Vital Stats:

Access method: WWW
To access: http://fullcoverage.yahoo.com/fc/US/Reform_Party

Yahoo! News: Republican Party

More than 100 news articles about the Republican Party, party leaders, and Republican candidates and office holders are available through this Yahoo! (p. 17) page. Stories are available from November 1998 to the present.

The news sources include the *Washington Post, New York Times, Los Angeles Times, San Jose Mercury News, San Francisco Chronicle, Christian Science Monitor, Philadelphia Daily News, Wired, Chicago Tribune, Seattle Times, The Times (United Kingdom), USA Today, Time, Business Week,* Associated Press, Reuters, ABC News, CNN, and the BBC, among others.

By clicking on Yahoo! News Search on the left side of the page, you will launch a search for news stories about the Republican Party published in recent days. A search usually returns well over 100 articles.

The page also has links to the official party site and to other sites and documents about the Republican Party.

Vital Stats:

Access method: WWW
To access: http://fullcoverage.yahoo.com/fc/US/Republican_Party

MILITIAS, ANTIGOVERNMENT GROUPS, AND THEIR OPPONENTS

Aryan Nations

The Aryan Nations, a white supremicist group located in Hayden Lake, Idaho, operates this site. It offers a list of the group's beliefs, pictures from Aryan Nations events, articles about a variety of subjects, and a catalog of books that can be ordered from the group.

Vital Stats:

Access method: WWW
To access: http://www.christian-aryannations.com

The Hate Directory: Hate Groups on the Internet

The Hate Directory lists hundreds of Web sites and other online forums operated by Ku Klux Klan groups, white power organizations, anti-Jewish groups, and other organizations. Opposition groups also are included. It's compiled and maintained by a private individual.

The directory is provided in Adobe Portable Document Format (PDF). To read it, you must have installed the free Adobe Acrobat Reader software on your computer.

Vital Stats:

Access method: WWW
To access: http://www.bcpl.net/~rfrankli/hatedir.htm

✓ HateWatch

This site offers links to hundreds of Web sites, mailing lists, and Usenet newsgroups operated by white supremacist organizations, neo-Nazis, anti-Semitic groups, anti-gay groups, Christian Identity organizations, anti-Arab groups, and Holocaust denial groups, among others. The links are particularly valuable because each has a paragraph-long quote from the site that gives an idea about its contents. The site is operated by HateWatch, a nonprofit group that monitors extremist activity on the Web.

The site also provides links to resources for people who actively oppose extremist groups, profiles of major extremist leaders and transcripts of interviews with some of them, articles about hate groups from various newspapers, and chat groups.

You also can sign up at the site to receive daily e-mail messages about activities of hate groups.

Vital Stats:

Access method: WWW
To access: http://hatewatch.org/frames.html

Imperial Klans of America Knights of the Ku Klux Klan

A twelve-point political program that calls for stopping all immigration, requiring drug tests of welfare recipients, placing people with AIDS in quarantine, and abolishing all gun control laws is outlined at this site. It's operated by the Imperial Klans of America Knights of the Ku Klux Klan, one of many Klan factions in the United States.

The site also offers articles about raids of IKA offices by law enforcement officers, pictures from IKA demonstrations and cross burnings, news about upcoming events, a list of "twenty reasons why you should join or support the IKA," and contact information for various IKA "realms" and links to their Web sites.

Vital Stats:

Access method: WWW
To access: http://www.kkkk.net/index.html

Militia of Montana Online Information Center

This site is run by the Militia of Montana, which is one of the best known militia groups in the United States.

Highlights include an article describing the militia's purpose, an archive of e-mail alerts distributed from August 1999 to the present, a calendar of events where Militia of Montana representatives will appear, a calendar of events around the country, a catalog of books and videotapes that can be ordered from the militia, and information about survival foods available from the militia.

The site also provides instructions for subscribing to an e-mail list that distributes alerts from the Militia of Montana.

Vital Stats:

Access method: WWW
To access: http://www.militiaofmontana.com

The Militia Watchdog: Links Page

Hundreds of annotated links to Web sites about militias and other groups are available through this page. It's part of the Militia Watchdog, a site operated by a private individual.

The links lead to sites operated by militias, common law organizations, white supremacist and hate groups, tax protesters, secessionist groups, and groups that oppose extremist organizations. Other links lead to articles about the militia movement and source material from various extremist organizations.

Vital Stats:

Access method: WWW
To access: http://www.militia-watchdog.org/m1.htm

---

misc.activism.militia

The very active misc.activism.militia newsgroup is filled with talk about militias and conspiracy theories. Most of the messages seem to be posted by militia members and sympathizers.

Vital Stats:

Access method: Usenet newsgroup
To access: news:misc.activism.militia

Open Directory Project: Militia Movement

Links to more than 100 sites about militias are provided through this page at the Open Directory Project (p. 11). The links are divided into five categories: articles, groups, information and news, survivalism, and watchdogs. Many of the links in the groups category are further divided by state.

Vital Stats:

Access method: WWW
To access: http://dmoz.org/Society/Issues/Militia_Movement

Southern Poverty Law Center: Intelligence Project

The Intelligence Project at the Southern Poverty Law Center monitors hundreds of Ku Klux Klan groups, militias, and other extremist groups around the United States.

The highlight of the project's Web site is the *Intelligence Report,* a quarterly magazine that profiles leaders of hate groups, reports on the activities of extremist groups, and chronicles bias incidents around the country.

The site also has a report titled *Ten Ways to Fight Hate: A Community Response Guide,* summaries of recent hate incidents reported to police around the country, and lists of hate groups and patriot groups throughout the United States. Both lists are arranged by state and include the group's name and the city where it's located.

Vital Stats:

Access method: WWW
To access: http://www.splcenter.org/intelligenceproject/ip-index.html

9

Voting and Elections

CAMPAIGN FINANCE

The Brookings Institution: Campaign Finance Reform

This page at the Brookings Institution's site (p. 152) provides the full text of *Campaign Finance Reform: A Sourcebook,* which examines the current state of campaign finance laws, First Amendment issues, political action committees, soft money, issue advocacy, the Federal Election Commission, and related topics.

The page also has updates about campaign finance legislation in Congress, analyses of recent court cases and administrative decisions in campaign finance cases, articles about various campaign finance issues, and links to related sites.

Vital Stats:

Access method: WWW
To access: http://www.brook.edu/GS/CF/CF_HP.HTM

The Buying of the President 2000: The Money Trail

Extensive financial information about each of the major presidential candidates in 2000 is available through databases accessible on this page, which is part of the site operated by the Center for Public Integrity (p. 153). All information in the databases was taken from official records.

For each candidate, the databases detail the financial assets, honoraria received for speeches while in public office, trips taken while in public office and who paid for them, the twenty-five largest donors over the candidate's entire political career, and investigations conducted by the Federal Election Commission of the candidate's previous federal campaigns, among other information.

Vital Stats:

Access method: WWW
To access: http://www.publicintegrity.org/reports/BOP2000/
                        financial.htm

Campaign Finance Information Center

The Campaign Finance Information Center site is aimed at journalists, but much of the information it offers will interest anyone who tracks campaign finance issues. The center is a project of two organizations for journalists—

Investigative Reporters and Editors and the National Institute of Computer-Assisted Reporting.

Highlights of the site include searchable databases containing campaign finance data for many states, a database containing stories about campaign finance from newspapers and magazines around the country, tip sheets from reporters, a directory of journalists who cover campaign finance, and a quarterly newsletter about reporting on money in politics.

Vital Stats:

Access method: WWW
To access: http://www.campaignfinance.org

✓ Campaign Finance Reform

This site is a fantastic directory of links to information about campaign finance across the Internet. It's operated by a private individual.

The links lead to proposals for campaign finance reform by major presidential candidates in 2000, databases of campaign contributions, legal decisions about campaign finance, studies by various interest groups and policy institutes, results of public opinion polls about campaign finance reform, newspaper articles, and information about reform efforts in specific states.

Vital Stats:

Access method: WWW
To access: http://www.campaignfinance.homestead.com/files/

Digital Sunlight: Disclosure Links Chart

This page provides links to agencies in each state that disclose campaign finance information to the public. It also provides links to agencies that disclose information about lobbyists and independent sources of state campaign finance information.

The page is part of Digital Sunlight, a Web site created by the California Voter Foundation.

Vital Stats:

Access method: WWW
To access: http://www.digitalsunlight.org/disclosurelinkschart.html

✓✓ FECInfo

Several sites offer federal campaign finance data, but FECInfo is one of the best—even better than the official site operated by the Federal Election Commission. FECInfo uses data from the FEC and other official sources, but it's operated by a private company called Netivation.com Inc.—which deserves three cheers from anyone interested in tracking money in politics.

FECInfo's searchable databases provide itemized information about receipts and expenditures for federal candidates, political action committees, and party committees. The data are extremely detailed. For example, you can search for contributions to individual candidates by the contributors' zip code. You also can search for contributors by name, occupation, or employer.

Other highlights include detailed information about political action committees and their contributions (including their soft money contributions), a report about the largest contributors of soft money to national parties, a list of recently registered corporate PACs, a list of the largest PACs, a list of contributors who gave money to candidates running outside of their home states, registration forms and reports that lobbyists file with the secretary of the Senate's Public Records Office, a searchable database of contributors to President Clinton's legal defense fund, and much, much more.

You can sign up to receive e-mail alerts when new data are added to the site.

Vital Stats:

Access method: WWW
To access: http://www.tray.com/fecinfo

Federal Election Commission

The Federal Election Commission, which regulates spending in federal elections, operates this site. It's badly organized and some of the type is so small it's almost unreadable, but the site nonetheless provides a huge amount of valuable data.

The highlight is a database of campaign finance reports filed from May 1996 to the present by House and presidential candidates, political action committees, and political party committees. Reports by Senate candidates are not included because they're filed with the secretary of the Senate. If you need help using the records, check out the *Guide to Researching Public Records* at the site.

Another valuable resource is the *Combined Federal/State Disclosure and Election Directory,* which provides detailed information about every federal and state office that collects campaign finance data or regulates election spending. For each office, the publication lists the types of data that are available and complete contact information, including a link to the office's Web site.

The site also provides summary financial data for House and Senate candidates in the current election cycle, a schedule of reports that must be filed with the FEC, a graph showing the number of political action committees in existence from 1974 to the present, summaries of campaign finance laws in each state, a collection of brochures that explain federal election laws, a form you can download to register to vote by mail, statistics about voting and elections, results from the most recent presidential and congressional elections, an explanation of how the electoral college works, FEC advisory opinions, a monthly newsletter, press releases, and more.

Vital Stats:

Access method: WWW
To access: http://www.fec.gov

The New York Times: Campaign Finance

Selected *New York Times* stories about campaign finance are provided through this page. The articles date from December 1996 to the present.

The page also has a chronology of campaign finance reform efforts from 1971 to the present and a few links to related sites.

Vital Stats:

Access method: WWW
To access: http://www.nytimes.com/library/politics/
                   fundraisingindex.html

✓✓ opensecrets.org

Whether you want raw data about money in politics or reports that analyze all the numbers for you, this site is a gold mine. It's operated by the Center for Responsive Politics, a nonprofit research group in Washington, D.C., that tracks money in politics.

Numerous databases contain detailed campaign finance data for federal candidates. One of the most interesting databases allows you to search for contributors by name, zip code, employer, or recipient.

Other databases offer information about contributions by political action committees to federal candidates, financial disclosure statements filed by all members of Congress, detailed campaign finance profiles of each member of Congress, information about travel expenses that House members received from private sources for attending meetings and other events, documents about activities of registered federal lobbyists, and documents about activities of foreign agents who are registered in the United States.

Three dozen reports available in full text provide detailed analyses of the influence of money in politics. Some of the available titles are *The Big Picture: The Money Behind the 1998 Elections; Influence Inc.: The Bottom Line on Washington Lobbyists; Digital Democracy: A 50-State Status Report on Electronic Filing; Why Do Donors Give?; The Politics of Sugar; High-Tech Influence: Computer Companies and Political Spending; Political Union: The Marriage of Labor and Spending; Speaking Freely: Former Members of Congress Talk about Money in Politics;* and *A Bag of Tricks: Loopholes in the Campaign Finance System.*

The site also has lists of the top federal contributors by industry, profiles of every political action committee registered with the Federal Election Commission, data about soft money contributions, links to sources of state campaign finance data, press releases, and excerpts from the *Follow the Money Handbook,* which is a step-by-step guide to investigating campaign money.

Vital Stats:

Access method:	WWW
To access:	http://www.opensecrets.org

Project Vote Smart: Campaign Finance

This page at Project Vote Smart (p. 15) provides links to two dozen sites about campaign finance. Each link is briefly annotated.

The sites are operated by the Alliance for Better Campaigns, the Brookings Institution Working Group on Campaign Finance Reform, the Campaign Finance Information Center, the Center for Public Integrity, the Center for Responsive Politics, Common Cause, the Congressional Accountability Project, the National Institute on Money in State Politics, the National Voting Rights Institute, and Public Campaign, among other groups.

Vital Stats:

Access method:	WWW
To access:	http://www.vote-smart.org/issues/CAMPAIGN_FINANCE

Reporters' Reference Center on Campaign Finance Reform

This site provides information about campaign finance reform efforts in thirty states. For each state, it describes current laws, lists bills that have been introduced in the state legislature, provides contact information for state campaign finance agencies, and offers detailed descriptions and contact information for state organizations involved in the issue. The site is operated by the Benton Foundation.

Other features include a lengthy overview of state and federal campaign finance reform efforts, discussions of various reform proposals, and links to other campaign finance sites.

Vital Stats:

Access method: WWW
To access: http://www.benton.org/neustadt/reporters

---

stateline.org: Campaign Finance

If you're tracking campaign finance reform efforts in states around the country, this page is a great place to start. Each day, summaries of newspaper articles about reform efforts in various states are posted. Each summary has a link to the full story.

You also can sign up to receive e-mail alerts when new campaign finance stories are posted, and you can search a database for campaign finance stories published in the past year. The site is a project of the Pew Center on the States.

Vital Stats:

Access method: WWW
To access: http://www.stateline.org/issue.cfm?issueid=306

USA Today: Campaign Finance

An archive of *USA Today* stories about campaign finance is provided at this page. The archive contains hundreds of stories dating from July 1997 to the present.

Vital Stats:

Access method: WWW
To access: http://www.usatoday.com/news/index/finance/ncfin000.htm

---

Washingtonpost.com: Campaign Finance Special Report

Dozens of stories about campaign finance from the *Washington Post* are available through this page. The stories date from March 1997 to the present.

The stories cover such topics as the Justice Department's investigation of the Clinton reelection campaign, accusations against Vice President Al Gore, campaign finance legislation, spending on campaigns, House and Senate hearings about campaign finance, and allegations of Chinese influence buying during the 1996 election. Also included are major *Post* series from 1997 and 1998 about campaign finance.

The page also offers editorials and opinion articles about campaign finance, profiles of major figures from various campaign finance investigations, lists of donors invited to White House coffees in 1995 and 1996, lists of donors and others who stayed overnight at the White House during President Clinton's first term, and links to numerous documents and Web sites about campaign finance.

Vital Stats:

Access method: WWW

To access: http://www.washingtonpost.com/wp-srv/politics/special/ campfin/campfin.htm

---

✓ Yahoo! News: Campaign Finance

Several hundred news stories about campaign finance are available through this Yahoo! (p. 17) page. The stories date from February 1997 to the present.

The articles are from a variety of media sources, including the *New York Times, USA Today, Washington Post, Miami Herald, Boston Globe, Christian Science Monitor, Denver Post, Time, Los Angeles Times, San Jose Mercury News, Wired, Philadelphia Inquirer, Baltimore Sun, Chicago Tribune, Business Week, Dallas Morning News,* Associated Press, Reuters, CNN, and ABC News.

The page also has links to a nice selection of Web sites and documents about campaign finance.

Vital Stats:

Access method: WWW

To access: http://fullcoverage.yahoo.com/fc/US/Campaign_Finance

---

Yahoo! Society and Culture: Campaign Finance

Links to nearly fifty sites about campaign finance are available through this Yahoo! (p. 17) page. Each link has a brief description.

The page provides links to general sites, sites about campaign finance reform, and sites with databases of contributions. Of particular interest are the links to campaign finance databases in various states.

Vital Stats:

Access method: WWW

To access: http://dir.yahoo.com/government/u_s__government/ politics/elections/campaign_finance

ELECTION LAWS AND ADMINISTRATION

Ballot Access News

The full text of the newsletter *Ballot Access News* from early 1994 to the present is available at this site. The newsletter publishes detailed stories about efforts around the country to overturn laws that restrict ballot access by candidates, court decisions in ballot access cases, and offices won by third-party candidates.

Vital Stats:

Access method: WWW
To access: http://www.ballot-access.org

Ballot Watch

Ballot Watch features a database with details about hundreds of initiatives and referendums that are moving toward qualification on state ballots or that have already qualified in states around the country. Ballot Watch is operated by the Initiative and Referendum Institute.

You can search the database by subject, status, state, and type of measure. The database provides extensive information about each measure, including a summary, whether the measure has qualified for the ballot or is still in process, the election where the measure is expected to appear, and contact information for proponents.

Vital Stats:

Access method: WWW
To access: http://www.ballotwatch.org

Commission on Presidential Debates

The Commission on Presidential Debates, which sponsors debates among presidential and vice presidential candidates, operates this site. It provides the criteria by which candidates will be selected for the 2000 debates and a list of sites and dates for the 2000 debates.

The site also has tips for hosting a candidate debate in your community, background information about the commission, and transcripts of selected presidential and vice presidential debates from the 1960, 1976, 1980, 1984, 1988, 1992, and 1996 elections.

Vital Stats:

Access method: WWW
To access: http://www.debates.org

ELECnet

ELECnet provides more than 400 links to Web sites operated by state, county, and city elections offices around the United States. The links are arranged by state.

It also has links to federal agencies that provide election-related information and national organizations that host election-oriented Web sites. The site is operated by a private individual.

Vital Stats:

Access method: WWW
To access: http://www.iupui.edu/~epackard/eleclink.html

Electoral College Home Page

Confused about what the electoral college is and what it does? A publication at this site titled *Procedural Guide to the Electoral College* should answer your questions. The site is operated by the National Archives and Records Administration.

The site also provides the popular votes and electoral college votes in presidential elections from 1789 to the present, state-level data about electoral votes in the 1992 and 1996 elections, and provisions of the U.S. Constitution and federal law pertaining to presidential elections.

Vital Stats:

Access method: WWW
To access: http://www.nara.gov/fedreg/ec-hmpge.html

Governments on the WWW: Institutions in the Area "Elections"

This page at the Governments on the WWW site (p. 46) has links to Web sites operated by national election offices in countries around the world. The links are arranged alphabetically by country.

Vital Stats:

Access method: WWW
To access: http://www.gksoft.com/govt/en/elections.html

✓ International Foundation for Election Systems (IFES)

One of the highlights of this site is the collection of links to Web sites operated by election commissions and other election-related organizations in countries around the world. The site also provides a worldwide elections calendar, links to news about current elections, and a newsletter titled *Elections Today*. The IFES receives much of its funding from the U.S. Agency for International Development.

Vital Stats:

Access method: WWW
To access: http://www.ifes.org/index.htm

National Association of State Election Directors

The National Association of State Election Directors operates this site, which has links to election offices in each state and a list of voting systems that have been approved by the NASED.

Vital Stats:

Access method: WWW
To access: http://www.nased.org

The Voting Integrity Project

A report titled *Are We Ready for Internet Voting?* highlights the site of the Voting Integrity Project, a nonprofit group that fights voter fraud.

The site also offers links to newspaper articles about Internet voting, news about a suit filed by the project to stop an online primary in Arizona, news about election fraud cases around the country, updates about court cases and state legislative activities involving voting, articles about problems with various voting machines, and press releases.

Vital Stats:

Access method: WWW
To access: http://www.voting-integrity.org

HISTORICAL ELECTION RESULTS

Election Statistics

Vote totals for every congressional candidate in elections from 1920 to the present are available at this page, which is part of the House of Representatives' Office of the Clerk On-line Information Center.

A separate document is provided for each election. Within each document, the vote totals are arranged alphabetically by state. Documents for the 1920 through the 1990 elections are available only in Adobe Portable Document Format (PDF), while documents for more recent elections are available in both PDF and HTML.

Vital Stats:

Access method: WWW
To access: http://clerkweb.house.gov/histrecs/history/elections/
                   elections.htm

State Vote '98

This site from the National Conference of State Legislatures has extensive results from 1998 state elections around the country. The site, which will be updated with each election, has maps showing partisan control of state legislatures, election profiles for each state, and a searchable database of results of state initiative and referendum votes around the country.

Vital Stats:

Access method: WWW
To access: http://www.ncsl.org/statevote98/statevote98.htm

U.S. Presidential Election Maps

Color-coded national maps at this site show which presidential candidate won the popular vote in each state in elections from 1860 to the present and also list the percentage of the popular vote that the candidate received.

A second set of maps show the number of electoral votes that candidates received in each state for elections from 1900 to the present. The site is operated by the Social Sciences Data Center at the University of Virginia.

Vital Stats:

Access method: WWW
To access: http://fisher.lib.virginia.edu/elections/maps

THE INTERNET IN ELECTIONS

Democracies Online Newswire (DO-WIRE)

The Democracies Online Newswire (DO-WIRE) is an e-mail announcement list that distributes items about "the convergence of democracies and the Internet around the world," according to its welcome message.

Many of the items concern electronic government and the use of the Internet in politics. The posts typically provide information about major news articles, conferences, new projects, online events and resources, research, and related topics.

The list is moderated by Steven Clift, a major figure in the electronic democracy movement.

Vital Stats:

Access method:	E-mail
To access:	Send an e-mail message to listserv@tc.umn.edu
Subject line:	
Message:	**SUBSCRIBE DO-WIRE** *firstname lastname place*

---

e-lection

The e-lection mailing list distributes news and information about electronic voting and related topics. Most of the messages are pointers to resources such as news stories, books, governmental and nongovernmental reports, Web sites, and conferences.

Vital Stats:

Access method:	E-mail
To access:	Send an e-mail message to majordomo@research.att.com
Subject line:	
Message:	**subscribe e-lection**

Electronic Voting Hot List

Links to dozens of documents and Web sites about various aspects of electronic voting are provided through this site. Each link is briefly described by Lorrie Cranor, a private individual who runs the site.

The links lead to information about available online voting systems, experimental electronic voting systems, the risks and reliability of electronic voting,

voting by phone or mail, electronic democracy, and voting equipment and services vendors, among other topics.

Vital Stats:

Access method: WWW

To access: http://www.ccrc.wustl.edu/~lorracks/sensus/hotlist.html

---

Hacktivism

Subscribers to this mailing list discuss hacktivism, which is generally defined as the fusion of political activism and computer hacking. Hacktivism can take many forms: defacing corporate or government Web sites, organizing community-based Web servers, or using mobile communications to create communications channels for the poor or oppressed, among many others.

Subscribers discuss everything from the precise definition of hacktivism to practical, tactical, and ethical issues. You can subscribe by e-mail or by going to the list's Web site (http://lists.tao.ca) and following the instructions.

Vital Stats:

Access method: E-mail

To access: Send an e-mail message to hacktivism-request@lists.tao.ca

Subject line:

Message: **subscribe**

NetElection.org

This site focuses on how politicians and others are using the Internet in elections. It's a joint project of the Annenberg Public Policy Center at the University of Pennsylvania, the Center for Public Integrity, and the Center for Government Studies; it is funded by a grant from the Pew Charitable Trusts.

The highlight is a collection of articles by NetElection.org staffers about such topics as the lack of interactive dialogue at presidential candidates' Web sites, regulation of online volunteers by the Federal Election Commission, online stores at presidential candidates' sites, privacy policies at presidential sites, and online fundraising.

The site also offers analytical articles, a comparison of features at the presidential candidates' Web sites, and bibliographic information for selected books, journal articles, and Web sites about cyberdemocracy and digital policy, among other subjects.

Vital Stats:

Access method: WWW
To access: http://netelection.org

The New York Times: The Internet and Political Campaigns

Dozens of *New York Times* articles about the Internet and politics are archived on this page at the newspaper's Web site. Most of the articles date from January 1999 to the present, although a few earlier stories also are available.

The articles report on such topics as use of the Internet by political candidates, online activism, and federal regulation of Internet campaigning.

Vital Stats:

Access method: WWW
To access: http://www.nytimes.com/library/tech/reference/
                  index-campaign.html

PoliSites

PoliSites is a free weekly e-mail newsletter about politics and the Internet. It provides descriptions of new political sites on the Internet and includes summaries of news stories, reports, and other documents about political use of the Internet. Links to the full documents are provided where available.

The newsletter, which is designed to update and supplement this book, is written by the book's author. You can subscribe by e-mail or at the newsletter's Web site (http://www.silverhammerpub.com).

Vital Stats:

Access method: E-mail
To access: Send an e-mail message to
                  join-polisites@lists.silverhammerpub.com
Subject line:
Message:

PoliticsOnline

The highlight of PoliticsOnline is its large collection of links to news stories about how the Internet is being used in politics and elections around the world.

The links archive goes back to May 1998. The site is operated by Phil Noble & Associates Inc., a political and public relations consulting firm.

Special collections of links lead to stories about use of the Internet in the war in Kosovo and the Federal Election Commission and online fundraising.

You also can subscribe at the site to two newsletters—the *Weekly PoliTicker* and *NetPulse*. Both include news about political use of the Internet and provide summaries and links to related news stories.

Vital Stats:

Access method: WWW
To access: http://www.politicsonline.com

✓✓ Vote Smart Web YellowPages

The *Vote Smart Web YellowPages* is a directory that lists thousands of political sites on the Internet. Most sites are very briefly described. The directory is basically a printed list of the links provided at the Project Vote Smart Web site (p. 15).

The links are divided into ten main categories: executive branch, judicial branch, Congresstrack, political parties, state political parties, state government and politics, research the issues, think tanks and research institutes, state think tanks and research institutes, and national and political news sources.

The directory, which runs just over 400 pages, is provided in Adobe Portable Document Format (PDF). To read it, you must have the Adobe Acrobat Reader software installed on your computer.

Vital Stats:

Access method: WWW
To access: http://www.vote-smart.org/about/services/
                  vswypupdate.phtml

VOTING

Federal Election Commission: About Elections and Voting

This page at the Federal Election Commission site (p. 276) offers historical data about voter registration and turnout. Separate documents provide statistics about national and state voter registration and turnout in the 1996 presidential election, voter registration and turnout in presidential elections from 1960 to 1992, voter registration and turnout in federal elections by gender from 1972 to 1996, and international voter turnout, among other subjects.

The page also has a report titled *The Impact of the National Voter Registration Act on Federal Elections 1995–1996.*

Vital Stats:

Access method: WWW
To access: http://www.fec.gov/elections.html

GoVote.com: Register to Vote

Extensive information about registering to vote is available through this page at GoVote.com.

The highlight is the National Voter Registration Application, which you can download. The application is in Adobe Portable Document Format (PDF), so you must have the Adobe Acrobat Reader software installed on your computer to read it. Once you fill out the application, you must mail it (by snail mail) to the address for your state listed on the form.

According to the site, two dozen states will accept the application printed off the Internet: Alabama, Alaska, Arizona, California, Colorado, Connecticut, Delaware, Hawaii, Iowa, Kansas, Louisiana, Michigan, Minnesota, Montana, Nebraska, New Jersey, New York, Oklahoma, Pennsylvania, South Carolina, Texas, Utah, Washington, and Wisconsin. Be sure to check the site for updates.

If your state doesn't accept the national application, you can:
- Send a written request for a state voter registration form to the address listed for your state on the national application; or
- Click on the link at GoVote.com for the Web site of your state election office. Some offices let you request a voter application form online.

Vital Stats:

Access method: WWW
To access: http://www.govote.com/resources/voter_registration.asp

U.S. Census Bureau: Voting and Registration Data

Extensive data about registration and voting by various demographic and socioeconomic groups are available through this page at the U.S. Census Bureau's Web site. Data are available from 1964 to the present.

Vital Stats:

Access method: WWW

To access: http://www.census.gov/population/www/
                              socdemo/voting.html

Voter Turnout from 1945 to 1998

Voter turnout figures for 171 countries are available at this site, which is operated by the International Institute for Democracy and Electoral Assistance.

The available data vary by country. However, statistics are usually provided for both presidential and parliamentary elections, and statistics are available for many countries from 1945 to 1998.

Vital Stats:

Access method: WWW

To access: http://www.idea.int/turnout

INDEX

Center for Government Studies, 10, 287
Center for Immigration Studies, 183
Center for International Environmental Law, 142
Center for Law and Social Policy, 245
Center for Media and Public Affairs, 207
Center for Media Education, 100
Center for Media Literacy, 207–208
Center for National Independence in Politics, 16
Center for Nonproliferation Studies, 159
Center for Policy Alternatives, 159
Center for Public Integrity, 153, 274, 278, 287
Center for Reproductive Law and Policy, 68
Center for Responsive Politics, 277, 278
Center for Science in the Public Interest, 168
Center for Security Policy, 114, 189
Center for the Study of American Business, 158
Center for Voting and Democracy, 159
Center on Budget and Policy Priorities, 124, 245
Centers for Disease Control and Prevention, 82, 173, 237
Central American Refugee Center, 183
Central Committee for Conscientious Objectors, 113
Central Intelligence Agency (CIA), 45, 106, 186, 188, 191
Century Foundation, 158
Chamber of Commerce, 95–96, 129
charter schools, 132, 134, 137–138
Chavez, Linda, 248
Chemical and Biological Arms Control Institute, 113
chemical and biological warfare, 109, 112, 113
chemical safety, 56
Cherokee Nation, 217
Chicago-Kent College of Law, 21, 37, 41
Chiefs of State and Cabinet Members of Foreign Governments, 45
children and families, 11, 12, 16, 35, 173, 211
    Administration for Children and Families, 173, 211
    child abuse, 104, 132
    child care, 200, 203
    child labor, 93, 179, 202, 203, 204
    child pornography, 73
    child protection online, 99, 101, 196, 199
    child support, 212
    childbearing, 66
    children's rights, 178
    Family and Medical Leave Act, 94, 203
    family planning, 66, 69, 71, 73, 74
    maternity-leave policy, 160
    National Partnership for Women & Families, 240
    vaccinations, 56
Children's Online Privacy Protection Act of 1998, 99
China, 94, 154, 157, 160, 176, 177, 192, 206, 257, 279–280
Chinese for Affirmative Action, 217
cholera, 56
Christian Coalition, 114, 136, 223, 233

Christian Identity, 268
Chronicle of Higher Education, 135
church arson, 215
church-state issues, 11, 17, 157, 222, 223, 224, 225, 226
CIA (Central Intelligence Agency), 45, 106, 186, 188, 191
CIA Electronic Document Release Center, 186
circus animals, 85, 86, 89, 90, 91
Citizens Against Government Waste, 130, 153–154, 159, 161, 173, 233
Citizens Clearinghouse for Hazardous Waste, 142
Citizens Committee for the Right to Keep and Bear Arms, 165
Citizens Flag Alliance Inc., 98
Citizens for a Sound Economy, 129
Citizens for Better Medicare, 171
Citizens for Health, 172
Citizens for REAL Retirement Security, 231
Citizens for Responsible Education Reform, 135
Citizens United Resisting Euthanasia, 227
city policy issues, 42, 43
city revitalization, 153
civil jury verdicts, 160
civil liberties, 11, 15, 97–101
    ACLU Action Network, 97
    ACLU NewsFeed, 97
    American Civil Liberties Union, 97–98
    Citizens Flag Alliance Inc., 98
    Electronic Privacy Information Center, 98–99, 100
    EPIC-News, 99
    Federal Trade Commission: Privacy, 99–100
    Free Expression Network Clearinghouse, 100
    free! The Freedom Forum Online, 100
    Open Directory Project: Civil Liberties, 101
    Privacy Rights Clearinghouse, 101
    Project Vote Smart: Civil Liberties, 101
civil rights, 11, 16, 22, 152, 155, 216, 217, 218
    American Civil Rights Coalition, 217
    Civil Rights Division (Justice Department), 215
    civilrights.org, 215
    for gays and lesbians, 158
    laws, enforcement of, 200
    Leadership Conference on Civil Rights, 215
    Project Vote Smart: Civil Rights/Human Rights, 217
    U.S. Commission on Civil Rights, 217, 218
    voting records on, 215
Civil Rights Act of 1964, 219
Civil Rights Act of 1991, 219
civil service, 20, 154
civilrights.org, 215
Claremont Institute, 114, 136, 173, 190, 248
class size, 134, 137
Clift, Steven, 286
climate, 17, 22, 46, 94, 139, 141, 146
Clinton, Bill, 31–32, 258, 260, 276, 279
Clinton, Hillary Rodham, 31, 256, 257

Maritime Municipal Training and Development Board, 42

Markle Foundation, 16

maternity-leave policy, 160

mathematics proficiency, 134, 136

mayors, 44

McCain 2000, 61

McCain, John, 61

McCullagh, Declan, 198

measles, 56

media and communications, 12, 15, 42, 206–209. *See also* political news
  alternative, 207
  confidential sources and information, 208
  corporate ownership of, 206
  diversity in media, 216
  Fairness & Accuracy in Reporting (FAIR), 206, 208
  gay and lesbian representation, 147, 148
  juvenile court access, 208
  Media Access Project, 197
  media advisories, 25
  Media Institute, 159
  media law, 197, 208
  media outlets, 12, 13
  Media Research Center, 114, 161, 190, 208, 248
  media watch organizations, 16
  Online Journalism Review, 206
  Open Directory Project: Media and Free Speech, 207
  Project for Excellence in Journalism, 207
  Project Vote Smart: Media & Communication, 207–208
  racism in media, 206
  Reporters Committee for Freedom of the Press, 208
  sexism in, 206
  society and media, 196
  violence in, 207, 209
  Yahoo! News: Media Watch, 208
  Yahoo! News: Violence in the Media, 209

Medicaid, 69, 124, 169, 171, 212, 231

medical malpractice litigation, 160

medical marijuana, 119–121, 123, 173

medical privacy, 99, 101, 170, 171, 173

medical records access, 170

Medicare, 125, 131, 152, 169, 174, 200, 230–231, 232, 234, 256
  MedicareWatch, 171
  reform, 35, 171, 230

MEDLINEplus: AIDS, 81

mental health and illness, 56–57, 94, 169, 170, 172

mentoring programs, 35

Mexico, 94

Michigan State University, 13

Microsoft antitrust litigation, 152

Middle East peace process, 192–193

Middle East Policy Council, 189

migrant workers, 178

military, 22, 160, 161
  alternatives to intervention, 109
  analysis of, 112
  base closures, 111, 160
  gays in, 147, 148
  international, 46, 48
  Military Spending Working Group, 113
  readiness, 153
  spending, 109, 110, 113, 152
  women in, 109, 161, 239

militias, antigovernment groups, and opponents, 11, 17, 268–271
  Aryan Nations, 268
  Hate Directory: Hate Groups on the Internet, 268
  HateWatch, 268–269
  Imperial Klans of America Knights of the Ku Klux Klan, 269
  Militia of Montana Online Information Center, 269
  Militia Watchdog: Links Page, 269
  misc.activism.militia, 270
  Open Directory Project: Militia Movement, 270
  Southern Poverty Law Center: Intelligence Project, 270–271

Mine Safety and Health Administration, 203

mineral resources, 22, 140

minimum wage, 94, 124, 128, 152, 200, 202, 203, 210, 224, 260

mining, 22, 94, 146, 180

minorities. *See also* race and ethnicity
  health issues, 169
  minority and women business development, 93
  Minority Business Development Agency, 96
  ownership of telecommunications companies, 197
  rights of, 178

misc.activism.militia, 270

missiles, 113
  missile defense programs, 114–115, 157, 161
  proliferation, 109, 112, 154, 159

missing in action, 112–113, 186

Missionaries to the Unborn, 70

monetary policy, 125

money laundering, 106

money supply, 128

Monthly Catalog of United States Government Publications, 28

Monthly Labor Review, 22, 201

Morbidity and Mortality Weekly Report, 82

Morris, Dick, 248

mortgages, 124

Mothers Against Drunk Driving, 104

MPPupdates, 120

MSNBC News: Politics, 246

multinational corporations, 95

Multinational Monitor, 95

multinational organizations, 52

multistate organizations, 36

municipal codes, 36
munisource, 42

NAACP (National Association for the Advancement of Colored People), 216, 217, 220
Nader, Ralph, 160
NAFTA (North American Free Trade Agreement), 160
naral-news, 70–71
Nation of Islam, 223
National Abortion and Reproductive Rights Action League (NARAL), 70, 71
National Abortion Federation, 71–72
National Academy of Social Insurance, 171
National Agricultural Library, 87
National Agricultural Statistics Service, 126
National Alliance for the Mentally Ill, 170, 172
National Antivivisection Society, 91
National Archives and Records Administration, 282
National Association for Bilingual Education, 183
National Association for the Advancement of Colored People (NAACP), 216, 217, 220
National Association of Broadcasters, 208
National Association of Chain Drug Stores, 96
National Association of Counties, 42–43
National Association of Latino Elected and Appointed Officials, 217–218
National Association of Manufacturers, 94
National Association of State Election Directors, 283
National Association of State Information Resource Executives, 40
National Association of Towns and Townships, 43
National Audubon Society, 142
National Bureau of Economic Research, 129
National Caucus and Center on Black Aged, 231
National Center for Education Statistics, 133–134
National Center for Policy Analysis, 217, 233
National Center for State Courts, 34
National Center for Tobacco Free Kids, 237
National Center on Addiction and Substance Abuse, 122
National Center on Institutions and Alternatives, 105
National Church Arson Task Force, 215
National Clearinghouse for Alcohol and Drug Information, 122
National Clearinghouse for Bilingual Education, 182–183
National Coalition Against Censorship, 100
National Coalition for Patient Rights, 170
National Coalition for the Homeless, 210, 212
National Coalition of Free Men, 241
National Coalition on Health Care, 171, 172
National Coalition to Abolish the Death Penalty, 104–105
National Commission for Economic Conversion and Disarmament, 113, 129

National Committee to Preserve Social Security and Medicare, 231
National Conference of Catholic Bishops, 224
National Conference of State Legislatures, 35, 284
National Congress of American Indians, 218
National Cooperative Business Association, 95
National Council of Churches, 224, 225
National Council of La Raza, 216, 218
National Council of Senior Citizens, 231
National Council on Disability, 116
National Criminal Justice Reference Service, 103, 104
national debt, 128
National Democratic Institute for International Affairs, 263
National Dropout Prevention Center, 135
National Education Association, 134, 135
National Election Studies, 256
National Environmental Scorecard, 140
National Federation of Independent Business, 95
National Gay and Lesbian Task Force, 149
National Governors' Association, 35–36
National Immigration Forum, 183
National Information Infrastructure, 198
National Institute for Literacy, 135
National Institute for Research Advancement, 10–11
National Institute of Computer-Assisted Reporting, 275
National Institute of Justice, 103
National Institute on Drug Abuse, 120
National Institute on Money in State Politics, 278
National Institutes of Health, 90, 173
National Institutes of Health Office of AIDS Research, 81
National Journal Group, 69, 80
National Labor Relations Board, 201–202
National Labor Relations Board Act, 201–202
National League of Cities, 43
National League of POW/MIA Families, 112–113
National Library of Medicine, 81
National Military Strategy of the United States, 23
National Neighborhood Coalition, 212
National Network for Immigration and Refugee Rights, 183
National Organization for the Reform of Marijuana Laws (NORML), 120–121
National Organization for Women (NOW), 74–75, 239–240, 241
National Organization for Women Political Action Committees, 240
National Organization of Physicians Who Care, 171
national origin discrimination, 219
National Park System, 140
National Parks and Conservation Association, 141
National Partnership for Women & Families, 240
National Prison Project of the ACLU, 105
National Pro-Choice Directory, 72
National PTA, 134–135

science, 33
  AAAS Science and Human Rights Program, 175
  American Association for the Advancement of
    Science, 175
  American Council on Science and Health, 172
  Center for Science in the Public Interest, 168
  and engineering, 22
  Federation of American Scientists, 112, 156–157,
    159, 188
  National Science Foundation, 126
  scientific and technical reports, 21
  scientific freedom, 175
  and technology, 11, 33
sci.med.aids, 82
sci.med.cannabis, 123
Scorecard, 143
search and seizure of computers, 107
search engines. *See* directories and search engines
secessionist groups, 270
Second Amendment, 164
Second Amendment Foundation, 165–166
secondhand smoke, 237
secrecy, 156–157, 160, 277–278
secretaries of state, 36
Senate, 27
  candidates for, 15, 260–261, 262–263
  committee meetings and hearings, 27
  Committee on Governmental Affairs, 154–155
  committee reports, 27
  Environment and Public Works Committee, 139–140
  floor schedules, 15
  Foreign Relations Committee, 190
  Joint Economic Committee, 126–127
  legislative calendar, 27
  races, 110
  rules, 29
  Special Committee on Aging, 234
  Standing Rules of the Senate, 27
  voting records, 27
senior issues, 160, 230–235
  AARP Webplace, 230
  Administration on Aging, 173, 230
  aging, 56, 173, 219, 230, 231, 234
  demographics, 230
  disabilities, 234
  Medicare, 230–231
  New York Times: Social Security, 231
  older adult services, 40
  Older Americans Act, 230
  Project Vote Smart: Seniors/Social Security, 231
  Public Agenda Online: Medicare, 232
  Public Agenda Online: Social Security, 232
  Social Security Online, 232–233
  Social Security Privatization, 233
  Town Hall: Social Security, 233
  U.S. Senate Special Committee on Aging, 234

Washingtonpost.com: Medicare Special Report, 234
Washingtonpost.com: Social Security Special Report,
  234
Yahoo! News: Social Security Debate, 235
sentencing, 102, 103–104, 105, 106
Sentencing Project, 105
separation of church and state, 11, 17, 157, 222, 223,
  224, 225, 226
sex education, 69, 135
sex offenses, 102, 103, 106
sexism in media, 206
sexual activity, 66–67
sexual harassment, 219
sexual health, 56, 69, 74, 169
sexual orientation. *See* gay and lesbian issues
sexually transmitted diseases, 54, 69, 82
shareholder engagement, 93
Sierra Club, 142, 143
60 Plus Association, 231
slavery, 178, 202
Small Business Survival Committee, 143, 173
smart growth, 35
smoking. *See* tobacco
Snow, Tony, 248
social beliefs, 257
social investment, 94
social issues, 33
social justice, 16
social promotion, 136
social research, 255
Social Security, 12, 61, 96, 116, 124, 131, 152, 155, 157,
  200, 224, 265
  National Committee to Preserve Social Security and
    Medicare, 231
  New York Times: Social Security, 231
  Project Vote Smart: Seniors/Social Security, 231
  Public Agenda Online: Social Security, 232
  reform, 17, 125, 126, 127, 128, 231, 233, 234, 257
  Social Security Administration, 232–233
  Social Security Education Center, 231
  Social Security Handbook, 22, 233
  Social Security numbers, 101, 194
  Social Security Online, 232–233
  Social Security Privatization, 233
  Social Security Reform Center, 233
  solvency, 230
  taxes, 153
  Town Hall: Social Security, 233
  Washingtonpost.com: Social Security Special Report,
    234
  Yahoo! News: Social Security Debate, 235
Socialist Workers Party, 261
society
  and politics, 248
  and values, 12
soft drinks, 168

Supreme Court decisions, 28, 29–30, 31, 156, 249
    abortion, 69, 73
    bilingual education, 182
    civil liberties, 98
    mental illness, 170
    syllabi of, 31
surveillance, 96, 99, 101, 194, 196
surveys. *See* political opinion
survivalism, 270
Susan B. Anthony List, 76
sustainable business practices, 93
sustainable development, 139, 142, 146
sustainable economics, 125
Sweatshop Watch, 203
sweatshops, 94, 95, 200, 203, 204

Taiwan, 152, 157
talk.abortion, 67
talk.euthanasia, 229
talk.politics.animals, 91
talk.politics.guns, 166
talk.politics.medicine, 173
TASH, 117
Task Force Online, 149–150
taxes, 15, 20, 63, 124, 128, 155, 157, 161. *See also* economic and tax policy
    analysis of, 125
    and budget, 39
    capital gains tax, 126
    flat income tax, 63
    Internet taxes, 127, 157, 198
    National Taxpayers Union, 114, 127, 129, 130, 143, 161, 173, 233
    National Taxpayers Union Foundation, 127
    per capita tax burden, 39
    reform, 17, 61, 94, 157
    Social Security taxes, 153
    stadium taxes, 17
    subsidies for education, 134, 222
    tax cuts, 127, 153, 257
    tax forms, 21, 36
    tax protesters, 270
    Taxpayer Assets Project, 159
    Town Hall: Budget and Tax, 130
    tuition tax credits, 132
T. C. Williams School of Law, 45
teachers
    hiring, 134
    qualifications of, 134
    quality of, 132, 134, 137
    resources for, 16
    salaries, 136
Teamsters, 202
Technology Administration, 96
teen alcohol misuse, 160
teen parents, 212

teen pregnancy, 69, 74, 132, 212
teen sexuality, 73
telecommunications. *See* Internet and telecommunications policy
telemarketing, 101, 106
telephony, 196
television news, 207
Ten Commandments, in schools and courthouses, 222
term limits, 17, 127, 161, 239
terrorism, 11, 46, 99, 189, 191, 194, 223, 254
Terrorism in the United States, 22
Test Ban Treaty, 257
think tanks, 12, 13, 14, 15, 16, 36, 157–158, 189, 289
    NIRA's World Directory on Think Tanks, 10–11
    Project Vote Smart: Think Tanks and Research Institutes, 159
Third Circuit Court of Appeals, 29
third parties, 261, 265, 281
3rd party Central, 265
THOMAS, 27
Thomas, Cal, 248
Tibet, 177
Time magazine, 244
tobacco, 15, 54, 56, 94, 157, 160, 236–238
    Action on Smoking and Health, 236, 237
    Alcohol, Tobacco, and Firearms Bureau, 162
    alt.smokers, 236
    Americans for Nonsmokers' Rights, 237
    Council for Tobacco Research, 237
    National Center for Tobacco Free Kids, 237
    New York Times: The Tobacco Debate, 236
    Open Directory Project: Tobacco, 237
    Project Vote Smart: Tobacco, 237
    secondhand smoke, 237
    tobacco companies, 254
    Tobacco Control Resource Center, 238
    Tobacco Institute, 237
    Tobacco Products Liability Project, 238
    tobacco settlement, 35
    TobaccoArchives.com, 237
    Yahoo! News: Tobacco, 238
torture, 175, 178
tourism and travel, 21, 37, 40
Town Hall
    Budget and Tax, 130
    Conservative Columnists, 248
    Defense Budget and Readiness, 113–114
    Education, 136
    Electronic Newsletters, 248
    Environment, 143–144
    Foreign Policy, 190–191
    Government Reform, 161
    Health Care, 173
    Missile Defense, 114
    Social Security, 233
towns and townships, 43